A HISTORY OF CHINA

A HISTORY OF CHINA

by

WOLFRAM EBERHARD

of the University of California

Illustrated

UNIVERSITY OF CALIFORNIA PRESS

BERKELEY AND LOS ANGELES

1950

CHINAS GESCHICHTE first published in Switzerland
1948

A HISTORY OF CHINA, translated by *E. W. DICKES*, first published in U.S.A. by
UNIVERSITY OF CALIFORNIA PRESS
Berkeley and Los Angeles
1950

Printed in Great Britain by
The Alcuin Press, Welwyn Garden City, Herts.

CONTENTS

Chapter VIII: THE EMPIRES OF THE SUI AND THE T'ANG

Chapter IX: THE EPOCH OF THE SECOND DIVISION OF CHINA

ILLUSTRATIONS

MAPS

INTRODUCTION

THERE are indeed enough Histories of China already: why yet another one? Because the time has come for new departures; because we need to clear away the false notions with which the general public is constantly being fed by one author after another; because from time to time syntheses become necessary for the presentation of the stage reached by research.

Histories of China fall, with few exceptions, into one or the other of two groups, pro-Chinese and anti-Chinese: the latter used to predominate, but today the former type is much more frequently found. We have no desire to show that China's history is the most glorious or her civilization the oldest in the world. The greatness of a civilization does not depend on its longevity; a thousand years ago China's civilization towered over those of the peoples of central and northern Europe! Today Europe leads; tomorrow China may lead again. The greatness of a civilization is measured by its achievements. China's history is as glorious as those of other peoples; we need to realize how China became what she is, and to note the paths pursued by the Chinese in human thought and action. And the lives of emperors, the great battles, this or the other famous deed, matter less to us than the discovery of the great forces that underlie these features and govern the human element. Only when we have knowledge of those forces and counter-forces can we realize the significance of the great personalities who have emerged in China; and only then will the history of China become intelligible even to those who have little knowledge of the Far East and can make nothing of a mere enumeration of dynasties and campaigns.

Views on China's history have radically changed in recent years. Until about twenty years ago our knowledge of the earliest times in China depended entirely on Chinese documents of much later date; now we are able to rely on many excavations which enable us to check the written sources. Ethnological, anthropological, and sociological research has begun for China and her neighbours; thus we are in a position to write with some confidence about the making of China, and about her ethnical development, where formerly we could only grope in the dark. The claim that "the Chinese race" produced the high Chinese civilization entirely by its own efforts, thanks to its special gifts, has become just as untenable as the other theory that immigrants from the West, some conceivably from Europe, carried civilization to the Far East. We know now that in early times there was no "Chinese race", there were not even "Chinese", and that the Chinese race resulted from the amalgamation of many separate peoples of different races in an enormously complicated and long-drawn-out process, as with all the other high civilizations of the world.

The picture of ancient and medieval China has also been entirely changed since it has been realized that the sources on which reliance has always been placed were not objective, but deliberately and emphatically represented a particular philosophy. The reports of the emperors and ministers of the earliest period are not historical at all, but served as examples of ideas of social policy or as glorifications of particular noble families. Myths such as we find to this day among China's neighbours were made into history; gods were made men and linked together by long family trees. We have been able to touch on all these things only briefly, and have had to dispense with any account of the complicated processes that have taken place here.

The later historical works apply to the course of Chinese history the criterion of Confucian ethics; for them history is a textbook of ethics. It shows by means of examples how the man of high character should behave or not behave. We have to go deeper, and try to extract the historic truth from these records. Many specialized studies by Chinese, Japanese, and European scholars on problems of Chinese history are now available and of assistance in this task, while Chinese writers still imagine that they are serving their country by yet again dishing up the old fables for the foreigner as history, and Europeans, knowing no better or aiming at setting alongside the unedifying history of Europe the shining example of the conventional story of China, continue in the old groove. To this day, of course, we are far from having really worked through every period of Chinese history; there are long periods on which scarcely any work has yet been done. Thus the picture we are able to give to-day has no finality about it and will need many modifications. But the time has come for a new synthesis, so that criticism may proceed along the broadest possible front and push our knowledge further forward.

The present work is intended for the general reader and not for the specialist, who will devote his attention to particular studies and to the original texts. In view of the wide scope of the work, I have had to confine myself to placing certain lines of thought in the foreground and paying less attention to others. I have devoted myself mainly to showing China's sociological development down to the present day. But I have also been concerned not to leave out of account China's relations with her neighbours. Now that we have a better knowledge of China's neighbours, the Turks, Mongols, Tibetans, Tunguses, Tai, not confined to the narratives of Chinese, who always speak only of "barbarians", we are better able to realize how closely China has been associated with her neighbours from the first day of her history to the present time; how greatly she is indebted to them, and how much she has given them. We no longer see a China surrounded by barbarians, but the great Chinese State coming to terms with its neighbours, who had a civilization of a quite different type but nevertheless a high one.

It is usual to split up Chinese history under the various dynasties that have ruled China or parts thereof. The beginning or end of a dynasty does not always indicate a definite period; the beginning and end of the Middle Ages cannot be fixed to a year. But inasmuch as every division is an arbitrary cut in a continuous development, the division by dynasties has been retained.

The account of Chinese history here given is based on the results of my own researches, which have been or will be published in various specialist periodicals. I have dispensed, however, with indications in footnotes of the particular source of every new opinion expressed. Instead, critical bibliographical notes are appended for each chapter, to give the reader the opportunity of seeking further information on the problems touched on, or consulting the evidence for the new views advanced. The bibliography takes account, however, as far as possible only of works accessible to the reader; works in non-European languages have therefore been cited only in exceptional cases.

THE EARLIEST TIMES

Chapter I

PREHISTORY

1 *Sources for the earliest history*

UNTIL recently we were dependent for the beginnings of Chinese history on the written Chinese tradition. According to this China's history began either about 4000 B.C. or about 2700 B.C. with a succession of wise emperors who "invented" the elements of a civilization, such as clothing, the preparation of food, marriage, and a state system; they instructed their people in these things, and so brought China, as early as in the third millennium B.C., to an astonishingly high cultural level. All we know, however, of the origin of civilizations makes this entirely improbable on the face of it; no other civilization in the world originated in any such way. Research has shown that the older historical sources make no mention of any rulers before 2400 B.C., no mention even of their names. The names first appear in documents of about 400 B.C., and the deeds attributed to their owners and the dates assigned to them do not appear until much later. As time went on, historians found more and more to say about primeval times. All these narratives were collected in the great imperial history that appeared at the beginning of the Manchu epoch. That book was translated into French, and all the works written in Western languages until recent years on Chinese history and civilization have been based in the last resort on that translation.

Modern research has not only demonstrated that all these accounts are inventions of a much later period, but has also shown *why* such narratives were composed. Finally, it has shown that the traditional chronology is wrong and another must be adopted, reducing all the dates for the more ancient history, before 900 B.C. All narratives and reports, however, from China's earliest period have been dealt a mortal blow by modern archaeology, with the excavations of recent years. It has been shown that there was no trace of any high civilization in the third millennium B.C., and, indeed, that we can only speak of a real "Chinese civilization" from 1000 B.C. onward. The peoples of the China of that time had come from the most varied sources; from 1000 B.C. they underwent a common process of development that welded them into a new unity. In this sense—as elements of a definite civilization—we are justified in using from then on a new name, "Chinese", for the peoples of China. Those sections, however, of their ancestral populations who played no part in the subsequent cultural and racial fusion, we may fairly call "non-Chinese", in spite of their descent. This distinction answers the question that continually crops up, whether the Chinese are "autochthonons". They are autochthonons in the sense that they formed a unit in the Far East, in the geographical region of the present China, and were not immigrants from the Middle East.

2 *The Peking Man*

Man makes his appearance in the Far East at a time when remains in other parts of the world are very rare and are disputed. He appears as the so-called Sinanthropus Pekinensis, the "Peking Man", whose bones were found in caves south of Peking. The Peking Man is vastly different from the men of to-day, and forms a special branch of the human race, closely allied to the Pithecanthropus of Java. The formation of later races of mankind from these types has not yet been traced, if it occurred at all. Anthropologists consider, however, that the Peking Man possessed already certain characteristics peculiar to the Yellow Race.

The Peking Man lived in caves; no doubt he was a hunter, already in possession of very simple stone implements and also of the art of making fire. As none of the skeletons so far found are complete, it is assumed that he buried certain bones of the dead in different places from the rest. This burial custom, which is found among primitive peoples in other parts of the world, suggests the conclusion that the Peking Man already had religious notions. We have no knowledge yet of the length of time the Peking Man may have inhabited the Far East. His first traces are attributed to a million years ago, and he may have flourished in 500,000 B.C.

3 *The Palaeolithic Age*

Here there comes a great gap in our knowledge. All that we know indicates that at the time of the Peking Man there must have been a warmer and especially a damper climate in North China and Inner Mongolia than today. Great areas of the Ordos region, now dry steppe, were traversed in that epoch by small rivers and lakes beside which men could live. There were elephants, rhinoceroses, extinct species of stag and bull, even tapirs and other wild animals. About 50,000 B.C. there lived by these lakes a hunting people whose stone implements (and a few of bone) have been found in many places. The implements are comparable in type with the palaeolithic implements of Europe (Mousterian type, and more rarely Aurignacian or even Magdalenian). They are not, however, exactly like the European implements, but have a character of their own. We do not yet know what the men of these communities looked like, because as yet no indisputable human remains have been found. All the stone implements have been found on the surface, where they have been brought to light by the wind as it swept away the loess. These stone age communities seem to have lasted a considerable time and to have been spread not only over North China but over Mongolia and Manchuria. It must not be assumed that the stone age came to an end at the same time everywhere. Historical accounts have recorded, for instance, that stone implements were still in use in Manchuria and eastern Mongolia at a time when metal was known and used in western Mongolia and northern China. It is an important fact that as yet no palaeolithic implements have been found in central or southern China. It must probably be assumed that in these regions there was no stone age but an age of wood or more probably bamboo, such as we still find among the most primitive races of remote parts of India. If all implements were made of bamboo, they naturally could not last until today.

About 25,000 B.C. there appears in North China a new human type, found in upper layers in the same caves that sheltered Peking Man. This type is beyond doubt not Mongolian, and may have been allied to the Ainu, a non-Mongol race still living in northern Japan. These, too, were a palaeolithic people, though some of their implements show technical advance. Later they disappear, probably because they were absorbed into various populations of central and northern Asia. Remains of them have been found in badly explored graves in northern Korea.

4 *The Neolithic age*

In the period that now followed, northern China must have gradually become arid, and the formation of loess seems to have steadily advanced. There is once more a great gap in our knowledge, until, about 4000 B.C., we can trace in North China a purely Mongolian people with a neolithic culture. In place of hunters we find cattle breeders, who are even to some extent agriculturists as well. This may seem an astonishing statement for so early an age. It is a fact, however, that pure pastoral nomadism is exceptional, that normal pastoral nomads have always added a little farming to their cattle-breeding, in order to secure the needed additional food, and above all fodder, in winter.

At this time, about 4000 B.C., the other parts of China come into view. The neolithic implements of the various regions of the Far East are far from being uniform; there are various separate cultures. In the north-west of China there is a system of cattle-breeding combined with agriculture, a distinguishing feature being the possession of axes of rectangular section, with a finely sharpened cutting edge. Farther east, in the north and reaching far to the south, is found a culture with axes of round or oval section; and especially in the south and in the coastal region, and reaching as far as the coasts of Korea and Japan, is a culture with so-called shoulder-axes,

All three of these cultures were at first independent. Later the shoulder-axe culture penetrated as far as eastern India. Its people are known to philological research as Austroasiatics, forming the original stock of the Australian aborigines, and remaining still in India as the Munda race, in Indo-China as the Mon-Khmer race, and in pockets in the islands of Indonesia and especially Melanesia. All these peoples had migrated from southern China. The peoples with the oval-axe culture are the so-called Papuan peoples in Melanesia; they, too, migrated from southern China, probably before the others. Both groups influenced the ancient Japanese culture. The rectangular-axe culture of north-west China spread widely, and moved southward, where the Austronesian peoples (from whom the Malays are descended) were its principal constituents, spreading that culture also to Japan.

Thus we see here, in this period around 4000 B.C., an extensive mutual penetration of the various cultures all over the Far East, including Japan, which in the palaeolithic age was apparently without or almost without settlers.

5 *The eight principal prehistoric cultures*

In the period roughly around 2500 B.C. the general historical view becomes much clearer. Thanks to a special method of working, making use of the ethnological sources available from later times together with the archaeological sources, much new knowledge has been gained in recent years. At this time there is still no trace of a Chinese realm or of saintly kings teaching a higher civilization; we find instead on Chinese soil a considerable number of separate local cultures, each developing on its own lines. The chief of these cultures, acquaintance with which is essential to a knowledge of the whole later development of the Far East, are as follows:

(a) *The north-east culture*, centred in the present provinces of Hopei (in which Peking lies), Shantung, and southern Manchuria. The people of this culture were ancestors of the Tunguses, probably mixed with an element that is contained in the present-day aboriginal Siberian races.

These men were mainly hunters, but probably soon developed a little primitive agriculture, and made coarse, thick pottery with certain basic forms which were long preserved in subsequent Chinese pottery (for instance, a type of the so-called tripods). Later, pig-breeding became typical of this culture.

(b) *The northern culture* existed to the west of that culture, in the region of the present Chinese province of Shansi and in the province of Jehol in Inner Mongolia. These people had been hunters, but then became pastoral nomads, depending mainly on cattle. The people of this culture were the tribes later known as Mongols, the so-called proto-Mongols. Anthropologically they belonged, like the Tunguses, to the Mongol race.

(c) The people of the culture farther west, the *north-west culture*, were not Mongols. They, too, were originally hunters, and later became a pastoral people, with a not inconsiderable agriculture (especially growing wheat and millet). Their chief animals, however, were not cattle but horses. The centre of this culture, so far as can be ascertained from Chinese sources, was the present provinces of Shensi and Kansu, but mainly only the plains. The people of this culture were undoubtedly ancestors of the later Turkish peoples. As early as the first recognizable period, the middle of the third millennium B.C., they show the same characteristics as later. It is not suggested, of course, that the original home of the Turks lay in the region of the Chinese provinces of Shensi and Kansu; one gains the impression, however, that this was a border region of the Turkish expansion; the Chinese documents concerning that period do not suffice to establish the centre of the Turkish territory.

(d) In the *west*, in the present provinces of Szechwan and in all the mountain regions of the provinces of Kansu and Shensi, lived the ancestors of the Tibetan peoples as another separate culture. They were simple shepherds, generally wandering with their flocks on the mountain heights.

(e) In the *south* we meet with four further cultures. One

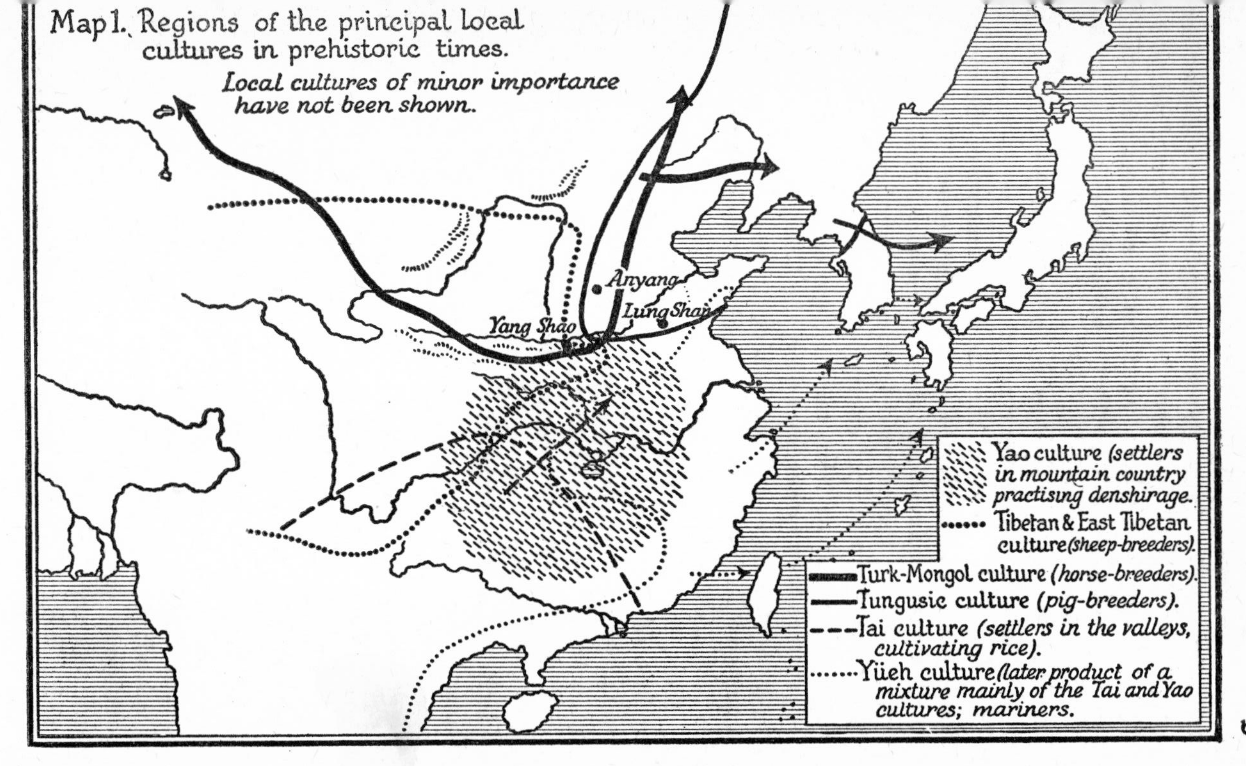

Map 1. Regions of the principal Local cultures in prehistoric times.

is very primitive, the Liao culture, the peoples of which are the Austroasiatics already mentioned. These are peoples who never developed beyond the stage of primitive hunters, some of whom were not even acquainted with the bow and arrow. Farther east is the Yao culture, an early Austronesian culture, the people of which also lived in the mountains, some as collectors and hunters, some going over to a simple type of agriculture (denshiring). They mingled later with the last great culture of the south, the Tai culture, distinguished by agriculture. The people lived in the valleys and mainly cultivated rice. In the course of time they spread farther and farther, and today they form the principal component of the Siamese people. Finally there arose from the mixture of the Yao with the Tai culture, at a rather later time, the Yüeh culture, another early Austronesian culture, which then spread over wide regions of Indonesia, and of which the axe of rectangular section, mentioned above, became typical.

Thus, to sum up, we may say that, quite roughly, in the middle of the third millennium we meet in the *north* of present-day China with a number of herdsmen cultures; of these the proto-Turkish culture was the most powerful, with the strongest influence on subsequent development. In the *south* there were a number of agrarian cultures, of which the Tai was the most powerful, becoming of most importance to the later China. We must assume that these cultures were as yet undifferentiated in their sociological composition, that is to say that as yet there were no classes, but at most the beginnings of class-formation, especially among the nomad herdsmen.

6 *The Yang Shao culture*

The various cultures here described gradually penetrated one another, especially at points where they met. Such a process does not yield a simple total of the cultural elements involved; the new combination produces entirely different conditions with correspondingly new results, which in turn represent the characteristics of the culture that supervenes. We can no longer follow this process of preparation

n detail; it need not by any means have been always war-
ke. One consequence of it, as a rule, was the formation of
. class division, the new society being made up of at least
one ruling and one ruled class. Thus there came into
existence around 2000 B.C. some new cultures, with which
archaeology has also made us now familiar. The most
important of these are the Yang Shao culture in the west
and the Lung Shan culture in the east. Our knowledge
of both these cultures is of quite recent date. The thoroughly
fantastic theories put forward after the first excavations
have since been abandoned; but there are many enigmas
still to be cleared up.

The *Yang Shao culture* takes its name from a prehistoric settlement in the west of the present province of Honan, where Swedish investigators discovered it. Typical of this culture is its wonderfully fine pottery, evidently used mainly as gifts to the dead. It is painted in three colours, white, red, and black. The patterns are all conventional, designs copied from nature being rare. The shapes are not found in later Chinese pottery. The people lived in open villages, for they were fairly active in agriculture, but cattle-breeding seems to have been the principal element of their economic system. Their implements were of stone with rare specimens of bone. The axes were of the rectangular type. Metal was as yet unknown.

After the discovery of this culture, its pottery was compared with the painted pottery of the Near East, and certain resemblances were found, especially with the pottery of the Lower Danube basin (Kukuteni) and that of Anau, in Turkestan. It was at once inferred that the Yang Shao pottery, and with it the oldest relatively high civilization, had come to China from the west, and some investigators went so far as to regard the Indo-Germanic race as the parents of that civilization. The closer study of the last five years has upset that theory. There are certain resemblances between the pottery of Anau and that of Yang Shao, but it is significant that it is not the earlier levels of the Yang Shao culture but its latest levels that are akin to Anau. The Yang Shao culture continued in the west

of China, in Kansu, for a long period, until well into th
bronze age, about 700 B.C.; and only pottery from layer
that can scarcely be older than 1400 B.C. has those re
semblances with Anau. Anau, however, is generally datec
about 3000 B.C. The resemblances must therefore, in al
probability, be fortuitous. It has also been discovered tha
the older layers of painted pottery are to be found in centra
China and only the later layers in the west; we shoulc
expect to find the opposite if this culture had come to Chin
from the Near East.

Who, then, were the people of this Yang Shao culture?
The first thing to note is that this culture appears only
toward the north of China, in North China itself, and in
western China, that is to say, only in mountain regions
and not in the plains. From our knowledge of primeval
settlement in China, Tibetan races, probably mixed with
Turkish races, must have lived in the whole region in question. The Yang Shao culture seems to have had a strong
Tibetan element, a smaller Turkish element, and in the
third place a slight element of the Tai race. This helps to
explain why some traces of painted pottery of the "Chinese"
type have been found in Eastern Turkestan: it must have
been made by Turkish peoples.

7 *The Lung Shan culture*

While the Yang Shao culture flourished in the mountain regions of northern and western China around 2000 B.C., there came into existence at latest at that time in the plains of eastern China another culture, which is called the Lung Shan culture, from the scene of the principal discoveries. Lung Shan is in the province of Shantung, near Tsinan-fu. This culture, discovered only about ten years ago, is distinguished by a black pottery of exceptionally fine quality and by a similar absence of metal. The pottery has a polished appearance on the exterior; it is never painted, and mostly without decoration; at most it may have incised geometrical patterns. The forms of the vessels are the same as have remained typical of Chinese pottery, and of Far Eastern pottery in general. To that extent the Lung

han culture may be described as one of the direct pre-
ecessors of the later Chinese civilization. The people of
ıe Lung Shan culture lived on mounds produced by
epeated building on the ruins of earlier settlements. They
vere therefore a long-settled population of agriculturists.
Their houses were of mud, and their villages were sur-
ounded with mud walls. There are unmistakable signs
hat their society was already divided into classes, and that
hey had a state organization at the head of affairs. So
ar as is known at present, this culture was spread over the
present provinces of Shantung, Kiangsu, Chekiang, and
Anhui, and some specimens of its pottery went as far as
Honan and Shansi, into the region of the painted pottery.
This culture lasted in the east until about 1700 B.C., with
clear evidence of rather longer duration only in the south.
According to our present knowledge the peoples of the
Lung Shan culture were mainly of Tai and Yao stocks,
together with some Tunguses.

Both in the west and the east of China, however, the
types of pottery in use were not confined to the two types
just mentioned; there was also a simple grey pottery out
of which vessels for everyday use were produced. This
primitive pottery seems to be connected with Tungus
peoples who lived in the north-east. The vessels were
ornamented in the style either of corded or of matted
ware.

8 *The first petty States in Shansi*

It must be realized that in addition to the two great cultural regions described above there were smaller ones,
especially where the two cultures met, in Shansi and eastern
Honan. Nothing can yet be said about these smaller
cultures from archaeological evidence. We believe, however, that the two semi-mythical figures Yao and Shun,
described in later Chinese historiography as kings, represent reminiscences of small States. It may be that
there existed in southern Shansi a small State under a
chieftain Yao, and in eastern Honan a small State under a
chieftain Shun, and that these States warred against each

other (as the older and unfalsified tradition tells), Yao's State being destroyed. Confucius, however, and the Confucian historians, made of Yao and Shun models of moral kingship, in order to be able to make use of them for their political purposes.

We first find an important element of advance, bronze, in China in traces in the middle layers of the Yang Shao culture, about 1800 B.C.; that element had become very widespread by 1400 B.C. The forms of the oldest weapons and their ornamentation show similarities with weapons from Siberia; and both mythology and other indications suggest that the bronze came into China from the north and was not produced in China itself. Thus, from the present state of our knowledge, it seems most correct to say that the bronze was brought to the Far East through the agency of peoples living north of China, such as the Turkish tribes who in historical times were China's northern neighbours (or perhaps only individual families, the so-called smith families with which we meet later in Turkish tradition), reaching the Chinese either through these people themselves or through the further agency of Mongols. At first the forms of the weapons were left unaltered. The bronze vessels, however, which made their appearance about 1450 B.C. are entirely different from anything produced in other parts of Asia; their ornamentation is recognizably southern (probably of the Tai culture), no doubt first applied to wooden vessels and vessels made from gourds, and then transferred to bronze. This implies that the art of casting bronze very soon spread from North China, where it was first practised by Turkish peoples, to the east and south, which quickly developed bronze industries of their own. There are few deposits of copper and tin in North China, while in South China both metals are plentiful and easily extracted, so that a trade in bronze from south to north soon set in.

The origin of the Hsia States may have been a consequence of the progress due to bronze. The Chinese tradition speaks of the Hsia *dynasty*, but can say scarcely anything about it. The excavations, too, yield no clear conclusions, so that we know virtually nothing beyond the names of the rulers. The dates assigned to them (2201-1760 B.C.) are demonstrably wrong. They belong to the period roughly between 1800 and 1500 B.C., when the petty State of Hsia made its appearance in southern Shansi as a late form of the Yang Shao culture. That culture maintained itself for a long time, as we know, in the mountain regions of the west and north.

Chapter II

THE SHANG DYNASTY (c. 1450-1050 B.C.)

1 *Period, origin, material culture*

All the cultures thus far referred to (the last appear to be correctly described in the allusions to them in ancient Chinese literature) were without the art of writing; and they made only limited use of bronze. About 1450 B.C. we come at last into the realm of history. Of the Shang dynasty which now followed, we have knowledge both from later texts and from excavations and the documents they have brought to light. The Shang civilization, an evident off-shoot of the Lung Shan culture (Tai, Yao, and Tunguses) was beyond doubt a high civilization. Of the origin of the Shang *State* we have no details, nor do we know how the Hsia culture passed into the Shang culture. There are still absent in the Shang period certain characteristic elements of Chinese civilization, so that we must still re-gard that period as pre-Chinese.

The central territory of the Shang realm lay in north-western Honan, alongside the Shansi mountains and ex-tending into the plains. It was a peasant civilization with towns. One of these towns has been excavated. It adjoined the site of the present town of Anyang, in the province of Honan. The town was surrounded by a mud wall, as were the settlements of the Lung Shan people. In the centre was what evidently was the ruler's palace. Round this were houses probably inhabited by artisans; for the artisans formed a sort of intermediate class, as dependents of the ruling class. The rectangular houses were built in a style still found in Chinese houses, except that their front did not face south as is now the general rule. Bronze implements and especially bronze vessels were cast in the town. We even know the trade marks of some famous bronze founders. The bronze weapons are still similar to those from Siberia, nd are often ornamented in the so-called "animal style", which was still used among all the nomad peoples between the Ordos region and Siberia until the beginning of the Christian era. On the other hand, the famous bronze vessels are of southern type, and reveal an advanced technique that has scarcely been excelled since. There can be no doubt that the bronze vessels were used for religious services and not for everyday life. For everyday use there were earthenware vessels. Even in the middle of the first millennium B.C., bronze was exceedingly dear, as we know from the records of prices. China has always suffered from scarcity of metal. For that reason metal was accumulated as capital, entailing a further rise in prices; when prices had reached a sufficient height, the stocks were thrown on the market and prices fell again. Later, when there was a metal coinage, this cycle of inflation and deflation became still clearer. The metal coinage was of its full nominal value, so that it was possible to coin money by melting down bronze implements. As the money in circulation was increased in this way, the value of the currency fell. Then it paid to turn coin into metal implements. This once more reduced the money in circulation and increased the value of the remaining coinage. Thus through the whole course of Chinese history the scarcity of metal and insufficiency of production of metal continually produced extensive fluctuations of the stocks and the value of metal, amounting virtually to an economic law in China. Consequently metal implements were never universally in use, and vessels were always of earthenware, with the further result of the early invention of porcelain. Porcelain vessels have many of the qualities of metal ones, but are cheaper.

The earthenware vessels used in this period are in many cases already very near to porcelain: there was a pottery of a brilliant white, lacking only the glaze which would have made it into porcelain. Patterns were stamped on the surface, often resembling the patterns on bronze articles. There was also a perfectly simple grey pottery.

Silk was already in use at this time. The invention of sericulture must therefore have dated from primeval times in China. It undoubtedly originated in the south of China, and at first not only the threads spun by the silkworm but those made by other caterpillars were used. The remains of silk fabrics that have been found show already an advanced weaving technique. In addition to silk, various plant fibres, such as hemp, were in use. Woollen fabrics do not seem to have been yet used.

2 *Writing and Religion*

Not only the material but the intellectual level attained in the Shang period was very high. We meet for the first time with writing—much later than in the Middle East and in India. Chinese scholars have succeeded in deciphering some of the documents discovered, so that we are able to learn a great deal from them. The writing is a rudimentary form of the present-day Chinese script, and like it a pictorial writing, but also makes use, as to-day, of many phonetic signs. There were, however, a good many characters that no longer exist, and many now used are absent. There were already more than 2,000 characters in use. (To-day newspapers use some 3,000 characters; scholars have command of up to 8,000; in the whole of Chinese literature, ancient and modern, some 50,000 characters are to be found.) With these 2,000 characters the Chinese of the Shang period were able to express themselves well.

The fragments of writing of this period which are still extant are found almost exclusively on tortoiseshells or on other bony surfaces, and represent oracles. As early as in the Lung Shan culture there was divination by means of "oracle bones", at first without written characters. In the earliest period any bones of animals (especially shoulder-bones) were used; later only tortoiseshell. For the purpose of the oracle a depression was burnt in the shell so that cracks were formed on the other side, and the future was foretold from their direction. Subsequently particular questions were scratched on the shells, and the answers to them; these are the documents that have come down to us. In Anyang tens of thousands of these oracle bones with inscriptions have been found.

The bronze vessels of later times often bear long inscriptions but those of the Shang period have at most one or two written characters. On the other hand, they are ornamented with pictures, as yet largely unintelligible, of countless deities, especially in the shape of animals or birds—pictures that demand interpretation. The principal form on these bronzes is that of the so-called T'ao-t'ieh, a hybrid with the head of a water-buffalo and tiger's teeth.

It is inferred from all this that the Shang period had a matriarchal element, and in harmony with it a religion with many nature deities, especially deities of fertility. There was no systematized pantheon, however, different deities being revered in each locality, often under the most varied names. These various deities were, however, similar in character , and later many of them were often combined by the priests into a single god. The composite deities thus formed were officially worshipped. Their primeval forms lived on, however, especially in the villages, many centuries longer than the Shang dynasty. The sacrifices associated with them became popular festivals, and so those gods or their successors were saved from oblivion; some of them have lived on in popular religions to the present day. The supreme god of the official worship was called Shang Ti; he was a god of vegetation, in human shape, who guided all growth and birth and was later conceived as a forefather of the races of mankind. The earth was represented as a mother goddess, who bore the plants and animals procreated by Shang Ti. In some parts of the Shang realm the two were conceived as a married couple who later were parted by one of their children. The husband went to heaven, and the rain is the male seed that creates life on earth. In other regions it was supposed that in the beginning of the world there was a world-egg, out of which a primeval god came, whose body was represented by the earth: his hair formed the plants, and his limbs the mountains and valleys. Every considerable mountain was also itself a god, and similarly the river god, the thunder god, cloud, lightning, and wind gods and many others were worshipped.

In order to promote the fertility of the earth, it was

believed that sacrifices must be offered to the earth. Consequently, in the Shang realm and the regions surrounding it there were many sorts of human sacrifices; often the victims were prisoners of war. But in some regions men lurked in the spring for people from other villages; they slew them, sacrificed them to the earth, and distributed portions of the flesh of the sacrifice to the various owners of fields, who buried them. At a later time all human sacrifices were prohibited, but we have reports down to the eleventh century A.D., and even later, that such sacrifices were offered secretly in certain regions of central China. In other regions a great boat festival was held in the spring, to which many crews came crowded in long narrow boats. At least one of the boats had to capsize; the people who were thus drowned were a sacrifice to the deities of fertility. This festival has maintained its fundamental character to this day, in spite of various changes. The same is true of other festivals, customs, and conceptions, vestiges of which are contained at least in folklore.

At the head of the Shang State was a "Ti", an emperor (the same word as in the name of the supreme god). We have found on bones the names of all the rulers of this dynasty; in addition there are lists in the ancient Chinese literature which are entirely in agreement with the record on the bones, so that there can be no doubt of the existence of these rulers. The emperor seems to have had no very great practical power; he was the high priest. Around him were many other priests. The central power does not seem to have extended very far. In the more distant parts of the realm were more or less independent lords, who recognized the emperor only as their supreme religious leader. We may describe this as an early form of the feudal system. The whole realm was still quite small, covering the southern part of the present province of Hopei, eastern and central Honan, eastern Shansi, and Shantung with the exception of its eastern part.

It was a population of peasants, who cultivated rice, wheat, millet, and other crops, were familiar with irrigation, and kept cattle, water-buffaloes, sheep, pigs, dogs, and in rare cases horses. They do not seem to have had a real plough, but only a sort of hoe and a spade that was held by one person and dragged through the soil by a second person by means of a rope.

3 *Transition to feudalism*

About the middle of the Shang period there were very interesting changes, under the influence of nomad peoples from the north-west, either Turks or Mongols. (The material as yet available is not enough to enable us to distinguish clearly, in regard to that period, between Mongol and Turk, though, of course, the two peoples and their cultures were not identical!) In religion there is evidence of star-worship; in the ornaments of bronze vessels there are strong traces of the animal style of the nomads, and horse-breeding becomes more and more evident; and with horse-breeding the wheeled vehicle makes its appearance in the form of the war chariot. The cart was not a Chinese invention, but came from the north, probably from Turkish peoples. It has been contended that it was connected with the war chariot of the Middle East; the fact, however, is that shortly before the Shang period there had been vast upheavals in western Asia through the appearance of peoples with lightly built two-wheeled war-chariots. Very soon the possessors of vehicles formed a privileged upper class in the Shang realm; they became a sort of nobility, and the constitution of the State steadily approximated to feudalism. The ruling house also adopted the chariot, and therewith a new military technique which made considerable conquests possible. Thus the Shang realm expanded further, after changes due to a northern (Turkish-Mongolian) influence that grew steadily stronger in the course of time; it covered the southern part of the province of Shansi and extended into the province of Shensi, that is to say into regions in which Turkish tribes had long lived together with Tibetans. Its conquests added more territory to the realm than could be coped with by the primitive communications of the time. Great rebellions occurred. One of these brought the dynasty to its end, about 1050 B.C.

ANTIQUITY

Chapter III

THE CHOU DYNASTY (c. 1050-247 B.C.)

1 *Cultural origin of the Chou and end of the Shang dynasty*

THE Shang culture lacked certain things that are typical of "Chinese" civilization. Especially the family system was not yet the patriarchal system of the later Chinese, but had pronounced matriarchal characteristics. The religion, too, in spite of certain other influences, was still a religion of agrarian fertility. And the feudal system was still primitive. In all these things there was development under the new Chou dynasty.

In the time of the Shang dynasty the Chou formed a small realm in the west, at first in central Shensi; then they must have pushed into eastern Shensi. Our present knowledge indicates that the Chou were originally a Turkish stock, and their small realm consisted mainly of Turks and Tibetans. Their culture was closely related to that of Yang Shao, described above (the painted-pottery culture), with, of course, the progress brought by time. They had bronze weapons, and especially the war-chariot. Their penetration into eastern Shensi took place perforce under the pressure of other peoples, who apparently also belonged to the Turkish race. This, however, brought them within the zone of the Shang culture, by which they were strongly influenced, so that the Chou culture lost more and more of its original Turkish character and increasingly resembled the Shang culture. The Chou were also brought into the political sphere of the Shang, as is shown by the fact that marriages took place between the ruling houses of Shang and Chou. In the end the Chou State became nominally dependent on the Shang State in the form of a fief with special prerogatives. Meanwhile the power of the Chou State steadily grew, while that of the Shang State diminished more and more through the disloyalty of its feudatories. Finally, about 1050 B.C., the Chou ruler, named Wu Wang ("the martial king"), crossed his eastern frontier and pushed into central Honan. His army was formed by an alliance between various tribes, in the same way as happened again and again in the building up of the armies of the rulers of the steppes. In the case of many of these tribes it can be seen to-day that they were Tibetan. Wu Wang forced a passage across the Yellow River and annihilated the Shang army. He pursued its vestiges as far as the capital, captured the last emperor of the Shang, and killed him. Thus was the Chou dynasty founded, and with it we begin the actual history of China. The Chou brought to the Shang culture strong elements of Turkish and also Tibetan culture, which were needed for the release of such forces as could create a new empire and maintain it through thousands of years as a cultural and generally also a political unit.

2 *Feudalism in the new empire*

A natural result of the situation thus produced was the turning of the country into a feudal State. The conquerors were an alien minority, so that they had to march out and spread over the whole country. Moreover, the allied tribal chieftains expected to be rewarded. The territory to be governed was enormous, but the communications in northern China at that time were similar to those still existing not long ago in southern China—narrow footpaths from one settlement to another. It is very difficult to build roads in the loess of northern China; and the war-chariots that required roads had only just been introduced. Under such conditions, the simplest way of administering the empire was to establish garrisons of the invading tribes in the various parts of the country under the command of their chieftains. Thus separate regions of the country were distributed as fiefs among the members of the Chou family and the leaders of the allied tribes. If a former subject of the Shang surrendered betimes with the territory under his rule, or if there was one who could not be overcome by force, the Chou recognized him as a feudal lord.

Thus we have this picture of the early Chou State: the imperial central power established in Shensi, near the present Sian; over a thousand feudal States, great and small, often consisting only of a small garrison, or sometimes a more considerable one, with the former chieftain as feudal lord over it. Around these garrisons the old population lived on, in the north the Shang population, farther east and south various other peoples and cultures. The conquerors' garrisons were like islands in a sea. Most of them formed new towns, walled, with a rectangular plan and central crossroads, similar to the Western towns subsequently formed out of Roman encampments. This town plan has been preserved to the present day.

This upper class in its garrisons formed the nobility; it was sharply divided from the indigenous population round the towns. The conquerors called the population "the black-haired people", and themselves "the hundred families".

3 *Fusion of Chou and Shang*

The conquerors brought with them, for their own purposes to begin with, their rigid patriarchate in the family system and their cult of Heaven, in which the worship of sun and stars took the principal place; a religion most closely related to that of the Turkish peoples and derived from them. Some of the Shang popular deities, however, were admitted into the official Heaven-worship. Popular deities became feudal lords under the Heaven-god. The Shang conceptions of the soul were also admitted into the Chou religion: the human body housed two souls, the personality-soul and the animal-soul. Death meant the separation of the souls from the body, the animal-soul also slowly dying. The personality-soul, however, could move about freely and lived as long as there were people who remembered it and kept it from hunger by means of sacrifices. The Chou systematized this idea and made it into the ancestor-worship that has endured down to the present time. The Chou officially abolished human sacrifices, especially since, as former pastoralists, they knew of better means of employing prisoners of war than did the agrarian Shang.

Elements of a living culture cannot, of course, be abolished out of hand by an official decree, so that at first there was a gap between theory and practice. In a State of small peasants like that of the Shang, slaves were not of much use, because they could produce little more than they consumed themselves. The Chou used slaves as domestic servants for their numerous nobility and as farm labourers on large estates; this became possible because soon after the coming of the Chou the plough was invented through the association of the old spade of the Shang age with the draught animal bred by the Chou.

From now on there were two moral codes, one for the noble ruling class, the other for the ruled, just as there were two religions and two family systems. In establishing these important innovations at the beginning of the Chou period the lead was taken by the duke of Chou, the brother of the first ruler, Wu Wang; the duke must be regarded as probably the greatest among the leading personalities of that period. After the death of Wu Wang the duke became regent during the minority of that emperor's son.

The old upper class of the Shang dynasty was not entirely set aside. It lived on and even attempted a widespread revolt. The Chou suppressed this revolt, and then transferred a large part of the population of the former capital of the Shang to Loyang. This population was there settled in a separate community, and vestiges of the Shang population were still to be found there in the fifth century A.D.: they were entirely impoverished potters, still making vessels in the old style.

The Chou capital, at Sian, was a double town. In one part lived the master-race of the Chou with the imperial court, in the other the subjugated population. At the same time, the Chou built a second capital, the Loyang just mentioned, in the present province of Honan. Loyang was just in the middle of the new State, and for the purposes of the Heaven-worship it was regarded as the centre of the universe, where it was essential that the emperor should reside. Loyang was another double town: in one part were the rulers' administrative buildings, in the other the transferred population of the Shang capital, probably artisans for the most part. The valuable artisans seem all to have been taken over, for the bronze vessels of the early Chou age are virtually identical with those of the Shang age. The shapes of the houses also remained unaltered, and probably also the clothing, though the Chou brought with them the novelties of felt and woollen fabrics, old possessions of their earlier period. The only fundamental change was in the form of the graves: in the Shang age house-like tombs were built underground; now great tumuli were constructed in the fashion preferred by all steppe peoples.

One professional class was severely hit by the changed circumstances—the Shang priesthood. The Chou had no priests. As with all the races of the steppes, the head of the family himself performed the religious rites. Beyond this there were only shamans for certain purposes of magic. And very soon Heaven-worship was combined with the family system, the ruler being declared to be the Son of Heaven; the mutual relations within the family were thus extended to the religious relations with the deity. If, however, the god of Heaven is the father of the ruler, the ruler as his son himself offers sacrifice, and so the priest becomes superfluous. Thus the priests became "unemployed". Some of them changed their profession. They were the only people who could read and write, and as an administrative system was necessary they obtained employment as scribes. Others withdrew to their villages and became village priests. They organized the religious festivals in the village, carried out the ceremonies connected with family events, and even conducted the exorcism of evil spirits with shamanistic dances; they took charge, in short, of everything connected with customary observances and morality. The Chou lords were great respecters of propriety. The Shang culture had, indeed, been a high one with an ancient and highly developed moral system, and the Chou as rough conquerors were impressed by the ancient forms and tried to imitate them. In addition, they had in their religion of Heaven a conception of the exist-tence of mutual relations between Heaven and Earth: all that went on in the skies had an influence on earth, and vice versa. Thus, if any ceremony was "wrongly" performed, it had an evil effect on Heaven—there would be no rain, or the cold weather would arrive too soon, or some such misfortune would come. It was therefore of great importance that everything should be done "correctly". Hence the Chou rulers were glad to call in the old priests as performers of ceremonies and teachers of morality. There thus came into existence in the early Chou empire a new social group, later called "scholars", men who were not regarded as belonging to the lower class represented by the subjugated population but were not included in the nobility; men who were not productively employed but belonged to a sort of independent profession. They became of very great importance in later centuries.

In the first centuries of the Chou dynasty the ruling house steadily lost power. Some of the emperors proved weak, or were killed at war; above all, the empire was too big and its administration too slow-moving. The feudal lords and nobles were occupied with their own problems in securing the submission of the surrounding villages to their garrisons and in governing them; they soon paid little attention to the distant central authority. In addition to this, the situation at the centre of the empire was more difficult than that of its feudal States farther east. The settlements around the garrisons in the east were inhabited by agrarian tribes, but the subjugated population around the centre at Sian was made up of nomad tribes of Turks and Mongols together with semi-nomad Tibetans. Sian lies in the valley of the river Wei; the riverside country certainly belonged still, though perhaps only insecurely, to the Shang empire, and was specially well adapted to agriculture; but its periphery—mountains in the south, steppes in the north—was inhabited (until a late period, to some extent to the present day) by nomads, who had also been subjugated by the Chou. The Chou themselves were by no means strong, as they had been only a small tribe and their strength had depended on auxiliary tribes, which had now spread over the country as a nobility and lived far from the Chou. The Chou emperors had thus to hold in check the subjugated but warlike tribes of Turks and Mongols who lived quite close to their capital. In the first centuries of the dynasty they were more or less successful, for the feudal lords still sent auxiliary forces. In time, however, these became fewer and fewer, because the feudal lords pursued their own policy; and the Chou were compelled to fight their own battles against tribes that continually rose against them, raiding and pillaging their towns. Campaigns abroad also fell mainly on the shoulders of the Chou, as their capital lay near the frontier.

It must not be simply assumed, as is done by the Chinese and some of the European historians, that the Turkish and Mongolian tribes were so savage or so pugnacious that they continually waged war just for the love of it. The problem is much deeper, and to fail to recognize this is to fail to understand Chinese history down to the Middle Ages. The conquering Chou established their garrisons everywhere, and these garrisons were surrounded by settlements of artisans and peasants, a process that ate into the pasturage of the Turkish and Mongolian nomads. These nomads, as already mentioned, pursued agriculture themselves on a small scale, but it occurred to them that they could get farm produce much more easily by barter or by raiding. Accordingly they gradually gave up cultiv-ation and became pure nomads, procuring the needed farm produce from their neighbours. This abandonment, however, of agriculture brought them into a dangerous situation: if for any reason the Chinese stopped supplying or demanded excessive barter payment, the nomads had to go hungry. They were then virtually driven to get what they needed by raiding. Thus there developed a mutual reaction that lasted for centuries. Some of the nomad tribes living between garrisons withdrew, to escape from the growing pressure, mainly into the province of Shansi, where the influence of the Chou was weak and they were not numerous; some of the nomad chiefs lost their lives in battle, and some learned from the Chou lords and turned themselves into petty rulers. Such is the changeful picture of the Chou period until 772 B.C.

The result of the three centuries that had passed was a symbiosis between the urban aristocrats and the country-people. The rulers of the towns took over from the general population almost the whole vocabulary of the language which from now on we may call "Chinese". They naturally took over elements of the material civilization. The subjugated population had, meanwhile, to adjust itself to its lord. In the organism that thus developed, with its unified economic system, the conquerors became an aristocratic ruling class, and the subjugated population became a lower class, with varied elements but mainly a peasantry. From now on we may call this society "Chinese"; it has endured to the present day. All later changes, however important, are the result of internal development and not of aggression from without.

4 *Limitation of the imperial power*

In 771 B.C. an alliance of northern feudal States attacked the ruler in his western capital; in a battle close to the city they overcame him and killed him. This campaign appears to have set in motion considerable groups from various tribes, so that almost the whole province of Shensi was lost. With the aid of some feudal lords who had remained loyal, a Chou prince was rescued and conducted eastward to the second capital, Loyang, which until then had never been the ruler's actual place of residence. In this rescue a lesser feudal prince, ruler of the feudal State of Ch'in, specially distinguished himself. Soon afterwards this prince, whose domain had lain close to that of the ruler, reconquered a great part of the lost territory, and thereafter regarded it as his own fief. The Ch'in family resided in the same capital in which the Chou had lived in the past, and five hundred years later we shall meet with them again as the dynasty that succeeded the Chou.

The new ruler, resident now in Loyang, was foredoomed to impotence. He was now in the centre of the country, and less exposed to large-scale enemy attacks; but his actual rule extended little beyond the town itself and its immediate environment. Moreover, attacks did not entirely cease; several times parts of the indigenous population living between the Chou towns rose against the towns, even in the centre of the country.

Now that the emperor had no territory that could be the basis of a strong rule, and, moreover, owed his position to the feudal lords and was thus under an obligation to them, he ruled no longer as the chief of the feudal lords but as a sort of sanctified overlord; and this was the position of all his successors. A situation was formed at first that may be compared with that of Japan at the beginning of the nineteenth century. The ruler was a symbol rather than an exerciser of power. There had to be a supreme ruler because, in the worship of Heaven which was recognized by all the feudal lords, the supreme sacrifices could only be offered by the Son of Heaven in person. There could not be a number of sons of heaven because there were not a number of heavens. The imperial sacrifices secured that all should be in order in the country, and that the necessary equilibrium between Heaven and Earth should be maintained. For in the religion of Heaven there was a close parallelism between Heaven and Earth, and every omission of a sacrifice, or failure to offer it in due form, brought down a reaction from Heaven. For these religious reasons a central ruler was a necessity for the feudal lords. They needed him also for practical reasons. In the course of centuries the personal relationship between the various feudal lords had ceased. Their original kinship and united struggles had long been forgotten. When the various feudal lords proceeded to subjugate the territories at a distance from their towns, in order to turn their city States into genuine territorial States, they came into conflict with each other. In the course of these struggles for power many of the small fiefs were simply destroyed. It may fairly be said that not until the eighth and seventh centuries B.C. did the old garrison towns become real States. In these circumstances the struggles between the feudal States called urgently for an arbiter, to settle simple cases, and in more difficult cases either to try to induce other feudal lords to intervene or to give his sanction to the new situation. These were the only governing functions of the ruler from the time of the transfer to the second capital.

5 *Changes in the relative strength of the feudal States*

In these disturbed times China also made changes in her outer frontiers. When we speak of frontiers in this connexion, we must take little account of the European conception of a frontier. No frontier in that sense existed in China until her conflict with the European Powers. In the dogma of the Chinese religion of Heaven, all the countries of the world were subject to the Chinese emperor, the Son of Heaven. Thus there could be no such thing as other independent States. In practice the dependence of various regions on the ruler naturally varied: near the centre, that is to say near the emperor's place of residence, it was most pronounced; then it gradually diminished in the direction of the periphery. The feudal lords of the inner territories were already rather less subordinated than at the centre, and those at a greater distance scarcely at all; at a still greater distance were territories whose chieftains regarded themselves as independent, subject only in certain respects to Chinese overlordship. In such a system it is difficult to speak of frontiers. In practice there was, of course, a sort of frontier, where the influence of the outer feudal lords ceased to exist. The development of the original feudal towns into feudal States with actual dominion over their territories proceeded, of course, not only in the interior of China but also on its borders, where the feudal territories had the advantage of more unrestricted opportunities of expansion; thus they became more and more powerful. In the south (that is to say, in the south of the Chou empire, in the present central China) the garrisons that founded feudal States were relatively small and widely separated; consequently their cultural system was largely absorbed into that of the aboriginal population, so that they developed into feudal States with a character of their

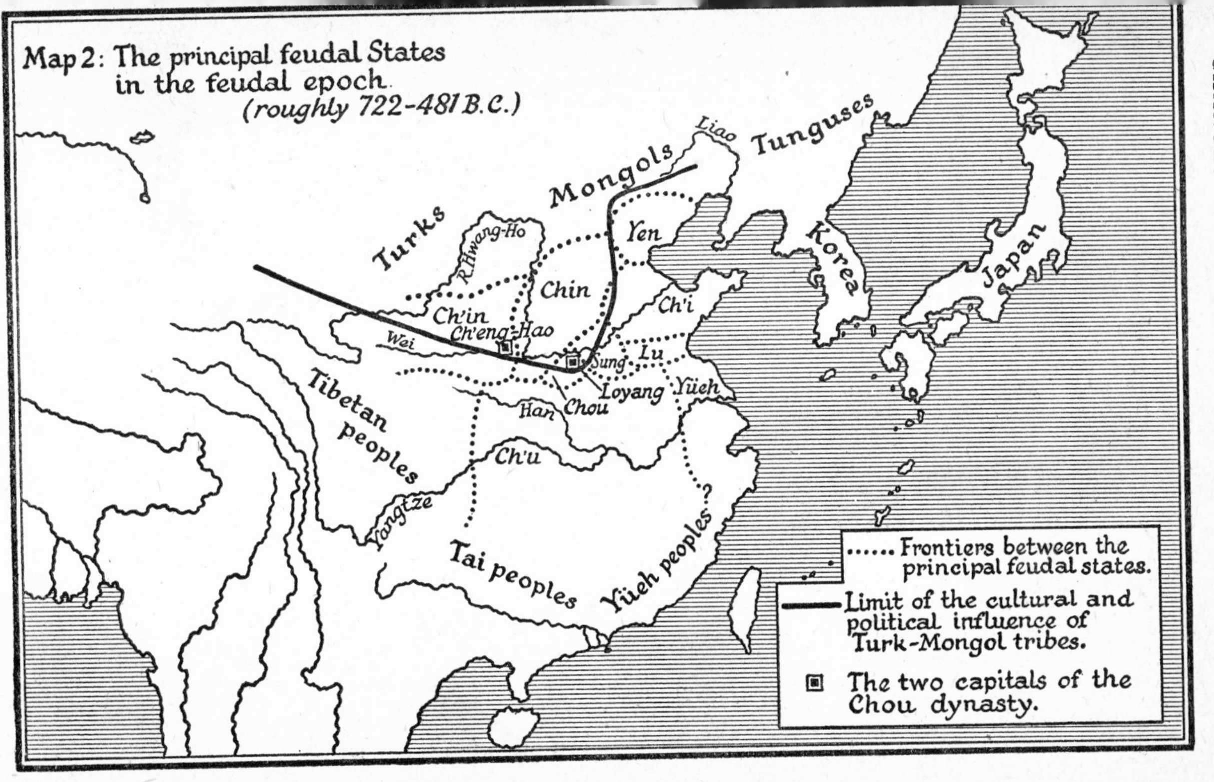

Map 2: The principal feudal States in the feudal epoch (roughly 722–481 B.C.)

own. Three of these attained special importance—(1) Ch'u, in the neighbourhood of the present Chungking and Hankow; (2) Wu, near the present Nanking; and (3) Yüeh, near the present Hangchow. In 704 B.C. the feudal prince of Wu proclaimed himself "Wang". "Wang", however, was the title of the ruler of the Chou dynasty. This meant that Wu broke away from the old Chou religion of Heaven, according to which there could be only one ruler (*wang*) in the world.

At the beginning of the seventh century it became customary for the ruler to unite with the feudal lord who was most powerful at the time. This feudal lord became a dictator, and had the military power in his hands, like the shoguns in nineteenth century Japan. If there was a disturbance of the peace, he settled the matter by military means. The first of these dictators was the feudal lord of the State of Ch'i, in the present province of Shantung. This feudal State had grown considerably through the conquest of the outer end of the peninsula of Shantung, which until then had been independent. Moreover, and this was of the utmost importance, the State of Ch'i was a trade centre. All the bronze, and later all the iron, for use in northern China came from the south in ships that went up the rivers to Ch'i, where it was distributed among the various regions of the north, north-east, and north-west. In addition to this, through its command of portions of the coast, Ch'i had the means of producing salt, with which it met the needs of great areas of eastern China. It was also in Ch'i that money was first used. Thus Ch'i soon became a place of great luxury, far surpassing the court of the Chou, and Ch'i also became the centre of the highest civilization.

After the feudal prince of Ch'i, supported by the wealth and power of his feudal State, became dictator, he had to struggle not only against other feudal princes, but also many times against risings among the most various parts of the population, and especially against the nomad tribes in the southern part of the present province of Shansi. In the seventh century not only Ch'i but the other feudal

States had expanded. The regions in which the nomad tribes were able to move had grown steadily smaller, and the feudal lords now set to work to bring the nomads of their country under their direct rule. The greatest conflict of this period was the attack in 660 B.C. against the feudal State of Wei, in northern Honan. The nomad tribes seem this time to have been Proto-Mongols; they made a direct attack on the garrison town and actually conquered it. The remnant of the population, no more than 730 in number, had to flee southward. It is clear from this incident that nomads were still living in the middle of China, within the territory of the feudal States, and that they were still decidedly strong, though no longer in a position to get rid entirely of the feudal lords of the Chou.

The period of the dictators came to an end after about a century, because it was found that none of the feudal States was any longer strong enough to exercise control over all the others. These others formed alliances against which the dictator was powerless. Thus this period passed into the next, which the Chinese call the period of the Contending States.

6 *Confucius*

After this survey of the political history we must consider the intellectual history of this period, for between 550 and 280 B.C. the enduring fundamental influences in the Chinese social order and in the whole intellectual life of China had their origin. We saw how the priests of the earlier dynasty of the Shang developed into the group of so-called "scholars". When the Chou ruler, after the move to the second capital, had lost virtually all but his religious authority, these "scholars" gained increased influence. They were the specialists in traditional morals, in sacrifices, and in the organization of festivals. The continually increasing ritualism at the court of the Chou called for more and more of these men. The various feudal lords also attracted these scholars to their side, employed them as tutors for their children, and entrusted them with the conduct of sacrifices and festivals.

China's best-known philosopher, Confucius (Chinese K'ung Fu-tzŭ), was one of these scholars. He was born in 551 B.C. in the feudal State in the present province of Shantung, son of a family descended from priests of the Shang dynasty. He acquired the knowledge which a scholar had to possess, and then taught in the families of nobles, also helping in the administration of their properties. He made several attempts to obtain advancement, either in vain or with only a short term of employment ending in dismissal. Thus his career was a continuing pilgrimage from one noble to another, from one feudal lord to another, accompanied by a few young men, sons of scholars, who were partly his pupils and partly his servants. Ultimately Confucius gave up his wanderings, settled in his home town of Lu, and there taught his disciples until his death in 479 B.C.

Such was briefly the life of Confucius. His enemies claim that he was a political intriguer, inciting the feudal lords against each other in the course of his wanderings from one State to another, with the intention of somewhere coming into power himself. There may, indeed, be some truth in that.

Confucius' importance lies in the fact that he built up a body of teaching, not of his own creation, and communicated it to a circle of disciples. His teachings were later set down in writing, and formed right down to the twentieth century the moral code of the upper classes of China. Confucius was fully conscious of his membership of a social class whose existence was bound up with that of the feudal lords. With their disappearance, his type of scholar would become superfluous. The common people, the lower class, was in his view in an entirely subordinate position. Thus his moral teaching is a code for the ruling class. Accordingly it retains almost unaltered the elements of the old cult of Heaven, following the old tradition inherited from the northern peoples. For him Heaven is not an arbitrarily governing divine tyrant, but the embodiment of a system of legality. Heaven does not act independently, but follows a universal law, the so-called "Tao"

Just as sun, moon, and stars move in the heavens in accordance with law, so man should conduct himself on earth in accord with the universal law, not against it. The ruler should not actively intervene in day-to-day policy, but should only act by setting an example, like Heaven; he should observe the established ceremonies, and offer all sacrifices in accordance with the rites, and then all else will go well in the world. The individual, too, should be guided exactly in his life by the prescriptions of the rites, so that harmony with the law of the universe may be established.

A second idea of the Confucian system came also from the old conceptions of the Chou conquerors, and thus originally from the northern peoples. This is the patriarchal idea, according to which the family is the cell of society, and at the head of the family stands the eldest male adult as a sort of patriarch. The State is simply an expansion of the family, "State", of course, meaning simply the class of the feudal lords. And the organization of the family is also that of the world of the gods. Within the family there are a number of ties, all of them, however, one-sided: that of father to son (the son having to obey the father unconditionally and having no rights of his own); that of husband to wife (the wife had no rights); that of elder to younger brother. An extension of these is the association of friend with friend, which is conceived as an association between an elder and a younger brother. The final link, and the only one extending beyond the family and uniting it with the State, is the association of the ruler with the subject, a replica of that between father and son. The ruler in turn is in the position of son to Heaven. Thus in Confucianism the cult of Heaven, the family system, and the State are welded into unity. The frictionless functioning of this whole system is effected by everyone adhering to the rites, which prescribe every important action. It is necessary, of course, that in a large family, in which there may often be a hundred persons living together, there shall be a precisely established ordering of relationships between individuals if there is not to be continual friction. Since the scholars of Confucius' type specialized in the knowledge and conduct of ceremonies, Confucius gave ritualism a correspondingly important place both in spiritual and in practical life.

So far as we have described it above, the teaching of Confucius was a further development of the old cult of Heaven. Through bitter experience, however, Confucius had come to realize that nothing could be done with the ruling house as it existed in his day. So shadowy a figure as the Chou ruler of that time could not fulfil what Confucius required of the "Son of Heaven". But the opinions of students of Confucius' actual ideas differ. Some say that in the only book in which he personally had a hand, the so-called *Annals of Spring and Autumn*, he intended to set out his conception of the character of a true emperor; others say that in that book he showed how he would himself have acted as emperor, and that he was only awaiting an opportunity to make himself emperor. He was called indeed, at a later time the "uncrowned ruler". In any case, the *Annals of Spring and Autumn* are simply a dry work of annals, giving the history of his native State of Lu on the basis of the older documents available to him. In his text, however, Confucius made small changes by means of which he expressed criticism or recognition; in this way he indirectly made known how in his view a ruler should act or should not act. He did not shrink from falsifying history, as can today be demonstrated. Thus on one occasion a ruler had to flee from a feudal prince, which in Confucius' view was impossible behaviour for the ruler; accordingly he wrote instead that the ruler went on a hunting expedition. Elsewhere he tells of an eclipse of the sun on a certain day, on which in fact there was no eclipse. By writing of an eclipse he meant to criticize the way a ruler had acted, for the sun symbolized the ruler, and the eclipse meant that the ruler had not been guided by divine illumination. The demonstration that the *Annals of Spring and Autumn* can only be explained in this way was the achievement some twenty years ago of Otto Franke, and through this discovery the work, which the old sinologists used to describe as a dry and inadequate book, has become of special value to us. The book ends with the year 481 B.C., and in spite of its distortions it is the principal source for the two-and-a-half centuries with which it deals.

Rendered alert by this experience, we are able to see and to show that most of the other official works of history follow the example of the *Annals of Spring and Autumn* in containing things that have been deliberately falsified. This is especially so in the work called *T'ung-chien kang-mu*, which was the source of the history of the Chinese empire translated into French by de Mailla.

Apart from Confucius' criticism of the inadequate capacity of the emperor of his day, there is discernible, though only in the form of cryptic hints, a fundamentally important progressive idea. It is that a country should not be ruled by a dynasty based on inheritance through birth, but by members of the nobility who show outstanding moral qualification for rulership. That is to say, the rule should pass from the worthiest to the worthiest, the successor first passing through a period of probation as a Minister. In an unscrupulous falsification of the tradition, Confucius declares that this principle was followed in early times. It is probably safe to assume that Confucius had in view here a possible justification of claims to rulership of his own.

Thus Confucius undoubtedly had ideas of reform, but he did not interfere with the foundations of feudalism. For the rest, his system consists only of a social order and a moral teaching. Metaphysics, logic, mental science, branches of philosophy which played so great a part in the West, are of no interest to him. Nor can he be described as the founder of a religion; for the cult of Heaven of which he speaks and which he takes over existed in exactly the same form before his day. He is merely the man who first systematized those notions. He had no successes in his lifetime and gained no recognition; nor did his disciples or their disciples gain any general recognition; his work did not become of importance until some three hundred years after his death, when in the second century B.C. his teaching was adjusted to the new social conditions: out of a moral system for the decaying feudal society of the past centuries developed the ethic of the rising social order of the gentry. The gentry (in much the same way as the European bourgeoisie) continually claimed that there should be access for every recognized member of their class to the highest places in the social pyramid; they regarded themselves as the heirs of the feudal aristocracy of the past. Thus the rules of Confucianism became binding on every member of their class, as a sort of code of gentlemanly behaviour. Only then did Confucianism develop into the imposing system that dominated China almost down to the present day. Confucianism did not become a religion. It was comparable to the later Japanese shintoism, or to a group of customs among us which we all observe, if we do not want to find ourselves excluded from our community, but which we should never describe as religion. We stand up when the national anthem is played, we give precedence to older people, we erect war memorials and decorate them with flowers, and by these and many other things show our sense of community. A similar but much more conscious and much more powerful part was played by Confucianism in the life of the average Chinese, though he was not interested in philosophical ideas.

While, however, Europe has set up the ideal of individualism, and is suffering now because it no longer has any ethical system to which individuals voluntarily submit; while for the Indians the social problem consisted in the solving of the question how every man could be enabled to live his life with as little disturbance as possible from his fellow-men, Confucianism solved the problem of enabling families with often hundreds of members to live together in peace and real co-operation in an overpopulated country. Everyone knew his position in the family, and so, in a broader sense, in the State; and this prescribed his rights and duties. We may feel that the rules to which he was subjected were pedantic; but there was no limit to their effectiveness: they reduced to a minimum the friction that always occurs when great masses of people live close together; they gave Chinese society the strength through which it has endured to this day. China's first real social crisis after the collapse of feudalism, that is to say, after the fourth or third century B.C., began only in the present century with the collapse of the social order of the gentry and the breakdown of the family system.

7 *Lao Tzŭ*

In eighteenth-century Europe Confucius was the only Chinese philosopher held in regard; in the last hundred years, the years of Europe's internal crisis, the philosopher Lao Tzŭ steadily advanced in repute, so that his book was translated almost a hundred times into various European languages. According to the general view among the Chinese, Lao Tzŭ was an older contemporary of Confucius; recent Chinese and Western research (A. Waley; H. H. Dubs) has contested this view and places Lao Tzŭ in the latter part of the fourth century B.C., or even later. Virtually nothing at all is known about his life; the oldest biography of Lao Tzŭ, written about 100 B.C., says that he lived as an official at the ruler's court, and one day became tired of the life of an official and withdrew from the capital to his estate, where he died in old age. This, too, may be legendary, but it fits well into the picture given to us by Lao Tzŭ's teaching and by the life of his later followers. From the second century A.D., that is to say at least four hundred years after his death, there are legends of his migrating to the far west. Still later narratives tell of his going to Turkestan (where a temple was actually built in his honour in the T'ang period); according to other sources he travelled as far as India or as the ancient province of Sogdiana (Samarkand and Bokhara), where according to some accounts he was the teacher or forerunner of Buddha, and according to others of Mani, the founder of Manichaeism. For all this there is not a vestige of documentary evidence.

Lao Tzŭ's teaching is contained in a small book, the *Tao Tê Ching*, the "Book of the World Law and its Power". The book is written in quite simple language, at times in rhyme, but the sense is so vague that countless versions, differing radically from each other, can be based on it, and just as many translations are possible, all philologically defensible. This vagueness is deliberate.

Lao Tzŭ's teaching is essentially an effort to bring man's life on earth into harmony with the life and law of the universe (Tao). This was also Confucius' purpose. But while Confucius set out to attain that purpose in a sort of primitive scientific way, by laying down a number of rules of human conduct, Lao Tzŭ tries to attain his ideal by an intuitive, emotional method. Lao Tzŭ is always described as a mystic, but perhaps this is not entirely appropriate; it must be borne in mind that in his time the Chinese language, spoken and written, still had great difficulties in the expression of ideas. In reading Lao Tzŭ's book we feel that he is trying to express something for which the language of his day was inadequate; and what he wanted to express belonged to the emotional, not the intellectual, side of the human character, so that any perfectly clear expression of it in words was entirely impossible. It must be borne in mind that the Chinese language lacks definite verbal categories like substantive, adjective, adverb, or verb; any word can be used now in one category and now in another, with a few exceptions; thus the understanding of a combination like "white horse" formed a difficult logical problem for the thinker of the fourth century B.C.: did it mean "white" plus "horse"? Or was "white horse" no longer a horse at all but something quite different? And so on.

Confucius' way of bringing human life into harmony with the life of the universe was to be a process of assimilating Man as a social being, Man in his social environment, to Nature, and of so maintaining his standard of activity within the bounds of the community. Lao Tzŭ pursues another path, the path for those who feel disappointed with life in the community. A Taoist, as a follower of Lao Tzŭ is called, withdraws from all social life, and carries out none of the rites and ceremonies which a man of the upper class should observe throughout the day. He lives in self-imposed seclusion, in an elaborate primitivity which is often described in vivid terms that pass the bounds of credibility. Far from the city, surrounded by Nature, he lives his own life, together with a few friends and his servants, entirely according to his nature. His own nature, like everything else, represents for him a part of the Tao, and the task of the individual consists in the most complete adherence to the Tao that is conceivable, as far as possible performing no act that runs counter to the Tao. This is the main element of Lao Tzŭ's doctrine, the doctrine of *wu-wei*, "passive achievement".

Lao Tzŭ seems to have thought that this doctrine could be applied to the life of the State. He assumed that an ideal life in society was possible if everyone followed his own nature entirely and no artificial restrictions were imposed. Thus he writes: "The more the people are forbidden to do this and that, the poorer will they be. The more sharp weapons the people possess, the more will darkness and bewilderment spread through the land. The more craft and cunning men have, the more useless and pernicious contraptions will they invent. The more laws and edicts are imposed, the more thieves and bandits there will be. 'If I work through Non-action,' says the Sage, 'the people will transform themselves.'"[1] Thus according to Lao Tzŭ, who takes the existence of a monarchy for granted, the ruler must treat his subjects as follows: "By emptying their hearts of desire and their minds of envy, and by filling their stomachs with what they need; by reducing their ambitions and by strengthening their bones and sinews; by striving to keep them without the knowledge of what is evil and without cravings. Thus are the crafty ones given no scope for tempting interference. For it is by Non-action that the Sage governs, and nothing is really left uncontrolled."[2]

Lao Tzŭ did not live to learn that that rule of good government could be followed by only one sort of rulers—dictators; and as a matter of fact the "Legalist theory" which provided the philosophic basis for dictatorship in the third century

[1] *The Way of Acceptance:* a new version of Lao Tzŭ's *Tao Tê Ching*, by Hermon Ould (Dakers, 1946,) Ch. 57. (Translator's note.)

[2] *The Way of Acceptance*, Ch. 3.

B.C. was attributable to Lao Tzŭ. He was not thinking however, of dictatorship; he was an individualistic anarchist believing that if there were no active government all men would be happy. Then everyone could attain unity with Nature for himself. Thus we find in Lao Tzŭ, and late in all other Taoists, a scornful repudiation of all social and official obligations. An answer that became famous wa given by the Taoist Chuang Tzŭ (see below) when it wa proposed to confer high office in the State on him (the story may or may not be true, but it is typical of Taois thought): "I have heard," he replied, "that in Ch'u there is a tortoise sacred to the gods. It has now been dead fo 3,000 years, and the king keeps it in a shrine with silken cloths, and gives it shelter in the halls of a temple. Which do you think that tortoise would prefer—to be dead and have its vestigial bones so honoured, or to be still alive and dragging its tail after it in the mud?" The officials replied "No doubt it would prefer to be alive and dragging it tail after it in the mud." Then spake Chuang Tzŭ "Begone! I, too, would rather drag my tail after me in the mud!" (Chuang Tzŭ 17, 10.)

The true Taoist withdraws also from his family. Typica of this is another story, surely apocryphal, from Chuang Tzŭ (Ch. 3, 3). At the death of Lao Tzŭ a disciple wen to the family and expressed his sympathy quite briefly and formally. The other disciples were astonished, and asked his reason. He said: "Yes, at first I thought that he was our man, but he is not. When I went to grieve, the old men were bewailing him as though they were bewailing a son, and the young wept as though they were mourning a mother. To bind them so closely to himself, he must have spoken words which he should not have spoken, and wept tears which he should not have wept. That, however is a falling away from the heavenly nature."

Lao Tzŭ's teaching, like that of Confucius, cannot be described as religion; like Confucius', it is a sort of social philosophy, but of irrationalistic character. Thus it was quite possible, and later it became the rule, for one and the same person to be both Confucian and Taoist. As an official and as the head of his family, a man would think and act as a Confucian; as a private individual, when he had retired far from the city to live in his little country house (often described as a cave or a thatched hut), or when he had been dismissed from his post or suffered some other trouble, he would feel and think as a Taoist. In order to live as a Taoist it was necessary, of course, to possess such an estate, to which a man could retire with his servants, and where he could live without himself doing manual work. This difference between the Confucian and the Taoist found a place in the works of many Chinese poets. I take the following quotation from an essay by the statesman and poet Ts'ao Chih, of the end of the second century A.D.:

"Master Mysticus lived in deep seclusion on a mountain in the wilderness; he had withdrawn as in flight from the world, desiring to purify his spirit and give rest to his heart. He despised official activity, and no longer maintained any relations with the world; he sought quiet and freedom from care, in order in this way to attain everlasting life. He did nothing but send his thoughts wandering between sky and clouds, and consequently there was nothing worldly that could attract and tempt him.

"When Mr. Rationalist heard of this man, he desired to visit him, in order to persuade him to alter his views. He harnessed four horses, who could quickly traverse the plain, and entered his light fast carriage. He drove through the plain, leaving behind him the ruins of abandoned settlements; he entered the boundless wilderness, and finally reached the dwelling of Master Mysticus. Here there was a waterfall on one side, and on the other were high crags; at the back a stream flowed deep down in its bed, and in front was an odorous wood. The master wore a white doeskin cap and a striped fox-pelt. He came forward from a cave buried in the mountain, leaned against the tall crag, and enjoyed the prospect of wild nature. His ideas floated on the breezes, and he looked as if the wide spaces of the heavens and the countries of the earth were too narrow for him; as if he was going to fly but had not yet left the ground; as if he had already spread his wings but wanted to wait a moment. Mr. Rationalist climbed up with the aid of vine shoots, reached the top of the crag, and stepped up to him, saying very respectfully:

" 'I have heard that a man of nobility does not flee from society, but seeks to gain fame; a man of wisdom does not swim against the current, but seeks to earn repute. You, however, despise the achievements of civilization and culture; you have no regard for the splendour of philanthropy and justice; you squander your powers here in the wilderness and neglect ordered relations between man. . . .' "

Frequently Master Mysticus and Mr. Rationalist were united in a single person. Thus, Shih Ch'ung wrote in an essay on himself:

" In my youth I had great ambition and wanted to stand out above the multitude. Thus it happened that at a little over twenty years of age I was already a court official; I remained in the service for twenty-five years. When I was fifty I had to give up my post because of an unfortunate occurrence. . . The older I became, the more I appreciated the freedom I had acquired; and as I loved forest and plain, I retired to my villa. When I built this villa, a long embankment formed the boundary behind it; in front the prospect extended over a clear canal; all around grew countless cypresses, and flowing water meandered round the house. There were pools there, and outlook towers; I bred birds and fishes. In my harem there were always good musicians who played dance tunes. When I went out I enjoyed nature or hunted birds and fished. When I came home, I enjoyed playing the lute or reading; I also liked to concoct an elixir of life and to take breathing exercises,[1] because I did not want to die, but wanted one day to lift myself to the skies, like an immortal genius. Suddenly I was drawn back into the official career, and became once more one of the dignitaries of the Emperor."

Thus Lao Tzŭ's individualist and anarchist doctrine was not suited to form the basis of a general Chinese social order, and its employment in support of dictatorship was

[1] Both Taoist practices.

certainly not in the spirit of Lao Tzŭ. Down to the present day, however, Taoism remained the philosophic attitude of individuals of the highest circle of society; its real doctrine never became popularly accepted; for the strong feeling for nature that distinguishes the Chinese, and their reluctance to interfere in the sanctified order of nature by technical and other deliberate acts, is not actually a result of Lao Tzŭ's teaching, but one of the fundamentals from which his ideas start.

If the date assigned to Lao Tzŭ by present-day research (the fourth instead of the sixth century B.C.) is correct, he was more or less contemporary with Chuang Tzŭ, who was probably the most gifted poet among the Chinese philosophers and Taoists. A thin thread extends from them as far as the fourth century A.D.: Huai-nan-Tzŭ, Chung-ch'ang T'ung, Yüan Chi (210-263), Liu Ling (221-300), and T'ao Ch'ien (365-427), are some of the most eminent names of Taoist philosophers. After that the stream of original thought dries up, and we rarely find a new idea among the late Taoists. These gentlemen living on their estates had acquired a new means of expressing their inmost feelings: they wrote poetry and, above all, painted. Their poems and paintings contain in a different outward form what Lao Tzŭ had tried to express with the inadequate means of the language of his day. Thus Lao Tzŭ's teaching has had the strongest influence to this day in this field, and has inspired creative work which is among the finest achievements of mankind. It became the opposite pole of Confucianism, containing with it the whole of the Chinese nature.

What are generally known as "Taoist writings" are a confused mass of shamanistic ideas, primitive conceptions, alchemy and superstition, clothed in a robe borrowed from Buddhism; this "popular Taoism" has little more than a few names and notions in common with philosophic Taoism. The Taoist monks and monasteries have equally little to do with Lao Tzŭ.

Chapter IV

THE CONTENDING STATES (481-256 B.C.): DISSOLUTION OF THE FEUDAL SYSTEM

1 *Social and military changes*

THE period following that of the Chou dictatorships is known as that of the Contending States. Out of over a thousand States, fourteen remained, of which, in the period that now followed, one after another disappeared, until only one remained. This period is the fullest, or one of the fullest, of strife in all Chinese history. The various feudal States had lost all sense of allegiance to the ruler, and acted in entire independence. As, however, no one of them was strong enough to control and subjugate the rest, alliances were formed. The most favoured union was the North-South Axis; it struggled against an East-West League. The alliances were not, however, stable, but broke up again and again through bribery or intrigue, which produced new combinations. We must confine ourselves to mentioning the most important of the events that took place behind this military façade.

Through the continual struggles more and more feudal lords lost their lands; and not only they, but the families of the nobles dependent on them, who had received so-called sub-fiefs. Some of the landless nobles perished; some offered their services to the remaining feudal lords as soldiers or advisers. Thus in this period we meet with a large number of migratory politicians who became competitors of the wandering scholars. Both these groups recommended to their lord ways and means of gaining victory over the other feudal lords, so as to become sole ruler. In order to carry out their plans the advisers claimed the rank of a Minister or Chancellor.

Realistic though these advisers and their lords were in

their thinking, they did not dare to trample openly on the old tradition. The emperor might in practice be a completely powerless figurehead, but he belonged nevertheless, according to tradition, to a family of divine origin, which had obtained its office not merely by the exercise of force but through a "divine mandate". Accordingly, if one of the feudal lords thought of putting forward a claim to the imperial throne, he felt compelled to demonstrate that his family was just as much of divine origin as the emperor's, and perhaps of remoter origin. In this matter the travelling "scholars" did good service as manufacturers of genealogical trees. Each of the old noble families already had its family tree, as an indispensable requisite for the sacrifices to ancestors. But in some cases this tree began as a branch of that of the imperial family: this was the case of the feudal lords who were of imperial descent and whose ancestors had been granted fiefs after the conquest of the country. Others, however, had for their first ancestor a local deity long worshipped in the family's home country, such as the ancient agrarian god Huang Ti, or the bovine god Shen Tung. Here the "scholars" stepped in, turning the local deities into human beings and "emperors". This suddenly gave the noble family concerned an imperial origin. Finally order was brought into this collection of ancient emperors. They were arranged and connected with each other in "dynasties" or in some other "historical" form. Thus at a stroke Huang Ti, who about 450 B.C. had been a local god in the region of southern Shansi, became the forefather of almost all the noble families, including that of the imperial house of the Chou. Needless to say, there would be discrepancies between the family trees constructed by the various scholars for their lords, and later, when this problem had lost its political importance, the commentators laboured for centuries on the elaboration of an impeccable system of "ancient emperors" —and to this day there are sinologists who try to present these humanized gods as historical personalities.

In the earlier wars fought between the nobles they were themselves the actual combatants, accompanied only by their retinue. As the struggles for power grew in severity, each noble hired such mercenaries as he could, for instance the landless nobles just mentioned. Very soon it became the custom to arm peasants and send them to the wars. This substantially increased the armies. The numbers of soldiers who fell in particular battles may have been greatly exaggerated (in a single battle in 260 B.C., for instance, the number who lost their lives was put at 450,000, a quite impossible figure); but there must have been armies of several thousand men, perhaps as many as 10,000. The population had grown considerably by that time.

The armies of the earlier period consisted mainly of the nobles in their war chariots; now came troops of infantry as well, drawn from the peasant population. To these, cavalry were first added in the fifth century B.C., by the northern State of Chao (in the present Shansi), following the example of its Turkish and Mongol neighbours. The general theory among ethnologists is that the horse was first harnessed to a chariot, and that riding came much later; but it is my opinion that riders were known earlier, but could not be efficiently employed in war because the practice had not begun of fighting in disciplined troops of horsemen, and the art had not been learnt of shooting accurately with the bow from the back of a galloping horse, especially shooting to the rear. In any case, its cavalry gave the feudal State of Chao a military advantage for a short time. Soon the other northern States copied it one after another—especially Ch'in, in north-west China. The introduction of cavalry brought a change in clothing all over China, for the former long skirt-like garb could not be worn on horseback. Trousers and the riding-cap were introduced from the north.

The new technique of war made it important for every State to possess as many soldiers as possible, and where it could to reduce the enemy's numbers. One result of this was that wars became much more sanguinary; another was that men in other countries were induced to immigrate and settle as peasants, so that the taxes they paid should provide the means for further recruitment of soldiers. In the State of Ch'in, especially, the practice soon started of using the whole of the peasantry simultaneously as a rough soldiery. Hence that State was particularly anxious to attract peasants in large numbers.

2 *Economic changes*

In the course of the wars much land became unoccupied through the expropriation of feudal princes and nobles and the death or migration of peasants. On this land the victorious feudal lord settled peasants, primarily for his own benefit. In earlier times there had been no trading in land; it had belonged to the nobles, who set peasants of the subjugated population to till it. The peasants gradually fell into serfdom. One of the results of the introduction of money was that land became an asset that could be bought and sold. In this period metal came more and more into general use, and iron began to make its appearance. The first metal agricultural implements were produced, and metal began to be used as currency. This greatly stimulated trade, which was largely trade in metals. But what were the traders to do with their profits? Even later in China, and almost down to recent times, it was never possible to hoard large quantities of money. Normally the money was of copper, and a considerable capital in the form of copper coin took up a good deal of room and was not easy to conceal. If anyone had much money, everyone in his village knew it. No one dared to hoard to any extent for fear of attracting bandits and creating lasting insecurity. On the other hand the merchants wanted to attain the standard of living which the nobles, the landowners, used to have. Thus they began to invest their money in land. This was all the easier for them since it often happened that one of the lesser nobles or a peasant fell deeply into debt to a merchant and found himself compelled to give up his land in payment of the debt.

Soon the merchants took over another function. So long as there had been many small feudal States, and the feudal lords had created lesser lords with small fiefs, it had been a simple matter for the taxes to be collected, in the form of grain, from the peasants through the agents of the lesser lords. Now, however, that there were only a few great States in existence, the old system was no longer effectual. This gave the merchants their opportunity. The rulers of the various States entrusted the merchants with the collection of taxes, and this had great advantages for the feudal prince: he could obtain part of the taxes at once, as the merchant usually had grain in stock, or was himself a landowner and could make advances at any time. Through having to pay the taxes to the merchant, the village population became dependent on him. Thus the merchants developed into the first administrative officials in the provinces.

The use of metal, including iron, spread more and more. Agricultural implements were improved by its use, and a plough, to be drawn by an animal, had been invented, becoming of great importance especially in the north. At that time the rice-fields, which could not make good use of a plough drawn by an animal, were of no economic importance. The basis of the economic system was wheat-growing, and the introduction of the plough made it possible to extend cultivation and increase the crop. In consequence of this, the population grew, and this made it possible for new areas to be brought under tillage, and for migrations to take place from one region to another, especially to the thinly settled south of China.

Gradually the centres of administration grew, so that the food produced in the neighbourhood of the towns no longer sufficed for their inhabitants. This led to the building of roads, which also facilitated the transport of supplies for great armies. These roads mainly radiated from the centre of consumption into the surrounding country, and they were less in use for communication between one administrative centre and another. For long journeys the rivers were of more importance, since transport by waggon was always expensive owing to the shortage of draught animals. Thus we see in this period the first important construction of canals and a development of communications. With the canal construction was united the construction of irrigation and drainage systems, which further promoted agricultural production.

So far nothing has been said in these chapters about China's foreign policy. Since the central ruling house was completely powerless, and the feudal princes were virtually independent rulers, little can be said, of course, about any "Chinese" foreign policy. There is less than ever to be said about it for this period of the "Contending States". Chinese merchants penetrated southwards, and soon settlers moved in increasing numbers into the plains, expelling or absorbing the indigenous population. The natives did not put up any very strong resistance. In the north, on the contrary there were continual struggles with Turkish and Mongol tribes, and about 300 B.C. the name of the Hsiung Nu (who are often described as "The Huns of the Far East") makes its first appearance. It is known that these northern peoples had mastered the technique of horseback warfare, and were far ahead of the Chinese, although the Chinese imitated their methods. The peasants of China, as they penetrated farther and farther north, had to be protected by their rulers against the northern peoples, and since the rulers needed their armed forces for their struggles within China, a beginning was made with the building of frontier walls, to prevent sudden raids of the northern peoples against the peasant settlements. Thus came into existence the early forms of the "Great Wall of China". This provided for the first time a real, fixed frontier between Chinese and non-Chinese. Along this frontier, just as by the walls of towns, great markets were held, at which Chinese peasants bartered their produce to non-Chinese nomads. Both partners in this trade became accustomed to it, and drew very substantial profits from it. We even know the names of several great horse-dealers, who bought horses from the nomads and sold them within China.

3 *Cultural changes*

Together with the economic and social changes in this period, came cultural changes. New ideas sprang up in exuberance, as would seem entirely natural, because in times of change and crisis men always come forward to offer solutions for pressing problems. We shall refer here only briefly to the principal philosophers of the period.

Mencius (c. 372-289 B.C.) and Hsün Tzŭ (c. 298-238 B.C.) were both followers of Confucianism. Both belonged to the so-called "scholars", and both came from the present Shantung, that is to say, from eastern China. Both elaborated the ideas of Confucius, but neither of them achieved personal success. Mencius (Meng Tzŭ) recognized that the removal of the ruling house of the Chou no longer presented any difficulty. The difficult question for him was when a change of ruler would be justified. And how could it be ascertained whom Heaven had destined as successor if the existing dynasty was brought down? Mencius replied that the voice of the "people", that is to say of the upper class and its following, would declare for the right man, and that this man would then be Heaven's nominee. This theory persisted throughout the history of China. Hsün Tzŭ's chief importance lies in the fact that he compressed and simplified the ideas of Confucius.

In the strongest contrast to this conservative tendency was the school of Mo Ti (at some time between 479 and 381 B.C.) The Confucian school held fast to the old feudal order of society, and was only ready to agree to a few superficial changes. The school of Mo Ti altered the fundamental principles of society. Family ethics must no longer be retained; the principles of family love must be extended to the whole upper class, which Mo Ti called the "people". One must love another member of the upper class just as much as one's own father. Then the friction between individuals and between States would cease. Instead of families, large groups of people friendly to one another must be created, much as the merchants and artisans had formed their organizations. The merchants of the various trades had formed guilds, and if a merchant travelled from the north to the south, his colleagues there welcomed him as a friend and relation, though they were unrelated to him and not even acquainted with him. Similarly all members of the upper class should join together. Further, and again an idea that sprang from commercial circles, one should live frugally and not expend endless money on effete rites, as the Confucianists demanded. The expenditure on weddings and funerals under the Confucianist ritual consumed so much money that many families fell into debt, and, if they were unable to pay off the debt, sank from the upper into the lower class. In order to maintain the upper class, therefore, there must be more frugality. Mo Ti's teaching won great influence. He and his successors surrounded themselves with a private army of supporters which was rigidly organized, and which could be brought into action at any time as its leader wished. Thus the Mohists came forward everywhere with an entirely different background to the isolated Confucians. When they offered their assistance to a ruler, they brought with them a group of technical and military experts who had been trained on the same principles. In consequence of its great influence. this teaching was naturally hotly opposed by the Confucianists.

The ideas of the Taoist teaching were elaborated especially by Chuang Tzŭ, toward the end of the fourth century B.C. He and the philosophers close to him were pure anarchist individualists, who withdrew from all public life and lived on their estates in the way they chose. They occupied themselves mainly with literature (Chuang Tzŭ left us the finest work of ancient times as regards form), and with mysticism and mystical puerilities. They soon adopted certain doctrines of magic from the popular shamanism, such as that of the artificial prolongation of life, and elaborated methods resembling those of the Indian Yoga. This school did not attain political importance. Allied to these philosophers was Yang Chu, who was contemporary with them or a little earlier: He carried anarchism and individualism to the utmost conceivable lengths.

At the same time as Chuang Tzŭ appeared the dialecticians. Here there are a number of names to mention: the most important are Kung-sun Lung and Hui Tzŭ, who are comparable with the ancient Greek dialecticians and Sophists. They saw their main task in the development of logic. Since, as we have mentioned, many "scholars" journeyed from one princely court to another, and other people came forward, each recommending his own method to the prince for the increase of his power, it was of great importance to be able to talk convincingly, so as to defeat a rival in a duel of words.

Unquestionably, however, the most important school of this period was that of the so-called Legalists, whose most famous representative was Shang Yang (or Shang Tzŭ). The supporters of this school came principally from old princely families that had lost their feudal possessions, and not from among the so-called scholars. They were people belonging to the upper class, who possessed political experience and now offered their knowledge to other princes who still reigned. These men had entirely given up the old conservative traditions of Confucianism; they were the first to make their peace with the new social order. They recognized that little or nothing remained of the old upper class of feudal lords and their following. The last of the feudal lords collected round the heads of the last remaining princely courts, or lived quietly on the estates that still remained to them. Such a class, with its moral and economic strength broken, could no longer lead. The Legalists recognized, therefore, only the ruler and next to him, as the really active and responsible man, the chancellor; under these there were to be only the common people, consisting of the richer and poorer peasants; the people's duty was to live and work for the ruler, and to carry out without question whatever orders they received. They were not to discuss or think, but to obey. The chancellor was to draft laws which came automatically into operation. The ruler himself was to have nothing to do with the government or with the application of the laws. He was only a symbol, a representative of the equally inactive Heaven. Clearly these theories were much the best suited to the conditions of the break-up of feudalism about 300 B.C. Thus they were first adopted by the State in which the old idea of the feudal State had been least developed, the State of Ch'in, in which alien peoples were most strongly represented. Shang Yang became the actual organizer of the State of Ch'in. It must be observed that these theories had little or nothing to do with the ideas of the old cult of Heaven or with family allegiance; on the other hand, the soldierly element, with the notion of obedience, was well suited to the militarized peoples of the west. The population of Ch'in, organized throughout on these principles, was then in a position to remove one opponent after another. In the middle of the third century B.C. the greater part of the China of that time was already in the hands of Ch'in, and in 256 B.C. the last emperor of the Chou dynasty was compelled, in his complete impotence, to abdicate in favour of the ruler of Ch'in.

Apart from these more or less political speculations, there came into existence in this period, by no mere chance, a school of thought which never succeeded in fully developing in China, concerned with natural science and comparable with the Greek natural philosophy. Several indications point to the conclusion that these ideas were influenced by Indian, Persian, and Sogdian thought, but it is probably too soon to assert that merchants from the Middle East imparted this knowledge, which may have been of practical economic importance, to their Chinese colleagues. The most important philosopher of this school was Tsou Yen; he, too, was a native of Shantung. His theories proceed from the doctrine that all that exists is to be explained by the positive, creative, or the negative, destructive action of the five elements, wood, fire, earth, metal, and water. Tsou Yen also considered the form of the world, and was the first to put forward the theory that the world consists not of a single continent with China in the middle of it, but of nine continents. The names of these continents sound like Indian names, and his idea of a central world-mountain may well have come from India. The "scholars" of his time were quite unable to appreciate this beginning of science, which actually led to the contention of this school, in the first century B.C., that the earth was of spherical shape. Tsou Yen himself was ridiculed as a dreamer; but very soon, when the idea of the reciprocal destruction of the elements was applied, perhaps by Tsou Yen himself, to politics, and when, in connexion with the astronomical calculations much cultivated by this school, the attempt was made to explain the duration and the supersession of dynasties, strong pressure began to be brought to bear against it. For hundreds of years its books were only distributed and read in secret, and many of its members were executed as revolutionaries, until in the second century A.D. its teachings were finally and completely extirpated.

Among the people the old religion of fertility lived on, hardly influenced at all by the philosophical systems. The fusion of individual gods proceeded further as local units of population were expanded by the growth of communications and by political organization. In this way certain gods gained increased importance. The various feudal princes and upstarts competing for the dignity of supreme ruler felt compelled to prove that they, too, were sons of Heaven. Under the influence of old totemistic notions, they traced their descent from particular gods, and accordingly supported the worship of those gods. Thus were formed elements of a pantheon, at the head of which was the god Shang Ti, who was able to maintain his position against various rivals. As Lao Tzŭ, too, had several times mentioned Shang Ti in such a way as to suggest that Shang Ti was an ancestor of his own, his name, and some of the notions he had originated, entered into the popular religion; these things, however, did not at once spread through the whole lower class, but found acceptance in various sects. These sects, whose main centre seems to have been in the present-day Hopei, also acquired pronounced shamanistic traits. There are indications that the first beginnings of the later secret societies (which first made their appearance about the beginning of our era as a typical reaction of an excessively oppressed peasant class) date from the third century B.C.; probably they already had the Messianic character which subsequently showed itself again and again. To this day this popular religion is called "Taoism", although in its form of worship and in the substance of its belief it has nothing, and could have nothing, in common with Lao Tzŭ's teaching, because it rests on a completely different foundation.

Chapter V

THE CH'IN DYNASTY (256-207 B.C.)

1 *Away from the unitary State*

IN 256 B.C. the last ruler of the Chou dynasty abdicated in favour of the feudal prince of the State of Ch'in. Some people place the beginning of the Ch'in dynasty in that year, 256 B.C.; others prefer the date 221 B.C., because it was only in that year that the remaining feudal States came to their end and Chi'n really ruled all China.

The territories of the State of Ch'in, the present Shensi and eastern Kansu, were, from a geographical point of view, transit regions, shut in on the north by steppes and deserts and on the south by almost impassable mountains. Only between these barriers, along the rivers Wei (in Shensi) and T'ao (in Kansu), is there a rich cultivable zone, which is also the only means of transit from east to west. All traffic from and to Turkestan had to take this route. It is assumed that the relations with Eastern Turkestan began in this period, and the State of Ch'in must have drawn big profits from its "foreign trade". The merchant class quickly gained more and more importance. The population was growing through immigration from the east, which the State encouraged. This growing population, with its increasing means of production (especially the great new irrigation systems), provided a welcome field for trade, which was also furthered by the roads, though these were actually built for military purposes.

The State of Ch'in had never been so closely associated with the feudal communities of the rest of China as the other feudal States, because a great part of its population, including the ruling class, was not purely Chinese but contained an admixture of Turks and Tibetans. The Chinese even called Ch'in a "barbarian State", and the foreign influence was, indeed, unceasing. This was a favourable soil for the overcoming of feudalism, and the process was furthered by the factors mentioned in the preceding chapter, which were leading to a change in the social structure of China. Especially the recruitment of the whole population, including the peasantry, for war was entirely in the interest of the influential nomad fighting peoples within the State. About 250 B.C., Ch'in was not only one of the economically strongest among the feudal States, but had already made an end of its own feudal system. The State was ruled on the principles of the Legalist School, which were best adapted to the new economic and social situation.

An illegitimate son of the penultimate feudal ruler of Ch'in was living as a hostage in the neighbouring State of Chao, in what is now northern Shansi. There he made the acquaintance of the merchant prince Lü Pu-wei, a man of education and of great political influence. Lü Pu-wei persuaded the feudal ruler of Ch'in to declare this son his successor. He also sold a girl to the prince to be his wife, and the son of this marriage was the famous and notorious Shih Huang Ti. Lü Pu-wei came with his protégé to Ch'in, where he became his Prime Minister, and after the prince's death in 247 B.C. Lü Pu-wei became the regent for his young son Shih Huang Ti (then called Cheng). For the first time in Chinese history a merchant, a commoner, had reached one of the highest positions in the State. It is not known what sort of trade Lü Pu-wei had carried on, but probably he dealt in horses, the principal export of the State of Chao. As horses were an absolute necessity for the armies of that time, it is easy to imagine that a horse-dealer might gain great political influence.

Soon after Shih Huang Ti's accession Lü Pu-wei was dismissed, and a new group of advisers, strong supporters of the Legalist school, came into power. These new men began an active policy of conquest instead of the peaceful course which Lü Pu-wei had pursued. One campaign followed another in the years from 230 to 222, until all the feudal States had been conquered, annexed, and brought under Shih Huang Ti's rule.

2 *Centralization in every field*

The main task of the now gigantic realm was the organization of administration. The Ministers then in office, as natives of Ch'in, were all opponents of the feudal system. One of their first acts after the conquest of the other feudal States was therefore to deport all the ruling families and other important nobles to the capital of Ch'in; they were thus deprived of the basis of their power, and their land could be sold. It was decided to set up a uniform system throughout the realm, one which had already been successfully introduced in Ch'in: the realm was split up into provinces and the provinces into prefectures; and an official was placed in charge of each province or prefecture. Originally the prefectures in Ch'in had been placed directly under the central administration, an official, probably very often a merchant, being responsible for the collection of taxes; the provinces, on the other hand, formed a sort of military command area, especially in the newly-conquered frontier territories. With the growing militarization of Ch'in, greater importance was assigned to the provinces, and the prefectures were made subordinate to them. Thus the officials of the provinces were originally army officers, but now, in the reorganization of the whole realm, the distinction between civil and military administration was abolished. At the head of the province were a civil and also a military governor, and both were supervised by a controller directly responsible to the emperor. Since there was naturally a continual struggle for power between these three officials, none of them was able to feel that he was supreme and to become a sort of feudal prince. In this system we can see the essence of the later Chinese administration. Shih Huang Ti's system broke down immediately after his death, not through any inadequacy but because there were not enough efficient men available.

Owing to the centuries of division into independent feudal States, the various parts of the country had developed differently. Each province spoke a different dialect, which also contained many words borrowed from the language of the indigenous population; and as these earlier populations sometimes belonged to different races with different languages, different words had found their way in each State into the Chinese language. This caused divergences not only in the spoken but in the written language, and even in the characters in use for writing. There exist to this day dictionaries in which the borrowed words of that time are indicated, and keys to the various old forms of writing also exist. Thus difficulties arose if, for instance, a man from the old territory of Ch'in was to be transferred as an official to the east: he could not properly understand the language, and could not read the borrowed words—if he could read at all! For a large number of the officials of that time, especially the officers who became military governors, were certainly unable to read. The government therefore ordered that the language of the whole country should be unified, and that a definite style of writing should be generally adopted. The words to be used were set out in lists, so that the first lexicography came into existence simply through the needs of practical administration, as had happened much earlier in Babylon.

The next requirement for the carrying on of the administration was the unification of weights and measures and, a surprising thing to us, of the gauge of the tracks for waggons. In the various feudal States there had been different weights and measures in use, and this had led to great difficulties in the centralization of the collection of taxes. The centre of administration, that is to say the new capital of Ch'in, had grown through the transfer of nobles, and through the enormous size of the administrative staff, into a thickly populated city with very large requirements of food. The fields of the former State of Ch'in could not alone feed the city; and the grain supplied in payment of taxation had to be brought in from far around, partly by cart. The only roads then existing consisted of deep cart-tracks. If the axles were not of the same length for all carts, the roads were simply unusable for many of them. Accordingly a fixed length was laid down for axles. The advocates of all these reforms were also their beneficiaries, the merchants.

The first principle of the Legalist school, a principle which had been applied in Ch'in and which was to be extended to the whole realm, was that of the training of the population in discipline and obedience, so that it should become a convenient tool in the hands of the officials. This requirement was best met by a people composed as far as possible only of peasants, industrious, uneducated, and—tax-paying. Scholars and philosophers were not wanted, in so far as they were not directly engaged on work commissioned by the State. The Confucianist writings came under special attack because they kept alive the memory of the old feudal conditions, preaching the ethic of the old feudal class which had just been destroyed and must not be allowed to rise again if the State was not to suffer fresh dissolution or the central administration to be weakened. In 213 B.C. there took place the great holocaust of books which destroyed the Confucianist writings with the exception of a copy of each for the State Library. Scientific books were not affected. In the fighting at the end of the Ch'in dynasty the State Library was burnt down, so that many of the old works have only come down to us in an imperfect state and with doubtful accuracy. The real loss arose, however, from the fact that the new generation was little interested in the Confucianist literature, so that when, fifty years later, the effort was made to restore the texts from the oral tradition, there no longer existed any scholars who really knew them by heart, as had been customary in the past.

In 221 B.C. Shih Huang Ti became emperor of all China. The judgments passed on him vary greatly: the official Chinese historiography rejects him entirely—naturally, for he tried to exterminate Confucianism, while every later historian was himself a Confucian. European scholars generally treat him as one of the greatest men in world history. Closer research has shown that Shih Huang Ti was evidently a very average man without any great gifts, and that he was superstitious and shared the tendency of his time to mystical and shamanistic notions. His own opinion was that he was the first of a series of ten thousand emperors of his dynasty (Shih Huang Ti means "First Emperor"), and this merely suggests megalomania. The basic principles of his administration had been laid down long before his time by the philosophers of the Legalist school, and were given effect by his Chancellor Li Ssŭ. Li Ssŭ was the really great personality of that period. The Legalists taught that the ruler must do as little as possible himself. His Ministers were there to act for him. He himself was to be regarded as a symbol of Heaven. In that capacity Shih Huang Ti undertook periodical journeys into the various parts of the empire, less for any practical purpose of inspection than for purposes of public worship. They corresponded to the course of the sun, and this indicates that Shih Huang Ti had adopted a notion derived from the old northern culture of the nomad peoples.

He planned the capital in an ambitious style, but although there was real need for extension of the city his plans can scarcely be regarded as of great service. His enormous palace, and also his mausoleum, which was built for him before his death, were constructed in accordance with astral notions. Within the palace the emperor continually changed his residential quarters, probably not only from fear of assassination but also for astral reasons. His mausoleum formed a hemispherical dome, and all the stars of the sky were painted on its interior.

3 *Frontier defence. Internal collapse*

When the empire had been unified by the destruction of the feudal States, the central government became responsible for the protection of the frontiers from attack from without. In the south there were only peoples in a very low state of civilization, who could offer no serious menace to the Chinese. The trading colonies that gradually extended to Canton and still farther south served as Chinese administrative centres for provinces and prefectures, with small but adequate armies of their own, so that in case of need they could defend themselves. In the north the position was much more difficult. In addition to their conquest within China, the rulers of Ch'in had pushed their frontier far to the north. The nomad tribes had been pressed back and deprived of their best pasturage, namely the Ordos region. When the livelihood of nomad peoples is affected, when they are threatened with starvation, their tribes often collect round a tribal leader who promises new pasturage and better conditions of life for all who take part in the common campaigns. In this way the first great union of tribes in the north of China came into existence in this period, forming the realm of the Hsiung Nu under their first leader, T'ouman. The Turkish people of the Hsiung Nu were ancestors of the Huns who later appeared in Europe. This first realm of the Hsiung Nu was not yet extensive, but its ambitious and warlike attitude made it a danger to Ch'in. It was therefore decided to maintain a large permanent army in the north. In addition to this, the frontier walls already existing in the mountains were rebuilt and made into a single great system. Thus came into existence in 214 B.C., out of the blood and sweat of countless pressed labourers, the famous Great Wall.

On one of his periodical journeys the emperor fell ill and died. His death was the signal for the rising of all reactionary elements. Nobles rose in order to regain power and influence; generals rose because they objected to the permanent pressure from the central administration and their supervision by controllers; men of the people rose as popular leaders because the people were more tormented than ever by forced labour, generally at a distance from their homes. Within a few months there were six different rebellions and six different "rulers". Assassinations became the order of the day; the young heir to the throne was removed in this way and replaced by another young prince. But as early as 206 B.C. one of the rebels, Liu Pang, entered the capital and dethroned the nominal emperor. Liu Pang at first had to retreat, and was involved in hard fighting with a rival, but gradually he succeeded in gaining the upper hand, and defeated not only his rival but the other eighteen States that had been set up anew in China in those years.

THE MIDDLE AGES

Chapter VI

THE HAN DYNASTY (206 B.C.–A.D. 220)

1 *Development of the gentry-State*

IN 206 B.C. Liu assumed the title of Emperor and gave his dynasty the name of the Han Dynasty. After his death he was given as emperor the name of Kao Tsu.[1] The period of the Han dynasty may be described as the beginning of the Chinese Middle Ages, while that of the Ch'in dynasty represents the transition from antiquity to the Middle Ages; for under the Han dynasty we meet in China with a new form of State, the gentry-State. The feudalism of ancient times has come definitely to its end.

Emperor Kao Tsu came from eastern China, and his family seems to have been a peasant family; in any case it did not belong to the old nobility. After his destruction of his strongest rival, the removal of the kings who had made themselves independent in the last years of the Ch'in dynasty was a relatively easy task for the new autocrat, although these struggles occupied the greater part of his reign. A much more difficult question, however, faced him: How was the empire to be governed? Kao Tsu's old friends and fellow-countrymen, who had helped him into power, had been rewarded by appointment as generals or high officials. Gradually he got rid of those who had been his best comrades, as so many upstart rulers have done before and after him in every country in the world. An emperor does not like to be reminded of a very humble past, and he is liable also to fear the rivalry of men who formerly were his equals. It is evident that little attention was paid to theories of administration; policy was determined mainly by practical considerations. Kao Tsu allowed

[1] From then on, every emperor was given after his death an official name as emperor, under which he appears in the Chinese sources. We have adopted the original or the official name according as either has come into the more general use in the European books.

many laws and regulations to remain in force, including the prohibition of Confucianist writings. On the other hand, he reverted to the allocation of fiefs, though not to old noble families but to his relatives and some of his closest adherents, generally men of inferior social standing. Thus a mixed administration came into being: part of the empire was governed by new feudal princes, and another part split up into provinces and prefectures and placed directly under the central power through its officials.

But whence came the officials? Kao Tsu and his supporters, as farmers from eastern China, looked down upon the trading population, to which farmers always regard themselves as superior. It may well be that the merchant class had already fallen at that time into the disrepute it suffered throughout later Chinese history, so that the emperor's enmity to the traders was in harmony with the popular attitude. In any case, the merchants were ignored as potential officials, although they had often enough held official appointments under the former dynasty. The second group from which officials had been drawn under the Ch'in was that of the army officers, but their military functions had now, of course, fallen to Kao Tsu's soldiers. The emperor had little faith, however, in the loyalty of officers, even of his own, and apart from that he would have had first to create a new administrative organization for them. Accordingly he turned to another class which had come into existence, the class later called the *gentry*, which in practice had the administration already in its hands.

The term "gentry" covers owners of substantial estates, who also held official positions and later were also literati. When the feudal system had collapsed, and landed property had become saleable, there began a great transformation in the countryside: the noble families disappeared, and their place was taken by new big landowners. Merchants who had grown wealthy invested their money in land; successful farmers, who had acquired wealth by marriage or inheritance, or by bringing waste land into cultivation, or in other ways, bought land from poorer farmers and accumulated large estates. But how were these big properties to be worked? One possibility was to make use of slaves. But slaves were always foreigners, who could only be acquired in the course of one of the few wars against foreign States, or by purchase at very high prices; and by no means all foreign captives were usable as slaves on farms. A Chinese could not be forced into slavery, because under the Chinese clan system his family, together with the families allied to it, would have avenged him. Thus there were few slaves. Hence the great landowners were compelled to lease their land, generally to the people from whom they had bought it. The great landowners lived on the high rents, reserving to themselves only a home farm occupied by part of their family, who supervised the collection of rents, while the remainder of their family could move into the nearest town. Such families not only had standing and power, but were the actual collectors of the taxes. It would have been very unwise if the new dynasty had set up an organization for tax collection independently of these people, so driving them into opposition. For the collection of taxes was at all times the basis of the administrative system. At the same time the members of the land-owning class who were living in the towns were rich enough to be able to occupy themselves with other things: social intercourse, education, and politics are pleasant in themselves, but are also means of gaining influence and power. In the course of time all who acquired wealth became members of the gentry, and so from now on that new class was the cradle of all the officials.

The mixed administration was bound to lead to a struggle for power between the new gentry and the new feudal lords. This struggle lasted nearly a hundred years, ending in favour of the gentry. The gentry-State began in the Han dynasty, under Kao Tsu; it lasted down to our own day. It is impossible to understand the history of medieval and modern China without a knowledge of the structure of the gentry and the gentry-State, just as it is impossible to understand ancient Chinese history without a knowledge of the feudal system. The fundamental difference between

Chinese and European society is clear: while China passed from the feudal State to the gentry-State, in Europe the feudal State gave place to the bourgeois State.

2 *Situation of the Hsiung Nu empire; its relation to the Han empire. Incorporation of South China*

In the time of the Ch'in dynasty there had already come into unpleasant prominence north of the Chinese frontier the tribal union, then relatively small, of the Hsiung Nu. Since then the Hsiung Nu empire had made all sorts of conquests, and had become a formidable power. Everything goes to show that it had close relations with the territories of northern China. Many Chinese seem to have migrated to the Hsiung Nu empire, where they were welcome as artisans, and probably also as farmers; but above all they were needed for the staffing of a new State administration. The scriveners in the newly introduced State secretariat were Chinese and wrote Chinese, for at that time the Hsiung Nu apparently had no written language. There were Chinese serving as administrators and court officials, and even as instructors in the army administration, teaching the art of warfare against non-nomads. But what was the purpose of all this? Mao Tun, the second ruler of the Hsiung Nu, and his first successors undoubtedly intended ultimately to conquer China, exactly as many other northern peoples after them planned to do and a few of them did. The main purpose of this was always to bring large numbers of peasants under the rule of the nomad rulers, and so to solve, once for all, the problem of the provision of additional winter food. Everything that was needed, and everything that seemed, as they grew more civilized, to be worth trying to get, would thus be obtained better and more regularly than by raids or by tedious commercial negotiations. But if China was to be conquered and ruled there must exist a State organization of equal authority to hers; the Hsiung Nu ruler must himself come forward as Son of Heaven and develop a court ceremonial similar to that of a Chinese emperor. Thus the basis of the organization of the Hsiung Nu State lay in its rivalry with the neighbouring China;

but the details naturally corresponded to the special nature of the Hsiung Nu social system. The young Hsiung Nu feudal State differed from the ancient Chinese feudal State not only in depending on a nomad economy instead of on agriculture, but also in possessing, in addition to a whole class of nobility and another of commoners, a stratum of slavery.

Thus Kao Tsu was faced in Mao Tun not with a mere nomad chieftain but with the most dangerous of enemies, and Kao Tsu's policy had to be directed to preventing any interference of the Hsiung Nu in North Chinese affairs, and above all to preventing alliances between Hsiung Nu and Chinese. Hsiung Nu alone, with their technique of horsemen's warfare, would scarcely have been equal to the permanent conquest of the fortified towns of the north and the Great Wall. But they might have succeeded with Chinese aid. Actually a Chinese opponent of Kao Tsu had already come to terms with Mao Tun, and in 200 B.C. Kao Tsu was very near suffering disaster in northern Shansi, as a result of which China would have come under the rule of the Hsiung Nu. But it did not come to that, and Mao Tun made no further attempt, although the opportunity came several times. Apparently the policy adopted by his court was not imperialistic but national, in the uncorrupted sense of the word. It was realized that a country so thickly populated as China could only be administered from a centre within China. The Hsiung Nu would thus have had to abandon their home territory and rule in China itself. That would have meant abandoning the flocks, abandoning nomad life, and turning into Chinese. The main supporters of the national policy, the first principle of which was loyalty to the old ways of life, seem to have been the tribal chieftains. Mao Tun fell in with their view, and the Hsiung Nu maintained their State as long as they adhered to that principle—for some seven hundred years. Other nomad peoples, Toba, Mongols, and Manchus, followed the opposite policy, and before long they were caught in the mechanism of the much more highly developed Chinese economy and culture, and each of them disappeared from the political scene in the course of a century or so.

The national line of policy of the Hsiung Nu did not at all mean an end of hostilities and raids on Chinese territory, so that Kao Tsu declared himself ready to give the Hsiung Nu the foodstuffs and clothing materials they needed if they would make an end of their raids. A treaty was concluded to this effect, and sealed by the marriage of a Chinese princess with Mao Tun. This was the first international treaty in the Far East between two independent Powers mutually recognized as equals. It was renewed at the accession of each new ruler, but was never adhered to entirely by either side. The needs of the Hsiung Nu increased with the expansion of their empire and the growing luxury of their court; the Chinese, on the other hand, wanted to give as little as possible, and no doubt they did all they could to cheat the Hsiung Nu. Thus in spite of the treaties the Hsiung Nu raids went on. With China's progressive consolidation, the voluntary immigration of Chinese into the Hsiung Nu empire came to an end, and the Hsiung Nu actually began to kidnap Chinese subjects. These were the main features of the relations between Chinese and Hsiung Nu almost until 100 B.C.

In the extreme south, around the present-day Canton, another independent empire had been formed in the years of transition, under the leadership of a Chinese. The narrow basis of this realm was no doubt provided by the trading colonies, but the indigenous population of Yüeh tribes was insufficiently civilized for the building up of a State that could have maintained itself against China. Kao Tsu sent a diplomatic mission to the ruler of this State, and invited him to place himself under Chinese suzerainty (196 B.C.). The ruler realized that he could offer no serious resistance, while the existing circumstances guaranteed him virtual independence, and he yielded to Kao Tsu without a struggle.

3 *Brief feudal reaction. Consolidation of the gentry*

Kao Tsu died in 195 B.C. From then to 179 the actual ruler was his widow, the empress Lü, while several children vere officially styled emperors. The empress tried to emove all the representatives of the emperor's family and o replace them with members of her own family. To secure ier position she revived the feudal system, but she met vith strong resistance from the dynasty and its supporters, vho already belonged in many cases to the new gentry, ind who did not want to find their position jeopardized oy the creation of new feudal lords.

On the death of the empress her opponents rose, under the leadership of Kao Tsu's family. Every member of the empress's family was exterminated, and a son of Kao Tsu, known later under the name of Wen Ti (Emperor Wen), came to the throne. He reigned from 179 to 157 B.C. Under him there were still many fiefs, but with the limitation which the emperor Kao Tsu had laid down shortly before his death: only members of the imperial family should receive fiefs, to which the title of King was attached. Thus all the more important fiefs were in the hands of the imperial family, though this did not mean that rivalries came to an end.

On the whole Wen Ti's period of rule passed in comparative peace. For the first time since the beginning of Chinese history, great areas of continuous territory were under unified rule, without unending internal warfare such as had existed under Shih Huang Ti and Kao Tsu. The creation of so extensive a region of peace produced great economic advance. The burdens that had lain on the peasant population were reduced, especially since under Wen Ti the court was very frugal. The population grew and cultivated fresh land, so that production increased and with it the exchange of goods. The most outstanding sign of this was the abandonment of restrictions on the minting of copper coin, in order to prevent deflation through insufficiency of payment media. This brought in more taxes, partly in kind, partly in coin, and this increased the power of the central government. The new gentry streamed into the towns, their standard of living rose, and they made themselves more and more into a class apart from the general population. As people free from material cares, they were able to devote themselves to scholarship. They went back to the old writings and studied them once more. They even began to identify themselves with the old nobles of feudal times, to adopt the rules of good behaviour and the rites inculcated in the Confucianist books, and very gradually, as time went on, to make these their textbooks of good form. From this point the Confucianist ideals first began to penetrate the official class recruited from the gentry, and then the State organization itself. It was expected that an official should be versed in Confucianism, and schools were set up for Confucianist education. This led about 100 B.C. to the introduction of the examination system, which gradually became the one method of selection of new officials. The system underwent many changes, but remained in operation in principle until 1904. The object of the examinations was to test not efficiency but command of the ideals of the gentry and knowledge of the literature inculcating them: this was regarded as sufficient qualification for any position in the service of the State.

In theory this path to training of character and to admission to the State service was open to every "respectable" citizen; that is to say, only "dishonourable" occupations, such as those of the soldier, the dancer, the musician, or the slave, were a disqualification. But in practice no one belonging to the peasantry had a chance to pass the examinations.[1] In the Han period the provincial officials had the right to propose suitable young persons for examination, and so for admission to the State service—and that makes it clear who had a chance to be proposed and who had not. In addition, schools had been instituted for the sons

[1] There is no statistical material for the normal examinations of this period. But the "extraordinary" examinations held from time to time have recently been investigated. In these, 65 persons came from the gentry, 8 are of uncertain origin, and 5 are stated to have come from families in "poor" circumstances. Most of the latter are shown by closer investigation to have belonged to families of the gentry, but to branches that were temporarily impoverished. This left their social standing unaffected, whereas it was of importance to European princes whether they were wealthy or had lost their domains. In the T'u Pa (Toba) period (385-550), out of all the successful candidates mentioned and all the later "professors" only one was found who did not come from the gentry.

of officials; the low level of the schooling is mentioned again and again. Through these schools all sons of officials, whatever their capacity or lack of capacity, could become officials in their turn. There was, it is true, no compulsion to attend these schools; a private tutor might be engaged instead. But if he did not want to sacrifice his good repute, a good tutor, one, that is, with the needed relations with the college of examiners and with other influential people, would not accept a peasant's son as a pupil. In spite of these weaknesses, the system had its good side. It inoculated a class of people with ideals that were unquestionably of high ethical value. The Confucian moral system gave a Chinese official or any member of the gentry a spiritual attitude and an outward bearing which in their best representatives has always commanded respect, an integrity that has always preserved its possessors, and in consequence Chinese society as a whole, from moral collapse, from spiritual nihilism, and has thus contributed to the preservation of Chinese cultural values in spite of all foreign conquerors.

In the time of Wen Ti, and especially of his successors, the revival at court of the Confucianist ritual and of the earlier Heaven-worship proceeded steadily. The sacrifices supposed to have been performed in ancient times, the ritual supposed to have been prescribed for the emperor in the past, all this was reintroduced. Obviously much of it was spurious: much of the old texts had been lost, and when fragments were found they were arbitrarily completed. Moreover, the old writing was difficult to read and difficult to understand; thus various things were read into the texts without justification. The new Confucians who came forward as experts in the moral code were very different men from their predecessors; above all, like all their contemporaries, they were strongly influenced by the shamanistic magic that had developed in the Ch'in period.

Wen Ti's reign had brought economic advance and prosperity; intellectually it had been a period of renaissance, but like every such period it did not simply resuscitate what was old, but filled the ancient moulds with an entirely new content. Sociologically the period had witnessed th consolidation of the new upper class, the gentry, wh copied the mode of life of the old nobility. This is seen mos clearly in the field of law. In the time of the Legalists th first steps had been taken in the codification of the crimina law; until then only a few quite primitive legal formula had existed. The great codifier of Chinese law was L K'uei, of whose career we know virtually nothing, no even the actual time when he lived. He clearly intende his laws to serve equally for all classes of the people: th old laws had been applicable only to the common people and never valid for the nobles. Li K'uei's code was use in the Han period, and was extensively elaborated b Siao Ho and others. His code consisted of two volumes o the chief laws for grave cases, one of mixed laws for the les serious cases, and six volumes on the imposition of penalties In the Han period "decisions" were added, so that abou A.D. 200 the code had grown to 26,272 paragraphs wit over 17,000,000 words. The collection then consisted o 960 volumes. This colossal code has been continuall revised, abbreviated, or expanded, and under its las name of "Collected Statutes of the Manchu Dynasty" i retained its validity down to the present century.

Alongside this collection there was another "statut book". The great Confucianist philosopher Tung Chung-shu (179-104 B.C.), a firm supporter of the ideology of th new gentry class, declared that the classic Confucianis writings, and especially the book *Ch'un-ch'iu*, "Annals o Spring and Autumn", attributed to Confucius himself were essentially books of legal decisions. They containe "cases" and Confucius' decisions in them. Consequentl any case at law that might arise could be decided by analog with the cases contained in those books. Only an educate person, of course, a member of the gentry, could clain that his action should be judged by the decisions of Con-fucius and not by the code compiled for the commo people, for Confucius had expressly stated that his rule were intended only for the upper class. Thus, right down t modern times an educated person could be judged unde

1 Painted pottery from Kansu: Neolithic.
In the collection of the Museum für Völkerkunde, Berlin.

2 Ancient bronze tripod found at Anyang.

From G. Ecke, *Frühe chinesische Bronzen aus der Sammlung Oskar Trautmann, Peking* 1939, *plate* 3.

a different code from that applicable to the common people.

Once more there came a reaction against the growing influence of the officials belonging to the gentry. It came as a reply to the attempt of a representative of the gentry to deprive the feudal princes of the whole of their power. In the time of Wen Ti's successor a number of feudal kings formed an alliance against the emperor, and even invited the Hsiung Nu to join them. The Hsiung Nu did not do so, because they saw that the rising had no prospect of success, and it was quelled. After that the feudal princes were steadily deprived of rights. It had become customary with the feudal rulers to administer their fiefs from the capital, and to devote themselves to some office at court, which offered further sources of power. Now, however, the feudal princes were divided into two classes, and only privileged ones were permitted to live in the capital, the others being required to remain in their domains. There the basis of their power was destroyed, the administration of the fief being placed in the hands of a controller, an official of the State. In the end the feudal princes became nothing more than a sort of pensioners of the State, with no official competence at all.

Soon after this the whole government was given the shape which it continued to have until A.D. 220, and which formed the point of departure for all later forms of government. At the head of the State was the emperor, in theory the holder of absolute power in the State. At his side were three counsellors who had, however, no active functions. The real conduct of policy lay in the hands of the "Chancellor", or of one of the "nine Ministers". Unlike the practice with which we are familiar in the West, the activities of the Ministries were concerned only with the imperial palace. As, however, the imperial secretariat was at the same time a sort of "Imperial Statistical Office", in which all economic, financial, and military statistical material was assembled, it may well have been possible for the decisions on issues of critical importance to come from it. Alongside it was an extensive administration of the capital with its military guards. The various parts of the country, including the lands given as fiefs to princes, had a local administration, entirely independent of the central government and more or less elaborated according to their size. There was at least a department for military questions, for each region had its own regional armies under the command of the governor. Often there was also a department for the education of the sons of the regional officials; later there was frequently a financial department or even an economic department. The regional administration was loosely associated with the central government through a sort of primitive "Ministry of the Interior", and similarly the Chinese representatives in the "protectorates", that is to say the foreign States which had submitted to Chinese protective overlordship, were loosely united with a sort of "Foreign Ministry" in the central government. When a rising or a local war broke out, that was the affair of the region concerned. If the regional troops were insufficient, those of the adjoining regions were drawn upon; if even these were insufficient, a real "state of war" came into being; that is to say, the emperor appointed eight generals-in-chief, mobilized the imperial troops, and intervened. This imperial army then had authority over the regional and feudal troops, the troops of the protectorates, the guards of the capital, and those of the imperial palace. At the end of the war the imperial army was demobilized and the generals-in-chief were transferred to other posts.

In all this there gradually developed a division into civil and military administration. A number of regions would make up a province with a military governor, who was in a sense the representative of the imperial army, and who was supposed to come into activity only in the event of war.

This administration of the Han period lacked the close organization that would make precise functioning possible. On the other hand, an extremely important institution had already come into existence in a primitive form. As the central statistical authority, the court secretariat had a special position within the Ministries, and supervised the administration of the other offices. Thus there existed alongside the executive a means of independent supervision of it, and the rivalry which naturally existed between the two authorities enabled the emperor or the chancellor to detect and eliminate excesses on the part of the administration. Later, in the system of the T'ang period (A.D. 618-906), this institution developed into an independent censorship, and the system was given a new form as a "State and Court Secretariat", in which the whole executive was comprised and unified. Toward the end of the T'ang period the permanent state of war necessitated the permanent commissioning of the imperial generals-in-chief and of the military governors, and as a result there came into existence a "Privy Council of State", which gradually took over the functions of the executive. The system of administration in the Han and in the T'ang period is shown in the following table:

Han epoch	*T'ang epoch*
1. Emperor	1. Emperor
2. Three counsellors to the emperor (with no active functions)	2. Three counsellors and three assistants (with no active functions)
3. Eight supreme generals (only appointed in time of war)	3. Generals and Governors-General (only appointed in time of war; but in practice continuously in office)
4. ———	4. (a) State secretariat (1) Central secretariat (2) Secretariat of the Crown (3) Secretariat of the Palace and imperial historical commission (b) Emperor's Secretariat (1) Private Archives (2) Court Adjutants' Office (3) Harem administration
5. Court administration (Ministries) (1) Ministry for State sacrifices (2) Ministry for imperial coaches and horses (3) Ministry for justice at court (4) Ministry for receptions (5) Ministry for ancestors' temples (6) Ministry for supplies to the court (7) Ministry for the harem (8) Ministry for the palace guards (9) Ministry for the court (State secretariat)	5. Court administration (Ministries) (1) Ministry for State sacrifices (2) Ministry for imperial coaches and horses (3) Ministry for justice at court (4) Ministry for receptions (i.e. foreign affairs) (5) Ministry for ancestors' temples (6) Ministry for supplies to the court (7) Economic and financial Ministry

Han epoch	*T'ang epoch*
	(8) Ministry for the payment of salaries
	(9) Ministry for armament and magazines
6. Administration of the capital:	6. Administration of the capital:
(1) Crown prince's palace	(1) Crown prince's palace
(2) Security service for the capital	(2) Palace guards and guards' office
(3) Capital administration:	
(a) Guards of the capital	(3) Arms production department
(b) Guards of the city gates	
(c) Building department	
	(4) Labour service department
	(5) Building department
	(6) Transport department
	(7) Department for education (of sons of officials!)
7. Ministry of the Interior (Provincial administration)	7. Ministry of the Interior (Provincial administration)
8. Foreign Ministry	8. ———————
	9. Censorship (Audit council)

There is no denying that according to our standard this whole system was still thoroughly primitive, and "personal", that is to say, attached to the emperor's person—though it should not be overlooked that we ourselves are not yet far from a similar phase of development. To this day the titles of not a few of the highest officers of State—the Lord Privy Seal, for instance—recall that in the past their offices were conceived as concerned purely with the personal service of the monarch.

The picture changes considerably to the advantage of the Chinese as soon as we consider the provincial administration. The governor of a province, and each of his district officers or prefects, had a staff often of more than a hundred officials. These officials were drawn from the province or prefecture and appointed by the governor or the prefect. The staff was made up of officials responsible for communications with the central or provincial administration (private secretary, controller, finance officer), and a group of officials who carried on the actual local administration. There were departments for transport, finance, education, justice, medicine (hygiene), economic and military affairs, market control, and presents (which had to be made to the higher officials at the New Year and on other occasions). In addition to these offices, organized in quite a modern style, there was an office for advising the governor and another for drafting official documents and letters.

The interesting feature of this system is that the provincial administration was *de facto* independent of the central administration, and that the governor and even his prefects could rule like kings in their regions, appointing and discharging as they chose. This was a vestige of feudalism, but on the other hand it was a healthy check against excessive centralization. It is thanks to this system that even the collapse of the central power or the cutting off of a part of the empire did not bring the collapse of the country. In a remote frontier town like Tun-huang, on the border of Turkestan, the life of the local Chinese went on undisturbed whether communication with the capital was maintained or was broken through the conquest of the district by Tibetans. The official sent from the centre would be liable at any time to be transferred elsewhere; and he had to depend on the practical knowledge of his subordinates, the members of the local families of the gentry. These officials had the local government in their hands, and carried on the administration of Tun-huang through a thousand years and more. The Hsin family, for instance, was living there in 50 B.C. and was still there in A.D. 950; and so were the Yin, Ling-hu, Li, and K'ang families.

All the officials of the various offices or Ministries were appointed under the State examination system, but they had no special professional training; only for the more important subordinate posts were there specialists, such as jurists, physicians, and so on. A change came toward the end of the T'ang period, when a Department of Commerce and Monopolies was set up; only specialists were appointed to it, and it was placed directly under the emperor. Except for this, any official could be transferred from any Ministry to any other without regard to his experience.

4 *Turkestan policy. End of the Hsiung Nu empire*

In the two decades between 160 and 140 B.C. there had been further trouble with the Hsiung Nu, though there was no large-scale fighting. There was a fundamental change of policy under the next emperor, Wu (or Wu Ti, 141-86 B.C.). The Chinese entered for the first time upon an active policy against the Hsiung Nu. There seem to have been several reasons for this policy, and several objectives. The raids of the Hsiung Nu from the Ordos region and from northern Shansi had shown themselves to be a direct menace to the capital and to its extremely important hinterland. Northern Shansi is mountainous, with deep ravines. A considerable army on horseback could penetrate some distance to the south before attracting attention. Northern Shensi and the Ordos region are steppe country, in which there were very few Chinese settlements and through which an army of horsemen could advance very quickly. It was therefore determined to push back the Hsiung Nu far enough to remove this threat. It was also of importance to break the power of the Hsiung Nu in the province of Kansu, and to separate them as far as possible from the Tibetans living in that region, to prevent any union between those two dangerous adversaries. A third point of importance was the safeguarding of caravan routes. The State, and especially the capital, had grown rich through Wen Ti's policy. Goods streamed into the capital from all quarters. Commerce with central Asia had particularly increased, bringing the products of the Middle East to China. The caravan routes passed through western Shensi and Kansu to eastern Turkestan, but at that time the Hsiung Nu dominated the approaches to Turkestan and were in a position to divert the trade to themselves or cut it off. The commerce brought profit not only to the merchants, most of whom were probably foreigners, but to the officials in the provinces and prefectures through which the routes passed. Thus the officials in western China were interested in the trade routes being brought under direct control, so that the caravans could arrive regularly and be immune from robbery. Finally, the Chinese government may well have regarded it as little to its honour to be still paying dues to the Hsiung Nu and sending princesses to their rulers, now that China was

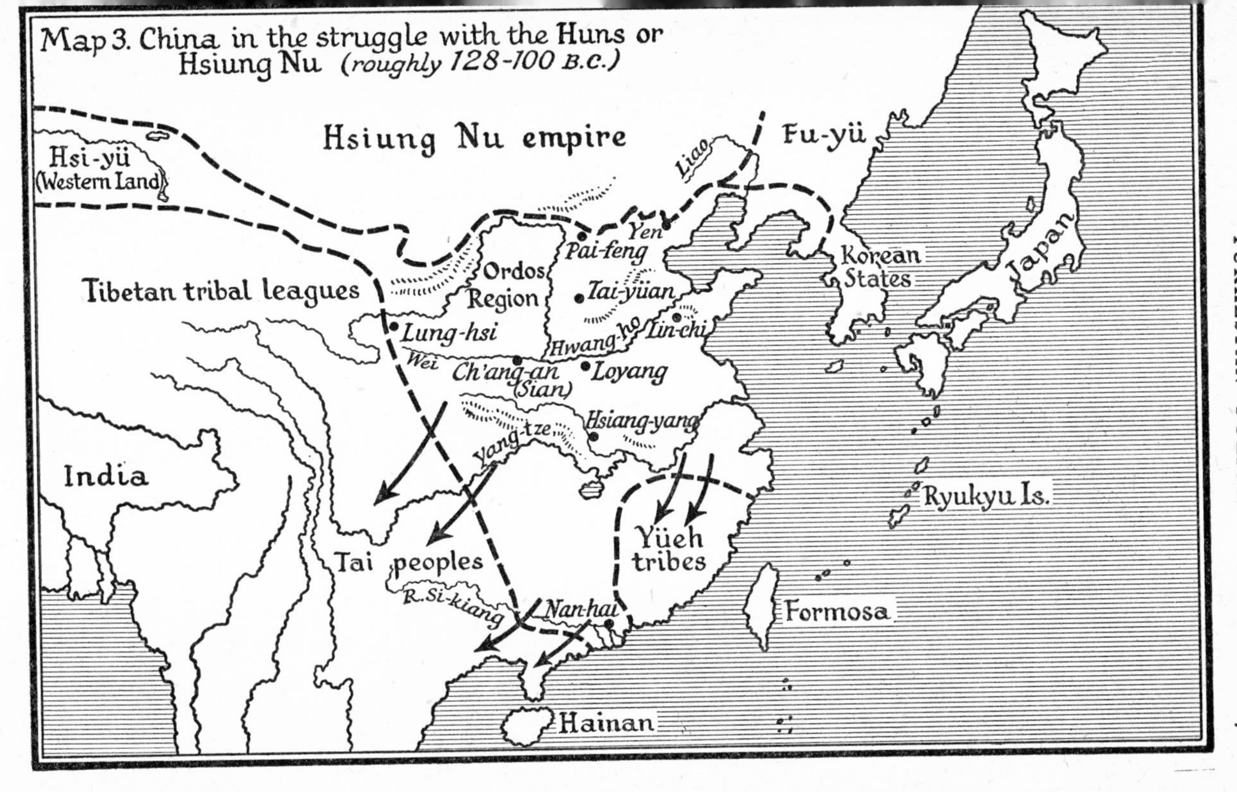

Map 3. China in the struggle with the Huns or Hsiung Nu (roughly 128-100 B.C.)

incomparably wealthier and stronger than at the time when that policy of appeasement had begun.

The first active step taken was to try, in 133 B.C., to capture the head of the Hsiung Nu State, who was called a *shan-yü*; but the *shan-yü* saw through the plan and escaped. There followed a period of continuous fighting until 119 B.C. The Chinese made countless attacks, without lasting success. But the Hsiung Nu were weakened, one sign of this being that there were dissensions after the death of the *shan-yü* Chün-ch'en, and in 127 B.C. his son went over to the Chinese. Finally the Chinese altered their tactics, advancing in 119 B.C. with a strong army of cavalry, which suffered enormous losses but inflicted serious loss on the Hsiung Nu. After that the Hsiung Nu withdrew further to the north, and the Chinese settled peasants in the important region of Kansu.

Meanwhile, in 125 B.C., the famous Chang Ch'ien had returned. He had been sent in 138 to conclude an alliance with the Yüeh Chih against the Hsiung Nu. The Yüeh Chih had formerly been neighbours of the Hsiung Nu as far as the Ala Shan region, but owing to pressure from the Hsiung Nu they had migrated to western Turkestan. Chang Ch'ien had followed them. Politically he had had no success, but he brought back accurate information about the countries in the far west, concerning which nothing had been known beyond the vague reports of merchants. Now it was learnt whence the foreign goods came and whither the Chinese goods went. Chang Ch'ien's reports (which are one of the principal sources for the history of central Asia at that remote time) strengthened the desire to enter into direct and assured commercial relations with those distant countries. The government evidently thought of getting this commerce into its own hands. The way to do this was to impose "tribute" on the countries concerned. The idea was that the missions bringing the annual "tribute" would be a sort of State bartering commissions. The State laid under tribute must supply specified goods at its own cost, and received in return agricultural produce, the value of which was to be roughly equal to the "tribute".

Thus Chang Ch'ien's reports had the result that, after the first successes against the Hsiung Nu, there was increased interest in a central Asian policy. The greatest military success was the campaigns of General Li Kuang-li to Ferghana in 104 and 102 B.C. The result of the campaigns was to bring under tribute all the small States in the Tarim basin and some of the States of western Turkestan.

In 108 B.C. the western part of Korea was also conquered. Korea was already an important transit region for the trade with Japan. Thus this trade also came under the direct influence of the Chinese government. Although this conquest represented a peril to the eastern flank of the Hsiung Nu, it did not by any means mean that they were conquered. The Hsiung Nu, although weakened, evaded the Chinese pressure, and in 104 B.C. and again in 91 they inflicted defeats on the Chinese. But the Hsiung Nu were indirectly threatened by Chinese foreign policy, for the Chinese concluded an alliance with old enemies of the Hsiung Nu, the Wu Sun, in the north of the Tarim basin. This made the Tarim basin secure for the Chinese, and threatened the Hsiung Nu with a new danger in their rear. Finally the Chinese did all they could through intrigue, espionage, and sabotage to promote disunity and disorder within the Hsiung Nu, though it cannot be seen from the Chinese accounts how far the Chinese were responsible for the actual conflicts and the continual changes of *shan-yü*. Hostilities against the Hsiung Nu continued incessantly, after the death of Wu Ti, under his successor, so that the Hsiung Nu were further weakened. In consequence of this it was possible to rouse against them other tribes who until then had been dependent on them—the Ting-ling in the north and the Wu Huan in the east. The internal difficulties of the Hsiung Nu increased further.

Wu Ti's active policy had not been directed only against the Hsiung Nu. After heavy fighting he brought southern China, with the region round Canton, and the south-eastern coast, firmly under Chinese dominion—in this case again on account of trade interests. No doubt there were already considerable colonies of foreign merchants in Canton and other coastal towns, trading in Indian and Middle East goods. The traders seem to have been Sogdians. The southern wars gave Wu Ti the control of the revenues from this commerce. He tried several times to advance through Yunnan in order to secure a better land route to India, but these attempts failed. Nevertheless, Chinese influence became stronger in the south-west.

In spite of his long rule, Wu Ti did not leave an adult heir, as the crown prince was executed, with many other persons, shortly before Wu Ti's death. The crown prince had been implicated in an alleged attempt by a large group of people to remove the emperor by various sorts of magic. It is difficult to determine to-day what lay behind this affair; probably it was a struggle between two cliques of the gentry. Thus a regency council had to be set up for the young heir to the throne; it included a member of a Hsiung Nu tribe. The actual government was in the hands of a general and his clique until the death of the heir to the throne, and at the beginning of his successor's reign.

At this time came the end of the Hsiung Nu empire—a foreign event of the utmost importance. As a result of the continual disastrous wars against the Chinese, in which not only many men but, especially, large quantities of cattle fell into Chinese hands, the livelihood of the Hsiung Nu was seriously threatened; and their troubles were increased by plagues and by unusually severe winters. To these troubles were added political difficulties, including unsettled questions in regard to the succession to the throne. The result of all this was that the Hsiung Nu could no longer offer effective military resistance to the Chinese. There were a number of *shan-yü* ruling contemporaneously, as rivals, and one of them had to yield to the Chinese in 58 B.C.; in 51 he came as a vassal to the Chinese court. The collapse of the Hsiung Nu empire was complete. After 58 B.C. the Chinese were freed from all danger from that quarter, and were able for a time to impose their authority in Central Asia.

5 *Impoverishment. Cliques. End of the Dynasty*

In other respects the Chinese were not doing as well as might have been assumed. The wars carried on by Wu Ti and his successors had been ruinous. The maintenance of large armies of occupation in the new regions, especially in Turkestan, also meant a permanent drain on the national funds. There was a special need for horses, for the people of the steppes could only be fought by means of cavalry. As the Hsiung Nu were supplying no horses, and the campaigns were not producing horses enough as booty, the Chinese peasants had to surrender those they had. Additional horses were bought at very high prices, and apart from this the general financing of the wars necessitated increased taxation of the peasants, a burden on agriculture no less serious than was the enrolment of many peasants for military service. Finally, the new external trade did not by any means bring the advantages that had been hoped for. The tribute missions brought tribute, but, to begin with, this meant an obligation to give presents in return; moreover, these missions had to be fed and housed in the capital, often for months, as the official receptions took place only on New Year's Day. Their maintenance entailed much expense, and meanwhile the members of the missions traded privately with the inhabitants and the merchants of the capital, buying things they needed and selling things they had brought in addition to the tribute. The tribute itself consisted mainly of "precious articles", which meant strange or rare things of no practical value. The emperor made use of them as elements of personal luxury, or made presents of some of them to deserving officials. The gifts offered by the Chinese in return consisted mainly of silk. Silk was received by the government in payment of taxes, and formed an important element of the revenue of the State. It now went abroad, without bringing in any corresponding return. The private trade carried on by the members of the missions was equally unserviceable to the Chinese. It, too, took from them goods of economic value, silk and gold, which went abroad in exchange for luxury articles of little or no economic importance, such as glass, precious stones, or stud horses, which in no way benefited the general population. Thus in this last century B.C. China's economic situation grew steadily and fairly rapidly worse. The peasants, more heavily taxed than ever, were impoverished, and yet the exchequer became not fuller but emptier, so that gold began even to be no longer available for payments.

Already under Wu Ti there had been signs of a development which now appeared constantly in Chinese history. Among the new gentry, families entered into alliances with each other, sealed their mutual allegiance by matrimonial unions, and so formed large cliques. Each clique made it its concern to get the most important government positions into its hands, so that it should itself control the government. Under Wu Ti, for example, almost all the important generals had belonged to a certain clique, which remained dominant under his two successors. Two of the chief means of attaining power were for such a clique to give the emperor a girl from its ranks as wife, and to see to it that all the eunuchs around the emperor should be persons dependent on the clique. Eunuchs came generally from the poorer classes; they were launched at court by members of the great cliques, or quite openly presented to the emperor.

The chief influence of the cliques lay, however, in the selection of officials. In the Han period candidates had to be recommended by the provincial officials. It is not surprising that the officials recommended only sons of people in their own clique—their family or its closest associates. On top of all this, the examiners were in most cases themselves members of the same families to which the provincial officials belonged. Thus it was made doubly certain that only those candidates who were to the liking of the dominant group among the gentry should pass.

Surrounded by these cliques, the emperors became in most cases powerless figureheads. At times energetic rulers were able to play off various cliques against each other, and so to acquire personal power; but the weaker emperors found themselves entirely in the hands of cliques. Not a few emperors in China were removed by cliques which they had attempted to resist; and various dynasties were brought to their end by the cliques; this was the fate of the Han dynasty.

The beginning of its fall came with the activities of the widow of the emperor Yüan Ti. She virtually ruled in the name of her eighteen-year-old son, the emperor Ch'eng Ti (32–7 B.C.), and placed all her brothers, and also her nephew, Wang Mang, in the principal government posts. They succeeded at first in either removing the strongest of the other cliques or bringing them into dependence. Within the Wang family the nephew Wang Mang steadily advanced, securing direct supporters even in some branches of the imperial family; these personages declared their readiness to join him in removing the existing line of the imperial house. When Ch'eng Ti died without issue, a young nephew of his (Ai Ti, 6–1 B.C.) was placed on the throne by Wang Mang, and during this period the power of the Wangs and their allies grew further, until all their opponents had been removed and the influence of the imperial family very greatly reduced. When Ai Ti died, Wang Mang placed an eight-year-old boy on the throne, himself acting as regent; four years later the boy fell ill and died, probably with Wang Mang's aid. Wang Mang now chose a one-year-old baby, but soon after that he felt that the time had come for officially assuming the rulership. In A.D. 8 he dethroned the baby, ostensibly at Heaven's command, and declared himself emperor and first of the Hsin ("new") dynasty. All the members of the old imperial family in the capital were removed from office and degraded to commoners, with the exception of those who had already been supporting Wang Mang. Only those members who held unimportant posts at a distance remained untouched.

6 *The pseudo-socialistic dictatorship. Revolution of the "Red Eyebrows"*

Wang Mang's dynasty lasted only from A.D. 9 to 23; but it was one of the most stirring periods of Chinese history.

He made use of every conceivable resource in order to secure power to his clique. As far as possible he avoided using open force, and he developed a sort of propaganda with which we are only too familiar to-day. Confucianism, the philosophic basis of the power of the gentry, served him as a bait; he made use of the so-called "Old Character school" for his purposes. When, after the holocaust of books, it was desired to collect the ancient classics again, texts were found, under strange circumstances, in the wall of Confucius' house; they were written in an archaic script. The people who occupied themselves with these books were called followers of the Old Character school. The texts came under suspicion; most scholars had little belief in their genuineness. Wang Mang, however, and his creatures energetically supported the cult of these ancient writings. The texts were edited and issued, and in the process, as can now be seen, certain things were smuggled into them that fitted in well with Wang Mang's intentions. He even had other texts reissued with falsifications. He now represented himself in all his actions as a man who did with the utmost precision the things which the books reported of rulers or ministers of ancient times. As regent he had declared that his model was the brother of the first emperor of the Chou dynasty; as emperor he took for his exemplar one of the mythical emperors of ancient China; of his new laws he claimed that they were simply revivals of decrees of the good old time. In all this he appealed to the authority of literature that had been tampered with to suit his aims. Such laws had never before been customary; either Wang Mang completely misinterpreted passages in an ancient text to suit his purpose, or he had dicta that suited him smuggled into the text. There can be no question that Wang Mang and his accomplices began by deliberately falsifying and deceiving. It becomes clear, however, that as time went on he began to believe in his own frauds.

Wang Mang's great series of laws has brought him the name of "the first Socialist on the throne of China". But closer consideration reveals that these measures, ostensibly aimed at the good especially of the poor, were in reality devised simply in order to fill the imperial exchequer and to consolidate the imperial power. When we read of the turning over of great landed estates to the State, do we not imagine that we are faced with a modern land reform? But this applied only to the wealthiest of all the landowners, who were to be deprived in this way of their power; the prohibition of private slave-owning had a similar purpose, the State reserving to itself the right to keep slaves. Moreover, landless peasants were to receive land to till, at the expense of those who possessed too much. This admirable law, however, was not intended to be seriously carried into effect, but the setting up of a system of State credits for peasants held out the promise, in spite of rather reduced interest rates, of important revenue. The peasants were never in a position to pay back their debts together with the usurious interest, but there were at least opportunities of coming to terms with a private usurer, whereas the State proved a merciless creditor. It could dispossess the peasant, and either turn his property into a communal farm, convey it to another owner, or make the peasant a State slave. Thus this measure worked against the interest of the peasants, as did the State monopoly of the exploitation of mountains and lakes. "Mountains and lakes" meant the uncultivated land around settlements, where the poorest people collected firewood or went fishing. They now had to pay money for fishing rights and for the right to collect wood—money for the emperor's exchequer. The same purpose lay behind the wine, salt, and iron tool monopolies. Enormous revenues came to the State from the monopoly of minting coin. Old metal coin of full value was called in and exchanged for debased coin. Another modern-sounding institution, that of the "equalization offices", was supposed to buy cheap goods in times of plenty, in order to sell them to the people in times of scarcity at similarly low prices, so preventing want and also preventing excessive price fluctuations. In actual fact these State offices formed a new source of profit, buying cheaply and selling as dearly as possible.

Thus the character of these laws was in no way socialistic; nor did they provide an El Dorado for the State finances, for Wang Mang's officials turned all the laws to their private advantage. The revenues rarely reached the capital; they vanished into the pockets of the subordinate officials. The result was a further serious lowering of the level of existence of the peasant population, with no addition to the financial resources of the State. Yet Wang Mang had great need of money, because he attached importance to display and because he was planning a new war. He aimed at the final destruction of the Hsiung Nu, so that access to central Asia should no longer be precarious and it should thus be possible to reduce the expense of the military administration of Turkestan. The war would also distract popular attention from the troubles at home. By way of preparation for war, Wang Mang sent a mission to the Hsiung Nu with dishonouring proposals, including a change in the name of the Hsiung Nu and in the title of the *shan-yü*. The name Hsiung Nu was to be given the insulting change to Hsiang Nu, meaning "subjugated slaves". The result was that risings of the Hsiung Nu took place. On this Wang Mang commanded that the whole of their country should be partitioned among fifteen *shan-yü*, and declared the country to be a Chinese province. Since this declaration had no practical result, it robbed Wang Mang of the increased prestige he had sought, and only further infuriated the Hsiung Nu. Wang Mang concentrated a vast army on the frontier. Meanwhile he lost the whole of the possessions in Turkestan.

But before Wang Mang's campaign against the Hsiung Nu could begin, the difficulties at home grew steadily worse. In A.D. 12 Wang Mang was reduced to abrogating all his reform legislation because it could not be carried into effect; and the economic situation proved more lamentable than ever. There were continual risings, which culminated in A.D. 18 in a great popular insurrection, a genuine revolutionary rising of the peasants, whose distress had grown beyond bearing through Wang Mang's ill-judged measures. The rebels called themselves "Red

Eyebrows"; they had painted their eyebrows red by way of badge and in order to bind their members indissolubly to their movement. The nucleus of this rising was a secret society. Such secret societies, usually led by large farmers, have existed in China down to the present day. In times of peace they are harmless, rather resembling the free-masons' lodges of Europe. But in emergency they may become an immensely effective instrument in the hands of the rural population. The secret societies then organize the peasants, in order to achieve a forcible settlement of the matter in dispute. Often, however, the movement grows far beyond its leaders' original objective, and becomes a popular revolutionary movement, directed against the whole ruling class. That is what happened on this occasion. Vast swarms of peasants marched on the capital, killing all officials and people of position on their way. The troops sent against them by Wang Mang either went over to the Red Eyebrows or copied them, plundering wherever they could and killing officials. Owing to the appalling mass murders and the fighting, the forces placed by Wang Mang along the frontier against the Hsiung Nu received no reinforcements, and, instead of attacking the Hsiung Nu, themselves went over to plundering, so that ultimately the army simply disintegrated. Fortunately for China, the *shan-yü* of the time did not take advantage of his opportunity, perhaps because the position within the Hsiung Nu empire was too insecure.

Scarcely had the popular rising begun when descendants of the deposed Han dynasty appeared and tried to secure the support of the upper class. They came forward as fighters against the usurper Wang Mang and as defenders of the old social order against the revolutionary masses. But the armies which these Han princes were able to collect were no better than those of the other sides. They, too, consisted of poor and hungry peasants, whose aim was to get money or goods by robbery; they, too, plundered and murdered more than they fought.

One prince, however, Liu Hsiu, gradually gained the upper hand. The prince's party conquered the capital,

Wang Mang, placing entire faith in his sanctity, did not flee; he sat in his robes in the throne-room and recited the ancient writings, convinced that he would overcome his adversaries by the power of his words. But a soldier cut off his head (A.D. 22). The skull was kept for two hundred years in the imperial treasury. The fighting, however, went on. Various branches of the prince's party fought one another, and all of them fought the Red Eyebrows. In those years millions of men came to their end. Finally, in A.D. 24, Liu Hsiu prevailed, becoming the first emperor of the second Han dynasty, also called the Later Han dynasty; his name as emperor was Kuang Wu Ti. (A.D. 25–57).

7 *Reaction and Restoration: the Later Han dynasty*

Within the country the period that followed was one of reaction and restoration. The massacres of the preceding years had so reduced the population that there was land enough for the peasants who remained alive. Moreover, their lords, and the moneylenders of the towns, were generally no longer alive, so that many peasants had become free of debt. The government was transferred from Sian to Loyang, in the present province of Honan. This brought it nearer the great corn-producing regions, so that the transport of corn and other taxes in kind to the capital was cheapened. Soon this cleared foundation was covered by a new stratum, a very sparse one, of great landowners—supporters and members of the new imperial house, largely descendants of the landowners of the earlier Han period. At first they were not much in evidence, but they gained power more and more rapidly. In spite of this, the first half-century of the Later Han period was one of good conditions on the land and economic recovery.

8 *Hsiung Nu policy*

In foreign policy the first period of the Later Han dynasty was one of extraordinary success, both in the extreme south and in the question of the Hsiung Nu. During the period of Wang Mang's rule and the fighting connected with it, there had been extensive migration to the south and south-west. Considerable regions of Chinese settlement had come into existence in Yunnan and even in Annam and Tongking, and a series of campaigns under General Ma Yüan now added these regions to the territory of the empire. These wars were carried on with relatively small forces, as previously in the Canton region, the natives being unable to offer serious resistance owing to their inferiority in equipment and civilization. The hot climate, however, to which the Chinese soldiers were unused, was hard for them to endure.

The Hsiung Nu, in spite of internal difficulties, had regained considerable influence in Turkestan during the reign of Wang Mang. But the king of the city-State of Yarkand had increased his power by shrewdly playing off Chinese and Hsiung Nu against each other, so that before long he was able to attack the Hsiung Nu. The small states in Turkestan, however, regarded the overlordship of the distant China as preferable to that of Yarkand or the Hsiung Nu, both of whom, being nearer, were able to bring their power more effectively into play. Accordingly many of the small States appealed for Chinese aid. Kuang Wu Ti met this appeal with a blank refusal, on the ground that order had only just been restored in China, and he now simply had not the resources for a campaign in Turkestan. Thus the king of Yarkand was able to extend his power over the remainder of the small States of Turkestan, since the Hsiung Nu had been obliged to withdraw. Kuang Wu Ti had had several frontier wars with the Hsiung Nu without any decisive result. But in the years around A.D. 45 the Hsiung Nu had suffered several severe droughts and also great plagues of locusts, so that they had lost a large part of their cattle. They were no longer able to assert themselves in Turkestan and at the same time to fight the Chinese in the south and the Hsien Pi and the Wu Huan in the east. These two peoples, apparently largely of Mongol origin, had been subject in the past to Hsiung Nu overlordship. They had spread steadily in the territories bordering Manchuria and Mongolia, beyond the eastern frontier of the Hsiung Nu empire. Living there in relative peace and at the same time in possession of very fertile pasturage, these two peoples had grown in strength. And since the great political collapse of 58 B.C. the Hsiung Nu had not only lost their best pasturage in the north of the provinces of Shensi and Shansi, but had largely grown used to living in co-operation with the Chinese. They had become much more accustomed to trade with China, exchanging animals for textiles and grain, than to warfare, so that in the end they were defeated by the Hsien Pi and Wu Huan, who had held to the older form of purely war-like nomad life. Weakened by famine and by the wars against Wu Huan and Hsien Pi, the Hsiung Nu split into two, one section withdrawing to the north.

The southern Hsiung Nu were compelled to submit to the Chinese in order to gain security from their other enemies. Thus the Chinese were able to gain a great success without moving a finger: the Hsiung Nu, who for centuries had shown themselves again and again to be the most dangerous enemies of China, were reduced to political insignificance. About a hundred years earlier the Hsiung Nu empire had suffered defeat; now half of what remained of it became part of the Chinese State. Its place was taken by the Hsien Pi and Wu Huan, but at first they were of much less importance.

In spite of the partition, the northern Hsiung Nu attempted in the years between A.D. 60 and 70 to regain a sphere of influence in Turkestan; this seemed the easier for them since the king of Yarkand had been captured and murdered, and Turkestan was more or less in a state of confusion. The Chinese did their utmost to play off the northern against the southern Hsiung Nu, and to maintain a political balance of power in the west and north. So long as there were a number of small States in Turkestan, of which at least some were friendly to China, Chinese trade caravans suffered relatively little disturbance on their journeys. Independent States in Turkestan had proved more profitable for trade than when a large army of occupation had to be maintained there. When, however, there appeared to be a danger of a new union of the two parts of the Hsiung Nu and so the restoration of a large empire, which would also comprise all Turkestan, the Chinese trading monopoly was endangered. Any great power would secure the best goods for itself, and there would be no good business remaining for China.

For these reasons a great Chinese campaign was undertaken against Turkestan in A.D. 73 under Tou Ku. Mainly owing to the ability of the Chinese deputy commander Pan Ch'ao, the whole of Turkestan was quickly conquered. Meanwhile the emperor Ming Ti (A.D. 58–75) had died, and under the new emperor Chang Ti (76–88) the "isolationist" party gained the upper hand against the clique of Tou Ku and Pan Ch'ao: the danger of the restoration of a Hsiung Nu empire, the isolationists contended, no longer existed; Turkestan should be left to itself, and the small States would favour trade with China of their own accord. Meanwhile, a considerable part of Turkestan had fallen away from China, for Chang Ti sent neither money nor troops to hold the conquered territories. Pan Ch'ao nevertheless remained in Turkestan (at Kashgar and Khotan), where he held on amid countless difficulties. Although he reported (A.D. 78) that the troops could feed themselves in Turkestan and needed neither supplies nor money from home, no reinforcements of any importance were sent; only a few hundred or perhaps a thousand men, mostly released criminals, reached him. Not until A.D. 89 did the Pan Ch'ao clique return to power, when the mother of the young emperor Ho Ti (89–105) took over the government during his minority: she was a member of the family of Tou Ku. She was interested in bringing to a successful conclusion the enterprise which had been started by members of her family and its followers. Accordingly, a campaign was started in 89 under her brother against the northern Hsiung Nu, and it decided the fate of Turkestan in China's favour. Turkestan remained firmly in Chinese possession until the death of Pan Ch'ao in 102. Shortly afterwards heavy fighting broke out again: the Tanguts advanced from the south in an attempt to cut off Chinese access to Turkestan. The Chinese drove back the Tanguts and maintained their hold on Turkestan, though no longer absolutely.

9 *Economic situation. Revolution of the "Yellow Turbans". Collapse of the Han dynasty*

The economic results of the Turkestan trade in this period were not so unfavourable as in the earlier Han period. The army of occupation was incomparably smaller, and under Pan Ch'ao's policy the soldiers were fed and paid in Turkestan itself, so that the cost to China remained small. Moreover, the drain on the national income was no longer serious, because in the intervening period regular Chinese settlements had been planted in Turkestan, with Chinese merchants, so that the trade no longer remained entirely in the hands of foreigners.

In spite of the economic consolidation at the beginning of the Later Han dynasty, and in spite of the more balanced trade, the political situation within China steadily worsened from A.D. 80 onwards. Although the class of great landowners was small, a number of cliques formed within it, and their mutual struggle for power soon went beyond the limits of court intrigue. New actors now came upon this stage, the eunuchs. With the economic improvement there had been a general increase in the luxury at the court of the Han emperors, and the court steadily increased in size. The many hundred wives and concubines in the palace made necessary a great army of eunuchs. As they had the ear of the emperor and so could influence him, the eunuchs formed an important political factor. For a time the main struggle was between the group of eunuchs and the group of scholars. The eunuchs served a particular clique, to which some of the emperor's wives belonged. The scholars, that is to say the Ministers, together with members of the ministries and the administrative staff, served the interests of another clique. The struggles grew more and more sanguinary in the middle of the second century A.D. It soon proved that the group with the firmest hold in the provinces had the advantage, because it was not easy to control the provinces from a distance. The result was that from about A.D. 150 events at court steadily lost importance, the lead being taken by the generals commanding the provincial troops. It would carry us too far to give the details of all these struggles. The principal generals were at first Ts'ao Ts'ao, Lü Pu, Yüan Shao, and Sun Ts'ê; later came Liu Pei. All were striving to gain control of the government, and all were engaged in mutual hostilities from about 180 onwards. Each general was also trying to get the emperor into his hands. Several times the last emperor of the Later Han dynasty, Hsien Ti (190–220), was captured by one or another of the generals. As the successful general was usually unable to maintain his hold on the capital, he dragged the poor emperor with him from place to place until he finally had to give him up to another general. The point of this chase after the emperor was that according to the ideas then current the first ruler of a new dynasty had to receive the imperial seals from the last emperor of the previous dynasty. The last emperor must abdicate in proper form. Accordingly each general had to get possession of the emperor to begin with, in order at the proper time to take over the seals.

By about A.D. 200 the new conditions had more or less crystallized. There remained only three great parties. The most powerful was that of Ts'ao Ts'ao, who controlled the north and was able to keep permanent hold of the emperor. In the west, in the province of Szechwan, Liu Pei had established himself, and in the south-east Sun Ts'ê's brother.

But we must not limit our view to these generals' struggles. At this time there were two other series of events of equal importance with those. The incessant struggles of the cliques against each other continued at the expense of the people, who had to fight them and pay for them. Thus after A.D. 150 the distress of the country population grew beyond all limits. Conditions were as disastrous as in the time of Wang Mang. And once more, as then, a popular movement broke out, that of the so-called "Yellow Turbans". This was the first of the two important events. This popular movement had a characteristic which from now on was typical of all these risings of the people. The intellectual leaders of the movement were members of a particular religious sect. This time they were leaders of the popular Taoism, that is to say, a sort of shamans who for nearly two hundred years had formed secret societies in the coastal regions of China and had organized the worship of the peasantry in little old temples. These priests of the people were instinctively opposed to the representatives of the official religion, that is to say the officials drawn from the gentry. In small towns and villages the temples of the gods of the fruits of the field, of the soil, and so on, were administered by the authorized local officials, and the officials also carried out the prescribed sacrifices. The old temples of the people were either done away with (we have many edicts of the Han period concerning the abolition of popular forms of religious worship), or their worship was converted into an official cult: the all-powerful gentry extended their domination over religion as well as all else. The peasants regarded these exponents of the popular Taoism as their natural leaders against the gentry and their forms of religion. The rising of the Yellow Turbans began in 184; all parties, cliques and generals alike, were equally afraid of the revolutionaries, since these were a threat to the gentry as such, and so to all parties. Consequently a combined army of considerable size was got together and sent against the rebels. The Yellow Turbans were beaten. During these struggles it became evident that Ts'ao Ts'ao with his troops had become the strongest of all the generals. His troops seem, however, to have consisted not of Chinese soldiers alone, but also of Hsiung Nu. It is understandable that the annals say nothing about this, and it can only be inferred from the facts. It appears that in order to reinforce their armies the generals recruited not only Chinese but foreigners. The generals operating in the region of the present-day Peking had soldiers of the Wu Huan and Hsien Pi, and even of the Ting Ling; Liu Pei, in the west, made use of Tanguts, and Ts'ao Ts'ao clearly went farthest of all in this direction; he seems to have been responsible for settling nineteen tribes of Hsiung Nu in the Chinese province of Shansi between 180 and 200, in return for their armed aid. In this way Ts'ao Ts'ao gained permanent power in the empire by means of these troops, so that immediately after his death his son Ts'ao P'ei, with the support of powerful allied families, was able to force the emperor to abdicate and to found a new dynasty, the Wei dynasty (A.D. 220).

This meant, however, that a part of China which for several centuries had been Chinese was given up to the Hsiung Nu. This was not, of course, what Ts'ao Ts'ao had intended; he had given the Hsiung Nu some areas of pasturage in Shansi with the idea that they should be controlled and administered by the officials of the surrounding districts. His plan had been similar to what the Chinese had often done with success: aliens were admitted into the territory of the empire in a body, but then the influence of the surrounding administrative centres was steadily extended over them, until the immigrants completely lost their own nationality and became Chinese. The nineteen tribes of Hsiung Nu, however, were much too numerous, and after the prolonged struggles in China the provincial administration proved much too weak to be able to carry out the plan. Thus there came into existence here, within China, a small Hsiung Nu realm ruled by several *shan-yü*. This was the second major development, and it became of the utmost importance to the history of the next four centuries.

10 *Literature and Art*

With the development of the new class of the gentry in the Han period, there was an increase in the number of those who were anxious to participate in what had been in the past an exclusively aristocratic possession—education. Thus it is by no mere chance that in this period many encyclopaedias were compiled. Encyclopaedias convey knowledge in an easily grasped and easily found form. The first compilation of this sort dates from the third century B.C. It was the work of Lü Pu-wei, the merchant prince who was prime minister and regent during the minority of Shih Huang Ti. It contains general information concerning ceremonies, customs, historic events, and other things the knowledge of which was part of a general education. Soon afterwards other encyclopaedias appeared, of which the best known is the "Book of the Mountains and Seas" (*Shan-hai-King*). This book, arranged according to regions of the world, contains everything known at the time about geography, natural philosophy, and the animal and plant world, and also about popular myths. This tendency to systemization is shown also in the historical works. The famous *Shih Chi*, one of our main sources for Chinese history, is the first historical work of the modern type, that is to say, built up on a definite plan, and it was also the model for all later official historiography. Its author, Ssŭ-ma Ch'ien, and his father made use of the material in the State archives and of private documents, old historical and philosophical books, inscriptions, and the results of their own travels. The philosophical and historical books of earlier times (with the exception of those of the nature of annals) consisted merely of a few dicta or reports of particular events, but the *Shih Chi* is a compendium of a mass of source-material. The documents were abbreviated, but the text of the extracts was altered as little as possible, so that the general result retains in a sense the value of an original source. In its arrangement the *Shih Chi* became a model for all later historians: the first part is in the form of annals, and there follow tables concerning the occupation of official posts and fiefs, and then biographies of various important personalities, though the type of the comprehensive biography did not appear till later. The *Shih Chi* also, like the later historical works, contains many monographs dealing with particular fields of knowledge, such as astronomy, the calendar, music, economics, official dress at court, and much else. The whole type of construction differs fundamentally from such works as those of Thucydides or Herodotus. The Chinese historical works have the advantage that the section of annals gives at once the events of a particular year, the monographs describe the development of a particular field of knowledge, and the biographical section offers information concerning particular personalities. The mental attitude is that of the gentry: shortly after the time of Ssŭ-ma Ch'ien an historical department was founded, in which members of the gentry worked as historians upon the documents prepared by representatives of the gentry in the government offices.

In addition to encyclopaedias and historical works, many books of philosophy were written in the Han period, but most of them offer no fundamentally new ideas. They were the product of the leisure of rich members of the gentry, and only three of them are of importance. One is the work of Tung Chung-shu, already mentioned. The second is the book by Liu An called *Huai-nan Tzŭ*. Prince Liu An occupied himself with Taoism and allied problems, gathered around him scholars of different schools, and carried on discussions with them. Many of his writings are lost, but enough is extant to show that he was one of the earliest Chinese alchemists. The question has not yet been settled, but it is probable that alchemy first appeared in China, together with the cult of the "art" of prolonging life, and was later carried to the West, where it flourished among the Arabs and in medieval Europe.

The third important book of the Han period was the *Lun Hêng* ("Critique of Opinions") of Wang Ch'ung, which appeared in the first century of the Christian era. Wang Ch'ung advocated rational thinking, and tried to pave the way for a free natural science, in continuation of the beginnings which the natural philosophers of the later Chou period had made. The book analyses reports in ancient literature and customs of daily life, and shows how much they were influenced by superstition and by ignorance of the facts of nature. From this attitude a modern science might have developed, as in Europe toward the end of the Middle Ages; but the gentry had every reason to suppress this tendency, which, with its criticism of all that was traditional, might have proceeded to an attack on the dominance of the gentry and their oppression especially of the merchants and artisans. It is fascinating to observe how it was the needs of the merchants and seafarers of Asia Minor and Greece that provided the stimulus for the growth of the classic sciences, and how on the contrary the growth of Chinese science was stifled because the gentry were so strongly hostile to commerce and navigation, though both had always existed.

There were great literary innovations in the field of poetry. The splendour and elegance at the new imperial court of the Han dynasty attracted many poets, who sang the praises of the emperor and his court and were given official posts and dignities. These praises were in the form of grandiloquent, overloaded poetry, full of strange similes and allusions, but with little real feeling. The many women singers and dancers at the court, mostly slaves from southern China, introduced at the court southern Chinese forms of song and poem, which were soon adopted and elaborated by poets. Poems and dance songs were composed which belonged to the finest that Chinese poetry can show—full of natural feeling, simple in language, moving in content.

Our knowledge of the plastic arts is drawn from two sources—literature, and the actual discoveries in the excavations. Thus we know that most of the painting was done on silk, of which plenty came into the market through the control of silk-producing southern China. Paper manufacture had meanwhile been introduced in the second century B.C., and brushes and china-ink came into use. Unfortunately nothing remains of the actual works that were the first examples of what the Chinese everywhere were beginning to call "art". "People", that is to say the gentry, painted as a social pastime, just as they assembled together for poetry, discussion, or performances of song and dance; they painted as an aesthetic pleasure and never as a means of earning. We find philosophic ideas or greetings, emotions, and experiences represented by pictures—pictures with fanciful or ideal landscapes; pictures representing the life and the environment of the cultured class in idealized form, never naturalistic either in fact or in intention. Until recently it was an indispensable condition in the Chinese view that an artist must be "cultured" and also a member of the gentry—distinguished, unoccupied, wealthy. Thus the painting that existed in China before the formation of the class of the gentry, especially the portrait-painting, was not regarded as art, but as the product of "painting workers", that is to say, craftsmen. Of this portrait-painting only literary evidence remains. We do possess, however, many of the works of other "craftsmen", which undoubtedly belong to the realm of art. In the tombs have been found reliefs whose technique is generally intermediate between simple outline engraving and intaglio. The lining-in is most frequently executed in scratched lines. The representations, mostly in strips placed one above another, are of lively historical scenes, scenes from the life of the dead, great ritual ceremonies, or adventurous scenes from mythology. Bronze vessels have representations in inlaid gold and silver, mostly of animals. The most important documents of the painting of the Han period consist of wooden tiles from tombs. We see especially ladies and gentlemen of society, with richly ornamented, elegant, expensive clothing that is very reminiscent of the clothing customary to this day in Japan. There are also artistic representations of human figures on lacquer caskets. These first evidences of the plastic arts in China show already such a degree of refinement that they must have been preceded by a considerable period of development.

With the end of the Han period a further epoch of Chinese history comes to its close. The Han period was that of the final completion and consolidation of the social order of the gentry. The period that followed was that of the conflicts of the Chinese with the populations on their northern borders.

Chapter VII

THE EPOCH OF THE FIRST DIVISION OF CHINA (A.D. 220-580)

(A) The three kingdoms (220-265)

1 *Sociological, intellectual, and economic problems during the first division*

The end of the Han period was followed by the three and a half centuries of the first division of China into several kingdoms, each with its own dynasty.[1] At the outset (220–280) there were three kingdoms (Wei, Wu, Shu Han); then came an unstable reunion during twenty-seven years (280–307) under the rule of the Western Chin. This was followed by a still sharper division between north and south: while a wave of non-Chinese nomad dynasties poured over the north, in the south one Chinese clique after another seized power, so that dynasty followed dynasty, until finally, in 580, a united China came again into existence, adopting the culture of the north and the traditions of the gentry.

This period from 220 to 580 cannot be simply dismissed as a "transition period", as was usually done by the older European works on China. The social order of the gentry, whose birth and development inside China we followed, had for the first time to defend itself against views and

[1] Sociologically regarded, the Chinese Middle Ages begin with the Han period, with the formation of the gentry-State, and end about the thirteenth century with the first appearance of a new class, the middle class of the towns. Politically, the Middle Ages divide into the following four periods: (a) the unified empire of the Han (Chapter VI, 206 B.C.-A.D. 220); (b) the period of the first division of China (Chapter VII, 220-580); (c) the unified empire of the Sui and T'ang (Chapter VIII, 580-906); (d) the period of the second division of China (Chapter IX, 907-1279). The division into periods hitherto customary did not treat the last period as a unit, but treated the decades of the "Five Dynasties" (907-960) as a transition stage and the Sung period (960-1279) as a continuation of the unified empire; the realms of the Kitan and the Djurdjen in the north were regarded as realms outside China.

systems entirely opposed to it; for the Turkish and Mongol peoples who ruled northern China brought with them their traditions of a feudal nobility with privileges of birth and all that they implied. Thus this period, socially regarded, is especially that of the struggle between the Chinese gentry and the northern nobility, the gentry being excluded at first as a direct political factor in the northern and more important part of China. In the south the gentry continued in the old style with a constant struggle between cliques, the only difference being that the class assumed a sort of "colonial" character through the formation of gigantic estates and through association with the merchant class.

To throw light on the scale of events, we need to have figures of population. There are no figures for the years around A.D. 220, and we must make do with those of 140; but in order to show the relative strength of the three States it is the ratio between the figures that matters. In 140 the regions which later belonged to Wei had roughly 29,000,000 inhabitants; those later belonging to Wu had 11,700,000; those which belonged later to Shu Han had a bare 7,500,000. (The figures take no account of the primitive native population, which was not yet included in the taxation lists.) The Hsiung Nu formed only a small part of the population, as there were only the nineteen tribes which had abandoned one of the parts, already reduced, of the Hsiung Nu empire. The whole Hsiung Nu empire at its zenith, under Mao Tun, had counted only some 3,000,000. At the time when the population of what became the Wei territory totalled 29,000,000 the capital with its immediate environment had over a million inhabitants. The figure is exclusive of most of the officials and soldiers, as these were taxable in their homes and so were counted there. It is clear that this was a disproportionate concentration round the capital.

It was at this time that both South and North China felt the influence of Buddhism, which had penetrated into China both by land and by sea in the first century B.C., but until A.D. 220 had no more real effect on China than the penetration of European civilization had between 1580 and 1842. Buddhism offered new notions, new ideals, foreign science, and many other elements of culture, with which the old Chinese philosophy and science had to contend. At the same time there came with Buddhism the first direct knowledge of the great civilized countries west of China. Until then China had been regarded as the only existing civilized country, and all other countries had been regarded as barbaric, for a civilized country was then taken to mean a country with urban industry and agriculture. In our present period, however, China's relations with the Middle East and with southern Asia were so close that the existence of civilized countries outside China had to be admitted. And when alien dynasties ruled in northern China and a new high civilization came into existence there, it was impossible to speak of its rulers as barbarians any longer. Even the theory that the Chinese emperor was the Son of Heaven and enthroned at the centre of the world was no longer tenable. Thus a vast widening of China's intellectual horizon took place.

Economically, our present period witnessed an adjustment in South China between the purely Chinese way of life, which had penetrated from the north, and that of the natives of the south. Large groups of Chinese had to turn over from wheat culture in dry fields to rice culture in wet fields, and from field culture to market gardening. In North China the conflict went on between Chinese agriculture and the cattle breeding of Central Asia. Was the will of the ruler to prevail and North China to become a country of pasturage, or was the country to keep to the agrarian tradition of the people under this rule? The Turkish and Mongol conquerers had recently given up their old supplementary agriculture, and had turned again into pure nomads, obtaining the agricultural produce they needed by raiding or trade. The conquerors of North China were now faced with a different question: if they were to remain nomads, they must either drive the peasants into the south, or make them into slave herdsmen, or exterminate them. There was one more possibility: they might install themselves as a ruling upper class, as nobles over the subjugated native peasants. The same question

3 Bronze plaque representing two horses fighting each other. Ordos region, animal style.

From V. Griessmaier, *Sammlung Baron Eduard von der Heydt, Vienna* 1936, *illustration no*. 6.

4 Hunting scene: detail from the reliefs in the tombs at Wu-liang-tz'u.

From a print in the author's possession.

5 Part of the 'Great Wall'.
Photo Eberhard.

was faced much later by the Mongols, and at first they answered it differently from the peoples of our present period. Only by attention to this problem shall we be in a position to explain why the rule of the Turkish peoples did not last, why these peoples were gradually absorbed and disappeared.

2 *Status of the two southern Kingdoms*

When the last emperor of the Han period had to abdicate in favour of Ts'ao P'ei, and the Wei dynasty began, China was in no way a unified realm. Almost immediately, in 221, two other army commanders, who had long been independent, declared themselves emperors. In the south-west of China, in the present province of Szechwan, the Shu Han dynasty was founded in this way, and in the south-east, in the region of the present Nanking, the Wu dynasty.

The situation of the southern kingdom of Shu Han (221–263) corresponded more or less to that of the Chungking régime in the second World War. West of it the high Tibetan mountains towered up; there was very little reason to fear any major attack from that direction. In the north and east the realm was also protected by difficult mountain country. The south lay relatively open, but at that time there were no Chinese living there, but only natives with a relatively low civilization. The kingdom could only be seriously attacked from two corners—through the north-west, where there was a negotiable plateau, between the Ch'in-ling mountains in the north and the Tibetan mountains in the west, a plateau inhabited by fairly highly developed Tibetan tribes; and through the south-east corner, where it would be possible to penetrate up the Yangtze. There was in fact incessant fighting at both the dangerous corners.

Economically, Shu Han was not in a bad position. The country had long been part of the Chinese wheat lands, and had a fairly large Chinese peasant population in the plain of Chengtu. There was also a wealthy merchant class, supplying grain to the surrounding mountain peoples and buying medicaments and other profitable Tibetan products. And there were trade routes from here through the present province of Yunnan to India.

Shu Han's difficulty was that its population was not large enough to be able to stand against the northern State of Wei; moreover, it was difficult to carry out an offensive from Shu Han, though the country could defend itself well. The first attempt to find a remedy was a campaign against the native tribes of the present Yunnan. The purpose of this was to secure man-power for the army, and also slaves for sale; for the south-west had for centuries been a main source for traffic in slaves. Finally it was hoped to gain control over the trade to India. All these things were intended to strengthen Shu Han internally, but in spite of certain military successes they produced no practical result, as the Chinese were unable in the long run to endure the climate or to hold out against the guerrilla tactics of the natives. Shu Han tried to buy the assistance of the Tibetans and with their aid to carry out a decisive attack on Wei, whose dynastic legitimacy was not recognized by Shu Han. The ruler of Shu Han claimed to be a member of the imperial family of the deposed Han dynasty, and therefore to be the rightful, legitimate ruler over China. His descent, however, was a little doubtful, and in any case it depended on a link far back in the past. Against this the Wei of the north declared that the last ruler of the Han dynasty had handed over to them with all due form the seals of the State and therewith the imperial prerogative. The controversy was of no great practical importance, but it played a big part in the Chinese Legalist school until the twelfth century, and contributed largely to a revision of the old conceptions of legitimacy.

The political plans of Shu Han were well considered and far-seeing. They were evolved by the premier, a man from Shantung named Chu-ko Liang; for the ruler died in 226 and his successor was still a child. But Chu-ko Liang lived only for a further eight years, and after his death in 234 the decline of Shu Han began. Its political leaders no longer had a sense of what was possible. Thus

Wei inflicted several defeats on Shu Han, and finally subjugated it in 263.

The situation of the State of Wu was much less favourable than that of Shu Han, though this second southern kingdom lasted from 221 to 280. Its country consisted of marshy, water-logged plains, or mountains with narrow valleys. Here Tai peoples had long cultivated their rice, while in the mountains Yao tribes lived by the chase and by simple denshiring. Peasants immigrating from the north found that their wheat and pulse did not thrive here: they had slowly to gain familiarity with rice cultivation. They were also compelled to give up their sheep and cattle and in their place to breed pigs and water buffaloes, as was done by the former inhabitants of the country. The lower class of the population was mainly non-Chinese; above it was an upper class of Chinese, at first relatively small, consisting of officials, soldiers, and merchants in a few towns and administrative centres. The country was poor, and its only important economic asset was the trade in metals, timber, and other southern products; soon there came also a growing overseas trade with India and the Middle East, bringing revenues to the State in so far as the goods were re-exported from Wu to the north.

Wu never attempted to conquer the whole of China, but endeavoured to consolidate its own difficult territory with a view to building up a State on a firm foundation. In general, Wu played mainly a passive part in the incessant struggles between the three kingdoms, though it was active in diplomacy. The Wu kingdom entered into relations with a man who in 232 had gained control of the present South Manchuria and shortly afterwards assumed the title of king. This new ruler of "Yen", as he called his kingdom, had determined to attack the Wei dynasty, and hoped, by putting pressure on it in association with Wu, to overrun Wei from north and south. Wei answered this plan by recourse to diplomacy, and very effectively. It began by arranging that Wu should have reason to fear an attack from its western neighbour Shu Han. A mission was also dispatched from Wei to negotiate with Japan.

Japan was then emerging from its stone age and introducing metals; there were countless small principalities and States, of which the State of Yamato, then ruled by a queen, was the most powerful. Yamato had certain interests in Korea, where it already ruled a small coastal strip in the east. Wei offered Yamato the prospect of gaining the whole of Korea if it would turn against the State of Yen in South Manchuria. Wu, too, had turned to Japan, but the negotiations came to nothing, since Wu, as an ally of Yen, had nothing to offer. The queen of Yamato accordingly sent a mission to Wei; she had already decided in favour of that State. Thus Wei was able to embark on war against Yen, which it annihilated in 237. This wrecked Wu's diplomatic projects, and no more was heard of any ambitious plans of the kingdom of Wu.

The two southern States had a common characteristic: both were condottiere States, not built up from their own population but conquered by generals from the north and ruled for a time by those generals and their northern troops. Natives gradually entered these northern armies and reduced their percentage of northerners, but a gulf remained between the native population, including its gentry, and the alien military rulers. This reduced the striking power of the southern States.

On the other hand, this period had its positive element. For the first time there was an emperor in South China, with all the organization that implied. A capital full of officials, eunuchs, and all the satellites of an imperial court provided incentives to economic advance, because it represented a huge supply market. The peasants around it were able to increase their sales and grew prosperous. The increased demand resulted in an increase of tillage and a thriving trade. Soon the transport problem had to be faced, as long ago in the north, and new means of transport, especially ships, were provided, and new trade routes opened, to last far longer than the three kingdoms; on the other hand, all this involved fresh taxation burdens for the population, to cover the costs of transport. The skilled staff needed for the business of administration came into the new capital from the surrounding districts, for the conquerers and new rulers of the territory of the two southern dynasties had brought with them from the north only uneducated soldiers and almost equally uneducated officers. The influx of scholars and administrators into the chief cities produced cultural and economic centres in the south, a circumstance of great importance to China's later development.

3 *The northern State of Wei*

The situation in the north, in the State of Wei (220–265) was anything but rosy. Wei ruled what at that time were the most important and richest regions of China, the plain of Shensi in the west and the great plain east of Loyang, the two most thickly populated areas of China. But the events of the end of the Han period had inflicted great economic injury on the country. The southern and southwestern parts of the Han empire had been lost, and though parts of Central Asia still gave allegiance to Wei, these, as in the past, were economically more of a burden than an asset, because they called for incessant expenditure. At least the trade caravans were able to travel undisturbed from and to China through Turkestan. Moreover, the Wei kingdom, although much smaller than the empire of the Han, maintained an undiminished court, at great expense, because the rulers, claiming to rule the whole of China, felt bound to display more magnificence than the rulers of the southern dynasties. They had also to reward the nineteen tribes of the Hsiung Nu in the north for their military aid, not only with cessions of land but with payments of money. Finally, they would not disarm, but maintained great armies for the continual fighting against the southern States. The Wei dynasty did not succeed, however, in closely subordinating the various army commanders to the central government. Thus the commanders, in collusion with groups of the gentry, were able to enrich themselves and to secure regional power. The inadequate strength of the central government of Wei was further undermined by the rivalries among the dominant gentry.

The imperial family (Ts'ao Pei, who reigned from 220 to 226, had taken as emperor the name of Wen Ti) was descended from one of the groups of great landowners that had formed in the later Han period. The nucleus of that group was a family named Ts'ui, of which there is mention from the Han period onward, and which maintained its power down to the tenth century; but it remained in the background and at first held entirely aloof from direct intervention in high policy. Another family belonging to this group was the Hsia-hou family, which was closely united to the family of Wen Ti by adoption; and very soon there was also the Ssŭ-ma family. Quite naturally Wen Ti, as soon as he came into power, made provision for the members of these powerful families, for he had only been able to ascend the throne, and to maintain his hold on the throne, thanks to their support. Thus we find many members of the Hsia-hou and Ssŭ-ma families in government positions. The Ssŭ-ma family especially showed great activity, and at the end of Wen Ti's reign their power had so grown that a certain Ssŭ-ma I was in control of the government, while the new emperor, Ming Ti (227–233), was completely powerless. This virtually sealed the fate of the Wei dynasty, so far as the dynastic family was concerned. The next emperor was installed and deposed by the Ssŭ-ma family; dissensions arose within the ruling family, leading to members of the family assassinating one another. In 264 a member of the Ssŭ-ma family declared himself king; when he died and was succeeded by his son Ssŭ-ma Yen, the latter, in 265, staged a formal act of renunciation of the throne of the Wei dynasty, and made himself the first ruler of the new Chin dynasty. There is nothing to gain by detailing all the intrigues that led up to this event: they all took place in the immediate environment of the court, and in no way affected the people, except that every item of expenditure, including all the bribery, had to come out of the taxes paid by the people.

With such a situation at court, with the bad economic situation in the country, and with the continual fighting against the two southern States, there could be no question of any far-reaching foreign policy. Parts of eastern Turkestan still showed some measure of allegiance to Wei, but only because at the time it had no stronger opponent. The Hsiung Nu beyond the frontier were suffering from a period of depression which was at the same time a period of reconstruction. They were beginning slowly to form, together with Mongol elements, a new unit, the Yüan Yüan, but at this time were still politically inactive. The nineteen tribes within North China held more and more closely together as militarily organized nomads, but did not yet represent a military power and remained loyal to the Wei. The only important element of trouble seems to have been furnished by the Hsien Pi tribes, who had joined with Wu Huan tribes and apparently also with vestiges of the Hsiung Nu in eastern Mongolia, and who made numerous raids over the frontier into the Wei empire. The State of Yen, in southern Manchuria, had already been destroyed by Wei in 238, thanks to Wei's good relations with Japan. Loose diplomatic relations were maintained with Japan in the period that followed; in that period many elements of Chinese civilization found their way into Japan and there, together with settlers from many parts of China, helped to transform the primitive neolithic culture of ancient Japan.

(B) The Western Chin dynasty (A.D. 265–317)

1 *Internal situation in the Chin empire*

The change of dynasty in the State of Wei did not bring any turn in China's internal history. Ssŭ-ma Yen, who as emperor was called Wu Ti (265–289), had come to the throne with the aid of his clique and his extraordinarily large and widely ramified family. To these he had to give offices as reward. There began at court once more the same spectacle as in the past, except that princes of the new imperial family now played a greater part than under the Wei dynasty, whose ruling house had consisted of a small family. It was customary, in spite of the abolition of the feudal system, for the imperial princes to receive large regions to administer, the fiscal revenues of which represented their income. The princes were not, however, to exercise full authority in the style of the former feudal lords: their courts were full of imperial control officials. In the event of war it was their duty to come forward, like other governors, with an army in support of the central government. The various Chin princes succeeded, however, in making other governors, beyond the frontiers of their regions, dependent on them, in collecting armies of their own independently of the central government, and in using those armies to pursue a personal policy. The members of the families allied with the ruling house, for their part, did all they could to extend their own power. Thus the first ruler of the dynasty was tossed to and fro between the conflicting interests, and was himself powerless. But though intrigue was piled on intrigue, the ruler, who had, of course, himself come to the head of the State by means of intrigues, was more watchful than the rulers of the Wei dynasty had been, and by shrewd counter-measures he repeatedly succeeded in playing off one party against another, so that the dynasty remained in power. Numerous widespread and furious risings nevertheless took place, usually led by princes. Thus during this period the history of the dynasty was of an extraordinarily dismal character.

In spite of this, the Chin troops succeeded in overthrowing the second southern State, that of Wu (A.D. 280), and in so restoring the unity of the empire, the Shu-Han realm having been already conquered by the Wei. After the destruction of Wu there remained no external enemy that represented a potential danger, so that a general disarmament was resolved on (280), in order to restore a healthy economic and financial situation. This disarmament applied, of course, to the troops directly under the orders of the dynasty, the troops of the court and the capital and the imperial troops in the provinces. Disarmament could not, however, be carried out in the princes' "feudal" regions, as the princes declared that they needed personal guards. The dismissal of the troops was accompanied by a decree ordering the surrender of arms. It may be assumed that the government proposed to mint money with the metal of the weapons surrendered, for coin (the old coin of the Wei dynasty) had become very scarce; money had largely been replaced by grain and silks for public payments, that is to say for the payment of salaries. Naturally the decree for the surrender of weapons remained a dead-letter. The discharged soldiers kept their weapons at first, and then preferred to sell them. A large part of them was acquired by the Hsiung Nu and the Hsien Pi in the north of China; apparently they usually gave up land in return. In this way many Chinese soldiers, though, of course, not all by any means, went as peasants to the regions in the north of China and beyond the frontier. They were glad to do so, for the Hsiung Nu and the Hsien Pi had not the efficient administration and rigid tax collection of the Chinese; and, above all, they had no great land-owners who could have organized the collection of taxes. For their part, the Hsiung Nu and the Hsien Pi had no reason to regret this immigration of peasants, who could provide them with the farm produce they needed. And at the same time they were receiving from them large quantities of the most modern weapons.

This ineffective disarmament was undoubtedly the most pregnant event of the period of the western Chin dynasty. The measure was intended to save the cost of maintaining the soldiers, and to bring them back to the land as peasants (and taxpayers); but the discharged men were not given land by the government. The disarmament achieved nothing, not even the desired increase in the money in circulation; what did happen was that the central government lost all practical power, while the military strength both of the dangerous princes within the country and also of the frontier peoples was increased. The results of these mistaken measures showed themselves at once, and compelled the government to arm anew.

2 *Effect on the frontier peoples*

Four groups of frontier peoples drew direct or indirect advantage from the demobilization law—the people of the Toba, the Tibetans, and the Hsien Pi in the north, and the nineteen tribes of the Hsiung Nu within the frontiers of the empire. In the course of time all sorts of complicated developments resulted in the mutual relations between those peoples, with their growing strength, and in their relations with the Chinese.

The Toba formed quite a small group in the north of the present province of Shansi, north of the present city of Tatung-fu, and were occupied in extending their small State edifice. They were primarily of Turkish origin, but had absorbed many tribes of the older Hsiung Nu and the Hsien Pi. In considering the ethnical relationships of all these northern peoples we must rid ourselves of our present-day notions of national unity. The Toba and all the other congeries of tribes were not nations. In each case there was a central stock round which various other stocks were grouped. Among the Toba the nucleus seems to have been Turkish, among the Hsien Pi Mongolian, among the Hsiung Nu Turkish. The Hsiung Nu belonged to a section of the Turkish peoples known in the Chinese tradition under the name "Huns"; and for simplicity we will call them Huns from now on. The other stocks belonging to these combinations were of all sorts of origin. Among the Toba there were many Turkish stocks, but also Mongol, and probably a Tungus stock and perhaps others, which we cannot yet analyse. These stocks may even have spoken different languages, much as later not only Mongol but also Turkish was spoken in the Mongol empire. The political units they formed were tribal unions, not national States.

The Tibetans were at first entirely without tribal allegiance; later they were a loosely associated group of peoples who fell apart into two sub-groups, the Ch'iang and the Ti. Both names appeared repeatedly as political conceptions, but the Tibetans, like all other State-forming groups of peoples, sheltered in their realms countless alien elements. In the course of the third and second centuries B.C. the group of the Ti, mainly living in the territory of the present Szechwan, had mixed extensively with remains of the Yüeh Chih; the others, the Ch'iang, were northern Tibetans or so-called Tanguts; that is to say, they were more strongly mingled with Turkish and Mongol elements.[1] In A.D. 296 began a great rising of the Ti, who made their leader, Ch'i Wan-nien, emperor. The Chi'ang rose with them, as it was not until later, from 312, that they pursued an independent policy. The Ti State, however, though it had a second emperor, very soon lost importance, so that we shall soon be occupied solely with the Ch'iang.

The Hsien Pi, according to our present knowledge, were a proto-Mongol people, with a strong admixture of Turkish Huns. Throughout the period during which they played a part in history, they never succeeded in forming any great political unit, in strong contrast to the Huns, who excelled in State formation. The separate groups of the Hsien Pi pursued a policy of their own; very frequently Hsien Pi fought each other, and they never submitted to a common leadership. Thus their history is entirely that of small groups. It has not so far been possible to determine why the Hsien Pi possessed no capacity for State-formation. As early as the Wei period there had been small-scale conflicts with the Hsien Pi tribes, and at times the tribes had had some success. The campaigns of the Hsien Pi against North China now increased, and in the course of them the various tribes formed firmer groupings, among which the Mu Yung tribe played a leading part. In 281, the year after the demobilization law, this group marched south into China, and occupied the region round Peking. After fierce fighting, in which the Mu Yung section suffered heavy losses, a treaty was signed in 289, under which the Mu Yung tribe of the Hsien Pi came under Chinese overlordship. The Mu Yung were driven to this step mainly because they had been continually attacked from southern

[1] It may, however, be assumed that at this time the admixture was only slight, increasing later.

Manchuria by another Hsien Pi tribe, the Yü Wen, the tribe most closely related to them. The Mu Yung made use of the period of their so-called subjection to organize their community in North China.

South of the Toba were the nineteen tribes of the Hsiung Nu or Huns, as we are now calling them. Their leader in A.D. 287, Liu Yüan, was one of the principal personages of this period. His name is purely Chinese, but he was descended from the Hun *shan-yü*, from the family and line of Mao Tun. His membership of that long-famous noble line and old ruling family of Huns gave him a prestige which he increased by his great organizing ability.

3 *Struggles for the throne*

We shall return to Liu Yüan later; we must now cast another glance at the official court of the Chin. In that court a family named Yang had become very powerful, a daughter of this family having become empress. When, however, the emperor died, the wife of the new emperor Hui Ti (290–306) secured the assassination of the old empress Yang and of her whole family. Thus began the rule at court of the Chia family. In 299 the family got rid of the heir to the throne, to whom they objected, assassinating this prince and another one. This event became the signal for large-scale activity on the part of the princes, supported by particular groups of families from time to time. The princes had not complied with the disarmament law of 280, and so had become militarily supreme. The generals newly appointed in the course of the imperial rearmament at once entered into alliance with the princes, and thus were quite unreliable as officers of the government. Both the generals and the princes entered into agreements with the frontier peoples, to assure their aid in the struggle for power. The most popular of these auxiliaries were the Hsien Pi, who were fighting for one of the princes whose territory lay in the east. Since the Toba were the natural enemies of the Hsien Pi, who were continually contesting their hold on their territory, the Toba were always on the opposite side to that supported by the Hsien Pi, so that they now supported generals who were ostensibly loyal to the government. The Huns, too, negotiated with several generals and princes, and received tempting offers. Above all, all the frontier peoples were now militarily well equipped, continually receiving new war material from the Chinese who from time to time were co-operating with them.

In A.D. 300 Prince Lun assassinated the empress Chia and removed her group. In 301 he made himself emperor, but in the same year he was killed by the prince of Ch'i. This prince was killed in 302 by the prince of Ch'angsha, who in turn was killed in 303 by the prince of Tunghai. The prince of Ho-chien rose in 302 and was killed in 306; the prince of Chengtu rose in 303, conquered the capital in 305, and then, in 306, was himself removed. I mention all these names and dates only to show the disunion within the ruling groups.

4 *Migration of Chinese*

All these struggles raged round the capital, for each of the princes wanted to secure full power and to become emperor. Thus the border regions remained relatively undisturbed. Their population suffered much less from the warfare than the unfortunate people in the neighbourhood of the central government. For this reason there took place a mass migration of Chinese from the centre of the empire to its periphery. This process, together with the shifting of the frontier peoples, is one of the most important events of that epoch. A great number of Chinese migrated especially into the present province of Kansu, where a governor who had originally been sent there to fight the Hsien Pi had created a sort of paradise by his good administration and maintenance of peace. The territory ruled by this Chinese, first as governor and then in increasing independence, was surrounded by Hsien Pi, Tibetans, and other peoples, but thanks to the great immigration of Chinese, and to its situation on the main caravan route to Turkestan, it was able to hold its own, to expand, and to become prosperous.

Other groups of Chinese peasants migrated southwards into the territories of the former State of Wu. A Chinese prince of the house of the Chin was ruling there, in the present Nanking. His purpose was to organize that territory, and then to intervene in the struggles of the other princes. We shall meet him again at the beginning of the Hun rule over North China in 317, as founder and emperor of the first South Chinese dynasty, which was at once involved in the usual internal and external struggles. For the moment, however, the southern region was relatively at peace, and was accordingly attracting settlers.

Finally, many Chinese migrated northward, into the territories of the frontier peoples, not only of the Hsien Pi but especially of the Huns. These alien peoples, although in the official Chinese view they were still barbarians, at least maintained peace in the territories they ruled, and they left in peace the peasants and craftsmen who came to them, even while their own armies were involved in fighting inside China. But not only peasants and craftsmen came in, but more and more educated persons. Members of families of the gentry that had suffered from the fighting, people who had lost their influence in China, were welcomed by the Huns and appointed teachers and political advisers of the Hun nobility.

5 *Victory of the Huns. The Hun Han dynasty* (*later renamed the Earlier Chao dynasty*)

With its self-confidence thus increased, the Hun council of nobles declared that in future the Huns should no longer fight now for one and now for another Chinese general or prince. They had promised loyalty to the Chinese emperor, but not to any prince. It was quite evident that the Chinese emperor was a complete nonentity and no longer played any part in the struggle for power. It was known that the murders would continue until one of the generals or princes overcame the rest and made himself emperor. Why should not the Huns have the same right? Why should not they join in this struggle for the Chinese imperial throne?

There were two arguments against this course, one of which was already out of date. The Chinese had for many centuries set down the Huns as uncultured barbarians; but the inferiority complex thus engendered in the Huns had virtually been overcome, because in the course of time their upper class had deliberately acquired a Chinese education, and so ranked culturally with the Chinese. Thus the ruler Liu Yüan, for example, had enjoyed a good Chinese education, and was able to read all the classical texts. The second argument was provided by the rigid conceptions of legitimacy held by the Turkish and Hun nobility. The Huns asked themselves: "Have we, as aliens, any right to become emperors and rulers in China, when we are not descended from an old Chinese family?" On this point Liu Yüan and his advisers found a good answer. They called Liu Yüan's dynasty the "Han dynasty", and so linked it with the most famous of all the Chinese dynasties, pointing to the pact which their ancestor Mao Tun had concluded five hundred years earlier with the first emperor of the Han dynasty, and which had described the two States as "brethren". They further recalled the fact that the rulers of the Huns were closely related to the Chinese ruling family, because Mao Tun and his successors had married Chinese princesses. Finally, Liu Yüan's Chinese family name, Liu, had also been the family name of the rulers of the Han dynasty. Accordingly the Hun Lius came forward not as aliens but as the rightful successors in continuation of the Han dynasty, as legitimate heirs to the Chinese imperial throne on the strength of relationship and of treaties.

Thus the Hun Liu Yüan had no intention of restoring the old empire of Mao Tun, the empire of the nomads; he intended to become emperor of China, emperor of a country of farmers. In this lay the fundamental difference between the earlier Hun empire and this new one. The question whether the Huns should join in the struggle for the Chinese imperial throne was therefore decided among the Huns themselves in 304 in the affirmative, by the founding of the "Hun Han dynasty". All that remained was the practical question of how to hold out with their small army of 50,000 men if serious opposition should be offered to the "barbarians" .

Meanwhile Liu Yüan provided himself with court ceremonial on the Chinese model, in a capital which, after several changes, was established at P'ing-ch'êng in southern Shansi. He attracted more and more of the Chinese gentry, who were glad to come to this rather barbaric but well-organized court. In 309 the first attack was made on the Chinese capital, Loyang. Liu Yüan died in the following year, and in 311, under his successor Liu Ts'ung (310–318), the attack was renewed and Loyang fell. The Chin emperor, Huai Ti, was captured and kept a prisoner in P'ing-ch'êng until in 313 a conspiracy in his favour was brought to light in the Hun empire, and he and all his supporters were killed. Meanwhile the Chinese clique of the Chin dynasty had hastened to make a prince emperor in the second capital, Ch'ang-an (Min Ti, 313–316) while the princes' struggles for the throne continued. Nobody troubled about the fate of the unfortunate emperor in his capital. He received no reinforcements, so that he was helpless in face of the next attack of the Huns, and in 316 he was compelled to surrender like his predecessor. Now the Hun Han dynasty held both capitals, which meant virtually the whole of the western part of North China, and the so-called "Western Chin dynasty" thus came to its end. Its princes and generals and many of its gentry became landless and homeless and had to flee into the south.

(C) The alien empires in North China, down to the Toba (A.D. 317–385)

1 *The Later Chao dynasty in eastern North China* (*Hun;* 329–352)

At this time the eastern part of North China was entirely in the hands of Shih Lo, a former follower of Liu Yüan. Shih Lo had escaped from slavery in China and had risen to be a tribal leader among the Huns. In 310 he had not only undertaken a great campaign right across China to the south, but had slaughtered more than 100,000 Chinese, including forty-eight princes of the Chin dynasty, who had formed a vast burial procession for a prince. This achievement added considerably to Shih Lo's power, and his relations with Liu Ts'ung, already tense, became still more so. Liu Yüan had tried to organize the Hun State on the Chinese model, intending in this way to gain efficient control of China; Shih Lo rejected Chinese methods, and held to the old nomad tradition, making raids with the aid of nomad fighters. He did not contemplate holding the territories of central and southern China which he had conquered; he withdrew, and in the two years 314–315 he contented himself with bringing considerable expanses in north-eastern China, especially territories of the Hsien Pi, under his direct rule, as a base for further raids. Many Huns in Liu Ts'ung's dominion found Shih Lo's method of rule more to their taste than living in a State ruled by officials, and they went over to Shih Lo and joined him in breaking entirely with Liu Ts'ung. There was a further motive for this: in States founded by nomads, with a federation of tribes as their basis, the personal qualities of the ruler played an important part. The chiefs of the various tribes would not give unqualified allegiance to the son of a dead ruler unless the son was a strong personality or gave promise of becoming one. Failing that, there would be independence movements. Liu Ts'ung did not possess the indisputable prestige of his predecessor Liu Yüan; and the Huns looked with contempt on his court splendour, which could only have been justified if he had conquered all China. Liu Ts'ung had no such ambition; nor had his successor Liu Yao (319–329), who gave the Hun Han dynasty retrospectively, from its start with Liu Yüan, the new name of "Earlier Chao dynasty" (304–329). Many tribes then went over to Shih Lo, and the remainder of Liu Yao's empire was reduced to a precarious existence. In 329 the whole of it was annexed by Shih Lo.

Although Shih Lo had long been much more powerful than the emperors of the "Earlier Chao dynasty", until their removal he had not ventured to assume the title of emperor. The reason for this seems to have lain in the conceptions of nobility held by the Turkish peoples in general and the Huns in particular, according to which only those could become *shan-yü* (or, later, emperor) who could show descent from the stock of Tu-ku, the rightful *shan-yü* stock. In accordance with this conception, all later Hun dynasties deliberately disowned Shih Lo. For Shih Lo, after his destruction of Liu Yao, no longer hesitated: ex-slave as he was, and descended from one of the non-noble stocks of the Huns, he made himself emperor of the "Later Chao dynasty" (329–352).

Shih Lo was a forceful army commander, but he was a man without statesmanship, and without the culture of his day. He had no Chinese education; he hated the Chinese, and would have been glad to make North China a grazing ground for his nomad tribes of Huns. Accordingly he had no desire to rule all China. The part already subjugated, embracing the whole of North China with the exception of the present province of Kansu, sufficed for his purpose.

The governor of that province was a loyal subject of the Chinese Chin dynasty, a man famous for his good administration, and himself a Chinese. After the execution of the Chin emperor Huai Ti by the Huns in 313, he regarded himself as no longer bound to the central government; he made himself independent and founded the "Earlier Liang dynasty", which was to last until 376. This mainly Chinese realm was not very large, although it had admitted a broad stream of Chinese emigrants from the dissolving Chin empire; but economically the Liang realm was very prosperous, so that it was able to extend its influence as far as Turkestan. During the earlier struggles Turkestan had been virtually in isolation, but now new contacts began to be established. Many traders from Turkestan set up branches in Liang. In the capital there were whole quarters inhabited only by aliens from western and eastern Turkestan and from India. With the traders came Buddhist monks; trade and Buddhism seemed to be closely associated everywhere. In the trading centres monasteries were installed in the form of blocks of houses within strong walls that successfully resisted many an attack. Consequently the Buddhists were able to serve as bankers for the merchants, who deposited their money in the monasteries, which made a charge for its custody; the merchants also warehoused their goods in the monasteries. Sometimes the process was reversed, a trade centre being formed around an existing monastery. In this case the monastery also served as a hostel for the merchants. Economically this Chinese State in Kansu was much more like a Turkestan city State that lived by commerce than the agrarian States of the Far East, although agriculture was also pursued under the Earlier Liang.

From this trip to the remote west we will return first to the Hun capital. From 329 onward Shih Lo possessed a wide empire, but an unstable one. He himself felt at all times insecure, because the Huns regarded him, on account of his humble origin, as a "revolutionary". He exterminated every member of the Liu family, that is to say the old *shan-yü* family, of whom he could get hold, in order to remove any possible pretender to the throne; but he could not count on the loyalty of the Hun and other Turkish tribes under his rule. During this period not a few Huns went over to the small realm of the Toba; other Hun tribes withdrew entirely from the political scene and lived with their herds as nomad tribes in Shansi and in the Ordos region. The general insecurity undermined the strength of Shih Lo's empire. He died in 333, and there came to the throne, after a short interregnum, another personality of a certain greatness, Shih Hu (334–349); he transferred the capital to the city of Yeh, in northern Honan, where the rulers of the Wei dynasty had reigned. There are many accounts of the magnificence of the court of Yeh. Foreigners, especially Buddhist monks, played a greater part there than Chinese. But the foundations of the State became more and more insecure. After Shih Hu's death there were fearful combats between his sons; ultimately a member of an entirely different family of Hun origin seized power, but was destroyed in 352 by the Hsien Pi, bringing to an end the Later Chao dynasty.

2 *Earlier Yen dynasty in the north-east* (*proto-Mongol; 352–370*), *and the Earlier Ch'in dynasty in all North China* (*Tibetan; 351–394*)

In the north, proto-Mongol Hsien Pi tribes had again made themselves independent; in the past they had been subjects of Liu Yüan and then of Shih Lo. A man belonging to one of these tribes, the tribe of the Mu Yung, became the leader of a league of tribes, and in 337 founded the State of Yen. This proto-Mongol State of the Mu Yung, which the historians call the "Earlier Yen" State, conquered parts of southern Manchuria and also the State of Kao-li in Korea, and there began then an immigration of Hsien Pi, which was still noticeable at a later date, into Korea. The conquest of Korea, which was still, as in the past, a Japanese market, and was very wealthy, enormously strengthened the State of Yen. Not until rather later, when Japan's trade relations were diverted to central China, did Korea's importance begin to diminish. Although this "Earlier Yen dynasty" of the Mu Yung officially entered on the heritage of the Huns, and its régime is therefore dated only from 352 (until 370), it failed either to subjugate the whole realm of the "Later Chao" or effectively to establish the State it had acquired. This old Hun territory had suffered economically from the anti-agrarian nomad tendency of the last of the Hun emperors; and unremunerative wars against the Chinese in the south had done nothing to improve its position. In addition to this, the realm of the Toba was dangerously gaining strength on the flank of the new empire. But the most dangerous enemy was in the west, on former Hun soil, in the province of Shensi—Tibetans, who finally came forward once more with claims to dominance. These were Tibetans of the P'u family, which later changed its name to Fu. The head of the family had worked his way up as a leader of Tibetan auxiliaries under the "Later Chao", gaining more and more power and following. When under that dynasty the death of Shih Hu marked the beginning of general dissolution, he gathered his Tibetans around him in the west, declared himself independent of the Huns, and made himself emperor in the "Earlier Ch'in dynasty" (351–394). He died in 355, and was followed after a short interregnum by Fu Chien (357–385), who was unquestionably one of the most important figures of the fourth century. This Tibetan empire ultimately defeated the "Earlier Yen dynasty" and annexed the realm of the Mu Yung. Thus the Mu Yung Hsien Pi came under the dominion of the Tibetans; they were distributed among a number of places as garrisons of mounted troops.

The empire of the Tibetans was quite differently built up from those of the Huns and the Hsien Pi tribes. The Turkish Huns and the proto-Mongol Hsien Pi had possessed a rigid tribal organization developed in the course of centuries. Within the tribe were freemen and slaves. If a tribe suffered defeat in war, the victor made captive all the members of the tribe and distributed them among its people as slaves; this meant the end of the defeated tribe as a unit. The slaves did the actual labour and left war and politics to the free. Among the Huns the various tribes were not of equal rank: there was at least one tribe of noble rank, which for some five hundred years had furnished the political leadership of the associated tribes, or had been supposed to do so. The various tribes had to supply soldiers to this leading tribe, but retained their tribal individuality. The Tibetans had virtually no tribal organization. There were not even the beginnings of it in the earliest times; later the custom grew up in times of war of a group choosing as its commander a man who was generally respected, and gathering round him for military purposes. This military unit was only of a temporary character, ceasing to exist the moment the fighting ended. Thus the Tibetans had never succeeded in forming strong States. In the Hun empires, however, they had been trained as soldiers. Tibetan army units had been created, with well-trained leaders of their own. Their organization was purely military and had nothing to do with the development of tribal organization. This had its advantages, for the leader of such a formation had no need to take account of tribal chieftains; he was answerable to no one and possessed considerable personal power. Nor was there any need for him to be of noble rank or descended from an old family. The Tibetan ruler Fu Chien organized all his troops, including the non-Tibetans, on this system, without regard to tribal membership.

Fu Chien's State showed another innovation: the armies of the Huns and the Hsien Pi had consisted entirely of cavalry, for the nomads of the north were, of course, horsemen; to fight on foot was in their eyes not only contrary to custom but contemptible. So long as a State consisted only of a league of tribes, it was simply out of the question to transform part of the army into infantry. Fu Chien, however, with his military organization that paid no attention to the tribal element, created an infantry in addition to the great cavalry units, recruiting for it large numbers of Chinese. The infantry proved extremely valuable, especially in the fighting in the plains of North China and in laying siege to fortified towns. Fu Chien thus very quickly achieved military predominance over the neighbouring States. As we have seen already, he annexed the "Earlier Yen" realm of the proto-Mongols (370), but he also annihilated the Chinese "Earlier Liang" realm, in 376, and in the same year the small Turkish Toba realm. This made him supreme over all North China, and stronger than any alien ruler before him. He had in his possession both the ancient capitals, Ch'ang-an and Loyang; the whole of the rich agricultural regions of North China belonged to him; he also controlled the routes to Turkestan. He himself had had a Chinese education, and attracted Chinese to his court; he protected the Buddhists; and he tried in every way to make the whole country culturally Chinese. As soon as Fu Chien had all North China in his power, as Liu Yüan and his Huns had done before him, he resolved, like Liu Yüan, to make every effort to gain the mastery over all China, to become emperor of China. Liu Yüan's successors had not had the capacity for which such a venture called; Fu Chien was to fail in it for other reasons. Yet, from a military point of view, his chances were not bad. He had far more soldiers under his command than the Chinese "Eastern Chin dynasty" which ruled the south, and his troops were undoubtedly better. In the time of the founder of the Tibetan dynasty the southern empire had been utterly defeated by his troops (354), and the South Chinese were no stronger now.

Against them the north had these assets: the possession of the best northern tillage, the control of the trade routes, and "Chinese" culture and administration. At the time, however, these represented only potentialities and not tangible realities. It would have taken ten to twenty years to restore the capacities of the north after its devastation in many wars, to reorganize commerce, and to set up a really reliable administration, and thus to interlock the various elements and consolidate the various tribes. As early, however, as 383 Fu Chien started his great campaign against the south, with an army of something like a million men. At first the advance went well. The horsemen from the north, however, were men of the mountain country, and in the soggy plains of the Yangtze region, cut up by hundreds of water-courses and canals, they suffered from climatic and natural conditions to which they were unaccustomed. Their main strength was still in cavalry; and they came to grief. The supplies and reinforcements for the vast army failed to arrive in time; units did not reach the appointed places at the appointed dates. The southern troops under the supreme command of Hsieh Hsüan, far inferior in numbers and militarily of no great efficiency, made surprise attacks on isolated units before these were in regular formation. Some they defeated, others they bribed; they spread false reports. Fu Chien's army was seized with widespread panic, so that he was compelled to retreat in haste. As he did so it became evident that his empire had no inner stability: in a very short time it fell into fragments. The South Chinese had played no direct part in this, for in spite of their victory they were not strong enough to advance far to the north.

3 *The fragmentation of North China*

The first to fall away from the Tibetan ruler was a noble of the Mu Yung, a member of the ruling family of the "Earlier Yen dynasty", who withdrew during the actual fighting to pursue a policy of his own. With the vestiges of the Hsien Pi who followed him, mostly cavalry, he fought his way northwards into the old homeland of the Hsien Pi and there, in central Hopei, founded the "Later Yen dynasty" (384–409), himself reigning for twelve years. In the remaining thirteen years of the existence of that dynasty there were no fewer than five rulers, the last of them a member of another family. The history of this Hsien Pi dynasty, as of its predecessor, is an unedifying succession of intrigues; no serious effort was made to build up a true State.

In the same year 384 there was founded, under several other Mu Yung princes of the ruling family of the "Earlier Yen dynasty", the "Western Yen dynasty" (384–394). Its nucleus was nothing more than a detachment of troops of the Hsien Pi which had been thrown by Fu Chien into the west of his empire, in Shensi, in the neighbourhood of the old capital Ch'ang-an. There its commanders, on learning the news of Fu Chien's collapse, declared their independence. In western China, however, far removed from all liaison with the main body of the Hsien Pi, they were unable to establish themselves, and when they tried to fight their way to the north-east they were dispersed, so that they failed entirely to form an actual State.

There was a third attempt in 384 to form a State in North China. A Tibetan who had joined Fu Chien with his followers declared himself independent when Fu Chien came back, a beaten man, to Shensi. He caused Fu Chien and almost the whole of his family to be assassinated, occupied the capital, Ch'ang-an, and actually entered into the heritage of Fu Chien. This Tibetan dynasty is known as the "Later Ch'in dynasty" (384–417). It was certainly the strongest of those founded in 384, but it still failed to dominate any considerable part of China and remained of local importance, mainly confined to the present province of Shensi. Fu Chien's empire nominally had three further rulers, but they did not exert the slightest influence on events.

With the collapse of the State founded by Fu Chien, the tribes of Hsien Pi who had left their homeland in the third century and migrated to the Ordos region proceeded to form their own State: a man of the Hsien Pi tribe of the Ch'i-fu founded the so-called "Western Ch'in dynasty" (385–431). Like the other Hsien Pi States, this one was of weak construction, resting on the military strength of a few tribes and failing to attain a really secure basis. Its territory lay in the east of the present province of Kansu, and so controlled the eastern end of the western Asian caravan route, which might have been a source of wealth if the Ch'i-fu had succeeded in attracting commerce by discreet treatment and in imposing taxation on it. Instead of this, the bulk of the long-distance traffic passed through the Ordos region, a little farther north, avoiding the Ch'i-fu State, which seemed to the merchants to be too insecure. The Ch'i-fu depended mainly on cattle-breeding in the remote mountain country in the south of their territory, a region that gave them relative security from attack; on the other hand, this made them unable to exercise any influence on the course of political events in western China.

Mention must be made of one more State that rose from the ruins of Fu Chien's empire. It lay in the far west of China, in the western part of the present province of Kansu, and was really a continuation of the Chinese "Earlier Liang" realm, which had been annexed ten years earlier (376) by Fu Chien. A year before his great march to the south, Fu Chien had sent the Tibetan Lü Kuang into the "Earlier Liang" region in order to gain influence over Turkestan. After the great Hun rulers, Fu Chien was the first to make a deliberate attempt to secure cultural and political overlordship over the whole of China. Although himself a Tibetan, he never fell into the error of pursuing a "Tibetan" policy; as the entirely legitimate ruler of China, he was concerned to prevent the northern peoples along the frontier from uniting with the Tibetan peoples of the west for political ends. The possession of Turkestan would avert that danger, which had shown signs of becoming imminent of late: some tribes of Hsien Pi had migrated as far as the high mountains of Tibet and had imposed themselves as a ruling class on the still very primitive Tibetans living there. From this symbiosis there began to be formed a new people. the so-called T'u-yü-hun, a hybridization of Mongol and Tibetan stock with a slight Turkish admixture. Lü Kuang had had considerable success in Turkestan; he had brought considerable portions of eastern Turkestan under Fu Chien's sovereignty, and administered those regions almost independently. When the news came of Fu Chien's end, he declared himself an independent ruler, of the "Later Liang" dynasty (386–403). Strictly speaking, this was simply a trading State, like the city-States of Turkestan: its basis was the transit traffic that brought it prosperity. For commerce brought good profit to the small States that lay right across the caravan route, whereas it was of doubtful benefit, as we know, to agrarian China as a whole, because the luxury goods which it supplied to the court were paid for out of the production of the general population.

This "Later Liang" realm was inhabited not only by a few Tibetans and many Chinese, but also by Hsien Pi and Huns. These heterogeneous elements, with their divergent cultures, failed in the long run to hold together in this long but extremely narrow strip of territory, which was almost incapable of military defence. As early as 397 a group of Huns in the central section of the country made themselves independent, assuming the name of the "Northern Liang" (397–439). These Huns quickly conquered other parts of the "Later Liang" realm, which then fell entirely to pieces. Chinese again founded a State, "West Liang", (400–421), in western Kansu, and the Hsien Pi founded "South Liang" (379–414) in eastern Kansu. Thus the "Later Liang" fell into three parts, more or less differing ethnically, though they could not be described as ethnically unadulterated States.

4 *Sociological analysis of the two great alien empires*

The two great empires of North China at the time of its division had been founded by non-Chinese—the first by the Hun Liu Yüan, the second by the Tibetan Fu Chien. Both rulers went to work on the same principle of trying to build up truly "Chinese" empires, but the traditions of Huns and Tibetans differed, and the two experiments turned out differently. Both failed, but not for the same reasons and not with the same results. The Hun Liu Yüan was the ruler of a league of feudal tribes, which was expected to take its place as an upper class above the unchanged Chinese agricultural population with its system of officials and gentry. But Liu Yüan's successors were national reactionaries who stood for the maintenance of the nomad life against that new plan of transition to a feudal class of urban nobles ruling an agrarian population. Liu Yüan's more far-seeing policy was abandoned, with the result that the Huns were no longer in a position to rule an immense agrarian territory, and the empire soon disintegrated. For the various Hun tribes this failure meant falling back into political insignificance, but they were able to maintain their national character and existence.

Fu Chien, as a Tibetan, was a war-maker and soldier, in accordance with the past of the Tibetans. Under him were grouped Tibetans (with no tribal chieftains), the great mass of Chinese, and dispersed remnants of tribes of Huns, Hsien Pi, and others. His organization was based entirely on soldiers and, outside the military sphere, on officials. The Chinese gentry, so far as they still existed, preferred to work with him rather than with the feudalist Huns. These gentry will have supported Fu Chien's southern campaign, for, in consequence of the wide ramifications of their families, it was to their interest that China should form a single economic unit. They were, of course, equally ready to work with another group, one of southern Chinese, to attain the same end by other means, if those means should prove more advantageous: thus the gentry were not a reliable asset, but were always ready to break faith.

Among other things, Fu Chien's southern campaign was wrecked by that faithlessness. When a purely military State suffers military defeat, it can only go to pieces. This explains the disintegration of that great empire within a single year into so many diminutive States, as already described.

5 *Sociological analysis of the petty States*

The States that took the place of Fu Chien's empire, those many diminutive States (the Chinese speak of the period of the Sixteen Kingdoms), may be divided from the economic point of view into two groups—trading States and warrior States; sociologically they also fall into two groups, tribal States and military States.

The small States in the west, in Kansu (the Later Liang and the Western, Northern, and Southern Liang), were trading States: they lived on the earnings of transit trade with Turkestan. The eastern States were warrior States, in which an army commander ruled by means of an armed group of non-Chinese and exploited an agricultural population. It is only logical that such States should be short-lived, as in fact they all were.

Sociologically regarded, during this period only the Southern and Northern Liang were still tribal States. In addition to these came the young Toba realm, which began in 385 but of which mention has not yet been made. The basis of that State was the tribe, not the family or the individual; after its political disintegration the separate tribes remained in existence. The other States of the east, however, were military States, made up of individuals with no tribal allegiance but subject to a military commandant. But where there is no tribal association, after the political downfall of a State founded by ethnical groups those groups sooner or later disappear as such. We see this in the years immediately following Fu Chien's collapse: the Tibetan ethnical group to which he himself belonged disappeared entirely from the historical scene. The two Tibetan groups that outlasted him, also forming military States and not tribal States, similarly came to an end shortly afterwards for all time. The Hsien Pi groups in the various fragments of the empire also continued, with the exception of the petty States in Kansu, only as tribal fragments led by a few old ruling families. They, too, after brief and undistinguished military rule, came to an end; they disappeared so completely that thereafter we no longer find the term Hsien Pi in history. Not that they had been exterminated. When the sociological structure produced by the traditional economic form falls to pieces, there remain only two alternatives for its individuals. Either they must go over to a new economic form, which in China could only mean that they became Chinese; many Hsien Pi in this way became Chinese in the decades following 384—or they could retain their old way of living in association with another stock of similar formation; this, too, happened in many cases. Both these courses, however, meant the end of the Hsien Pi as an independent ethnical unit. We must keep this process and its reasons in view if we are to understand how a great people can disappear once and for all.

The Huns, too, so powerful in the past, were suddenly scarcely to be found any longer. Among the many petty States there were many Hsien Pi kingdoms, but only a single, quite small, Hun State, that of the Northern Liang. The disappearance of the Huns was, however, only apparent; at this time they remained in the Ordos region and in Shansi as separate nomad tribes with no integrating political organization; their time had still to come.

6 *Spread of Buddhism*

According to the prevalent Chinese theory, nothing of importance was achieved during this period in North China in the intellectual sphere; there was no culture in the north, only in the south. This is natural: for a Confucian this period, the fourth century, was one of degeneracy in North China, for no one came into prominence as a celebrated Confucian. Nothing else could be expected, for in the north the gentry, which had been the class that maintained Confucianism since the Han period, had largely been destroyed; from political leadership especially it had been shut out during the periods of alien rule. Nor could we expect to find Taoists in the true sense, that is to say followers of the teaching of Lao Tzŭ, for these, too, had been dependent since the Han period on the gentry. Until the fourth century, however, these two remained the dominant philosophies.

What could take their place? The alien rulers had left little behind them. Most of them had been unable to write Chinese, and in so far as they were warriors they had no interest in literature or in political philosophy, for they were men of action. Few songs and poems of theirs remain extant in translations from their language into Chinese, but these preserve a strong alien influence in their mental attitude and in their diction. They are the songs of fighting men, songs that were sung on horseback, songs of war and its sufferings. These songs have nothing of the excessive formalism and aestheticism of the Chinese, but give expression to simple emotions in unpolished language with a direct appeal. The epic of the Turkish peoples had clearly been developed already, and in North China it produced a rudimentary ballad literature, to which four hundred years later no less attention was paid than to the emotional world of contemporary songs.

The actual literature, however, and the philosophy of this period are Buddhist. How comes it that Buddhism had gained such influence?

It will be remembered that Buddhism came to China overland and by sea in the earlier Han epoch, mainly during the first century B.C. In China it had interested a few cultured people, not for its religious or philosophical content, but on account of the scientific knowledge that accompanied it. The missionary monks who came from abroad with the foreign merchants found little approval among the Chinese gentry. They were regarded as second-rate persons, belonging, according to Chinese notions, to an inferior social class. Thus the monks had to turn to the middle and lower classes in China. Among these they found widespread acceptance, not of their profound philosophic ideas, but of their doctrine of the after life. This doctrine was in a certain sense revolutionary: it declared that all the high officials and superiors who treated the people so unjustly, and who so exploited them, would in their next reincarnation be born in poor circumstances or into inferior rank, and would have to suffer punishment for all their ill deeds. The poor who had to suffer undeserved evils would be born in their next life into high rank, and would have a good time. This doctrine brought a ray of light, a promise, to the country people who had suffered so much since the later Han period of the second century A.D. Their situation remained unaltered down to the fourth century; and under their alien rulers the Chinese country population became Buddhist.

The merchants made use of the Buddhist monasteries as banks, stock exchanges, and warehouses. Thus they, too, were well inclined toward Buddhism, and gave money and land for its temples. The temples were able to settle peasants on this land as their tenants. In those times a temple was a more reliable landlord than an individual alien, and the poorer peasants readily became temple tenants; this increased their inclination toward Buddhism.

The Indian, Sogdian, and Turkestan monks were readily allowed to settle by the alien rulers of China, who had no national prejudice against other aliens. The monks were educated men, and brought much useful knowledge from abroad. Educated Chinese were scarcely to be found, for the gentry retired to their estates, which they protected as well as they could from their alien ruler. So long as the gentry had no prospect of regaining control of the threads of political life that extended throughout China, they were not prepared to provide a class of officials and scholars for the anti-Confucian foreigners, who showed interest only in fighting and trading. Thus educated persons were needed at the courts of the alien rulers, and Buddhists were therefore engaged. These foreign Buddhists had all the important Buddhist writings translated into Chinese, and so made use of their influence at court for religious propaganda.

This does not mean that every Indian text was translated; especially in the later period many works appeared which came not from India but from Sogdia or Turkestan, or had even been written in China by Sogdians or other natives of Turkestan, and were then translated into Chinese. In Turkestan, Khotan in particular became a centre of Buddhist culture. Buddhism was influenced by vestiges of indigenous cults, so that Khotan developed a special religious atmosphere of its own; deities were honoured there (for instance, the king of Heaven of the northerners) to whom little regard was paid elsewhere. This "Khotan Buddhism" had special influence on the Buddhist Turkish peoples.

Big translation bureaux were set up for the preparation of these translations into Chinese, in which many copyists simultaneously took down from dictation a translation made by a "master" with the aid of a few native helpers. The translations were not at first precise, but were paraphrases, most of them greatly reduced in length; glosses were introduced when the translator thought fit for political or doctrinal reasons, or when he thought that in this way he could better adapt the texts to Chinese feeling.

Buddhism, quite apart from the special case of "Khotan Buddhism", underwent extensive modification on its way from India to China. Its original Indian form (Hinayana), as a purely individualistic religion of salvation without God—related in this respect to genuine Taoism—was no more able to gain a footing in China than elsewhere; only traces of it are to be found later in the meditative Buddhism of the south. At all times the Hinayana doctrine found acceptance only among rulers or merchants; according to that doctrine the true Buddhist is forbidden all productive activity and has to support himself by begging or on gifts received. Mahayana Buddhism, on the other hand, developed into a true popular religion of salvation. It did not interfere with the indigenous deities, and did not discountenance life in human society; it did not recommend Nirvana at once, but placed before it a future life with all the joys worth striving after. In this form Buddhism was certain of

6 Sun Ch'üan, ruler of Wu.
From a painting by Yen Li-pen (*c.* 640-680).

7 General view of the Buddhist cave-temples of Yün-kang. In the foreground, the present village; in the background, the rampart.

success in Asia. On its way from India to China it divided into countless separate streams, each characterized by a particular book. Every nuance, from profound philosophical treatises to the most superficial little tracts written for the simplest of souls, and even a good deal of Turkestan shamanism and Tibetan belief in magic, was to be found in the Buddhist writings, so that some Buddhist monks had a knowledge of shamanistic practices.

In spite of the rivalry of Buddhism, the old shamanistic religion of the peasants (wrongly called the "Taoist Church", for it had nothing to do with the Taoism of Lao Tzu's teaching) retained its vitality, especially because it closely copied Buddhism and its religious observances.

The Chinese cult of Heaven, saturated with Confucianism, was the third still living form of religion; and finally the alien rulers had brought their own mixture of worship of Heaven and shamanism. Their worship of Heaven was the official, "representative" religion; shamanism the private religion of daily life. Accordingly the alien rulers showed great interest both in Buddhist and in Chinese shamans. Not infrequently competitions were arranged between priests of the two religions, who often competed for the possession of monks who were particularly skilled in magic or soothsaying. Thus the "private" religion of the aliens consorted perfectly with shamanist Buddhism and with the shamanist popular Taoism.

But what was the position of the "official" religion? Were the aliens to hold to their own worship of Heaven, or were they to take over the official Chinese cult, or what else? This problem posed itself already in the fourth century, but it was left unsolved.

(D) The Toba empire in North China (A.D. 385–550)

1 *The rise of the Toba State*

On the collapse of Fu Chien's empire one more State made its appearance; it has not yet been dealt with, although it was the most important one. This was the empire of the

Toba, in the north of the present province of Shansi. Fu Chien had brought down the small old Toba State in 376, but had not entirely destroyed it. Its territory was partitioned, and part was placed under the administration of a Hun: in view of the old rivalry between Toba and Huns, this seemed to Fu Chien to be the best way of preventing any revival of the Toba. A descendant, however, of the old ruling family of the Toba succeeded, with the aid of related families, in regaining power and forming a small new kingdom. Very soon many tribes which still lived in North China, and which had not been broken up into military units, joined him. Of these there were ultimately 119, including many Hun tribes from Shansi, and also many Hsien Pi tribes. Thus the question who the Toba were is not easy to answer. The ruling family itself had migrated southward in the third century from the frontier territory between northern Mongolia and northern Manchuria. After this migration the first Toba State, the so-called Tai State, was formed (338–376); not much is known about it. The tribes that grouped themselves round this ruling house from 385, after the break-up of the Tibetan empire, were both Turkish and Mongol; but from the culture and language of the Toba we think it must be inferred that the ruling element and many of the tribes were Turkish; in any case, the Turkish element seems to have been stronger than the Mongolian.

Thus the new Toba kingdom was a tribal State, not a military State. But the tribes were no longer the same as in the time of Liu Yüan a hundred years earlier. Their total population must have been quite small; we must assume that they were but the remains of 119 tribes rather than 119 full-sized tribes. Only part of them were still living the old nomad life; others had become used to living alongside Chinese peasants and had assumed leadership among the peasants. These Toba now faced a difficult situation. The country was arid and mountainous, and did not yield much agricultural produce. For the many people who had come into the Toba State from all parts of the former empire of Fu Chien, to say nothing of the needs of a capital and a court which since the time of Liu Yüan had been regarded as the indispensable entourage of a ruler who claimed imperial rank, the local production of the Chinese peasants was not enough. All the government officials, who were Chinese, and all the slaves and eunuchs, needed corn to eat. Attempts were made to settle more Chinese peasants round the new capital, but without success; something had to be done. It seemed necessary to embark on a campaign to conquer the fertile plain of eastern China. In the course of a number of battles the Hsien Pi of the "Later Yen" were annihilated and eastern China conquered (409).

Now a new question arose: what should be done with all those people? Nomads used to enslave their prisoners and use them for watching their flocks. Some tribal chieftains had adopted the practice of establishing captives on their tribal territory as peasants. There was an opportunity now to subject the millions of Chinese captives to servitude to the various tribal chieftains in the usual way. But as the captives were mainly peasants, who could not be taken away from their fields without robbing the country of its food, it would have been necessary to spread the tribes over the whole of eastern China, and this would have added immensely to the strength of the various tribes and would have greatly weakened the central power. The administration accordingly followed the advice of Chinese officials at the court. Almost all these Chinese officials had come originally from the territories just conquered. They had come from there about a hundred years earlier, and still had all their relatives in the east. If the eastern territories had been placed under the rule of separate tribes, and the tribes had been distributed in this way, the gentry in those territories would have been destroyed as a class, being reduced to the position of enslaved peasants. The Chinese officials accordingly persuaded the Toba emperor not to place the new territories under the tribes, but to leave them to be administered by officials of the central administration. These officials must have a firm footing in their territory, for only they could extract from the peasants the corn required for the support of the capital. Consequently the Toba government did not enslave the Chinese in the eastern territory, but made the gentry who had long lived there into government officials, instructing them to collect as much corn as possible for the capital. The Chinese gentry worked in close collaboration with the Chinese officials at the court, and this determined the whole fate of the Toba empire.

The Hsien Pi of the newly conquered east no longer belonged to any tribe, but only to military units. They were transferred as soldiers to the Toba court and placed directly under the government, which was thus notably strengthened, especially as in addition to this millions of peasants under the administration of the Chinese officials were also directly dependent on the central power. The government now proceeded to convert its own Toba tribes into military formations. The tribal families of noble rank were brought to court as a soldiery, and so separated from the generality and the slaves who had to remain with the herds. This change, which robbed the tribes of all means of independent action, was not carried out without bloodshed. There were revolts of tribal chieftains, which were ruthlessly suppressed. The central power had triumphed, but it realized that more reliance could be placed on Chinese than on its own people, who were used to independence. Thus the Toba were glad to employ more and more Chinese, and the Chinese pressed more and more into the administration. In this the differing social organization of Toba and Chinese played an important part: the Chinese have a patriarchal system of wide family ramifications. When a member of a family obtains a good position, he is obliged to make provision for the other members of his family and to secure good positions for them too; and not only the members of his own family but those of other families related to it or allied with it by marriage! The Toba had a patriarchal family system, but as nomad warriors with no fixed abode, they were unable to form large family groups. Among them the individual was much more independent; each one tried to do his best for himself. No Toba thought of collecting a large clique around himself; each was the artificer of his own fortune. Thus, when a Chinese obtained an official post, he was followed by countless others; when a Toba had a position he remained alone, and so the sinification of the Toba empire went on incessantly.

2 *The Hun kingdom of the Hsia* (407–431)

At the rebuilding of the Toba empire, however, a good many Hun tribes withdrew westward into the Ordos region, beyond the reach of the Toba, and there formed the Hun "Hsia" kingdom. Its ruler, Ho-lien P'o-p'o, belonged to the family of Mao Tun, and originally, like Liu Yüan, bore the sinified family name Liu, but he altered this to a Hun name, taking the family name of Ho-lien. This one fact resulted in the Hsia rejecting the Chinese element and becoming a Hun nation. Thus there were now two realms in North China, one undergoing progressive sinification, the other falling back to the old traditions of the Huns.

3 *Rise of the Toba to a great Power*

The present province of Szechwan, in the west, had belonged to Fu Chien's empire. At the break-up of the Tibetan State that province had passed to the southern Chinese empire. This gave the southern Chinese access, though it was very difficult access, to the caravan route leading to Turkestan. The small States in Kansu, which dominated the route, now passed on the traffic along two routes, one northward to the Toba and the other alien States in North China, the other through north-west Szechwan to South China. In this way the Kansu States were strengthened both economically and politically, for they were able to direct the commerce either to the northern States or to South China as suited them. When the South Chinese saw the break-up of Fu Chien's empire into numberless fragments, Liu Yüan, who was then all-powerful at the South Chinese court, made an attempt to conquer the whole of western China. A great army was sent from South

China into the province of Shensi, where the Tibetan empire of the "Later Ch'in" was situated. The Ch'in appealed to the Toba for help, but the Toba were themselves too hotly engaged to be able to spare troops. They also considered that South China would be unable to maintain these conquests, and that they themselves would find them later an easy prey. Thus in 417 the State of "Later Ch'in" received a mortal blow from the South Chinese army. Large numbers of the upper class fled to the Toba. As had been foreseen, the South Chinese were unable to maintain their hold over the conquered territory, and it was annexed with ease by the Hun Ho-lien P'o-p'o. But why not by the Toba?

Toward the end of the fourth century, vestiges of Hun, Hsien Pi, and other tribes had united in Mongolia to form the new people of the Yüan Yüan. Scholars disagree as to whether the Yüan Yüan were Turks or Mongols; European investigators believe them to have been identical with the Avars who migrated to Europe, and are inclined, on the strength of a few vestiges of their language, to regard them as Mongols. Investigations concerning the various tribes, however, show that among the Yüan Yüan there were both Mongol and Turkish tribes, and that the question cannot be decided in favour of either race. Some of the tribes belonging to the Yüan Yüan had formerly lived in China. Others had lived farther north or west, and came now for the first time into the history of the Far East.

This Yüan Yüan people threatened the Toba in the rear, from the north. It made raids into the Toba empire for the same reasons for which the Huns in the past had raided agrarian China; for agriculture had made considerable progress in the Toba empire. Consequently, before the Toba could attempt to expand southward, the Yüan Yüan peril must be removed. This was done in the end, after a long series of hard and not always successful struggles. That was why the Toba had played no part in the fighting against South China, and had been unable to take immediate advantage of that fighting.

After 429 the Yüan Yüan peril no longer existed, and in

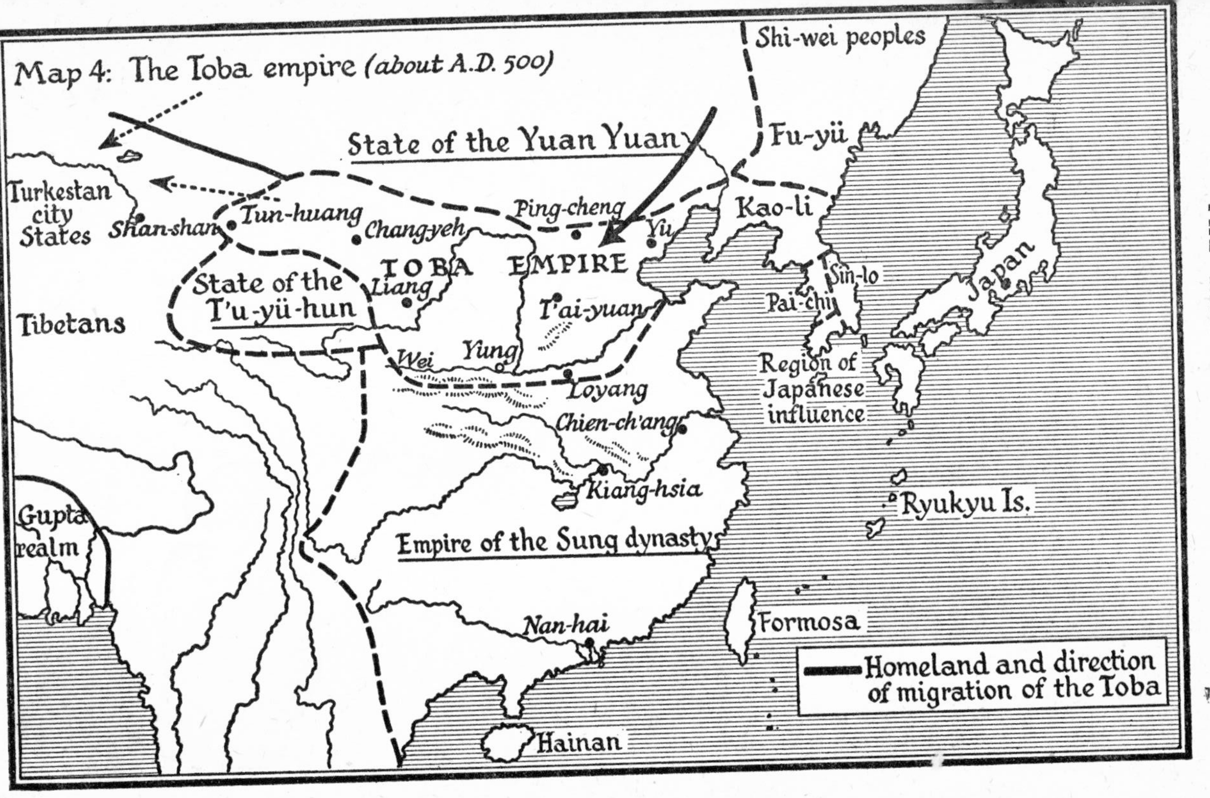

Map 4: The Toba empire (*about A.D. 500*)

the years that followed the whole of the small States of the west were destroyed, one after another, by the Toba—the "Hsia kingdom" in 431, bringing down with it the "Western Ch'in", and the "Northern Liang" in 439. The non-Chinese elements of the population of those countries were carried northwards and served the Toba as soldiers; the Chinese also, especially the remains of the Kansu "Western Liang" State (conquered in 420), were enslaved, and some of them carried to the north. Here again, however, the influence of the Chinese gentry made itself felt after a short time. The Chinese of "Western Liang" in Kansu had originally migrated there from eastern China. Their eastern relatives, who had come under Toba rule through the conquest of eastern China, and who through their family connexions had found safety as Chinese officials of the Toba empire, brought their influence to bear on behalf of the Chinese of Kansu, so that many families regained office and social standing.

Their expansion into Kansu gave the Toba control of the commerce with Turkestan, and there are many mentions of tribute missions to the Toba court in the years that followed, some even from India. The Toba also spread in the east. And finally there was fighting with South China (430–431), which brought to the Toba empire a large part of the province of Honan with the old capital, Loyang. Thus about 440 the Toba must be described as the most powerful State in the Far East, ruling the whole of North China.

4 *Economic and social conditions*

The internal changes of which there had only been indications in the first period of the Toba empire now proceeded at an accelerated pace. There were many different factors at work. The whole of the civil administration had gradually passed into Chinese hands, the Toba retaining only the military administration. But the wars in the south called for the services of specialists in fortification and in infantry warfare, who were only to be found among the Chinese. The growing influence of the Chinese was further promoted by the fact that many families of Toba were exterminated in the revolts of the tribal chieftains, and others were wiped out in the many battles. Thus the Toba lost ground also in the military administration.

The wars down to A.D. 440 had been large-scale wars of conquest, lightning campaigns that had brought in a great deal of booty. With their loot the Toba developed great magnificence and luxury. The campaigns that followed were hard and long-drawn-out struggles, especially against South China, where there was no booty, because the enemy retired so slowly that they could take everything with them. The Toba therefore began to be impoverished, because plunder was the main source of their wealth. In addition to this, their herds gradually deteriorated, for less and less use was made of them; for instance, horses were little required for the campaign against South China, and there was next to no fighting in the north. In contrast with the impoverishment of the Toba, the Chinese gentry grew not only more powerful but more wealthy.

Thus in the years between 440 and 490 there were great changes not only in the economic but in the sociological sphere. The Toba declined in number and influence. Many of them married into rich families of the Chinese gentry and regarded themselves as no longer belonging to the Toba. In the course of time the court was completely sinified.

The Chinese at the court now formed the leading element, and they tried to persuade the emperor to claim dominion over all China, at least in theory, by installing his capital in Loyang, the old centre of China. This transfer had the advantage for them personally that the territories in which their properties were situated were close to that capital, so that the corn they produced found a ready market. And it was indeed no longer possible to rule the great Toba empire, now covering the whole of North China, from North Shansi. The administrative staff was so great that the transport system was no longer able to bring in sufficient corn. For the existing capital did not lie on a navigable river, and all the corn had to be carted, an expensive and unsafe mode of transport. Ultimately, in 493–4, the Chinese gentry officials secured the transfer of the capital to Loyang. In the years 490 to 499 the Toba emperor Wen Ti (471–499) took further decisive steps required by the stage reached in internal development. All aliens were prohibited from using their own language in public life. Chinese became the official language. Chinese clothing and customs also became general. Owing to his bringing up, the emperor no longer regarded himself as Toba but as Chinese; he adopted the Chinese culture, acting as he was bound to do if he meant to be no longer an alien ruler in North China. Already he regarded himself as emperor of all China, so that the South Chinese empire was looked upon as a rebel State that had to be conquered. While, however, he succeeded in everything else, the campaign against the south failed except for some local successes.

The transfer of the capital to Loyang was a blow to the Toba nobles. Their herds became valueless, for animal products could not be carried over the long distance to the new capital. In Loyang the Toba nobles found themselves parted from their tribes, living in an unaccustomed climate, and with nothing to do, for all important posts were occupied by Chinese. The government refused to allow them to return to the north. Those who did not find their way into Chinese families and become Chinese grew visibly poorer and poorer.

5 *Victory and retreat of Buddhism*

What we said in regard to the religious position of the other alien peoples applied also to the Toba. As soon, however, as their empire grew, they, too, needed an "official" religion of their own. For a few years they had continued their old sacrifices to Heaven; then another course opened to them. The Toba, together with the Chinese living in the Toba empire, were all captured by Buddhism, and especially by its shamanist element. Throughout the early period of Buddhism in the Far East, the question had been discussed what should be the relations between the Buddhist monks and the emperor, whether they were subject to him or not. This was connected, of course, with the fact that most of the Buddhist monks were foreigners, who, in the view prevalent in the Far East, owed only a limited allegiance to the ruler of the land. The Buddhist monks at the Toba court now submitted to the emperor, regarding him as a reincarnation of Buddha. Thus the emperor became protector of Buddhism and a sort of god. This combination was a good substitute for the old Chinese theory that the emperor was the Son of Heaven; it increased the prestige and the splendour of the dynasty. At the same time the old shamanism was legitimized under a Buddhist reinterpretation. Thus Buddhism became a sort of official religion. The emperor appointed a Buddhist monk as head of the Buddhist Church, and through this "Pope" he conveyed endowments on a large scale to the Church.

Like all Turkish peoples, the Toba possessed a myth, according to which their ancestors came into the world from a sacred grotto. The Buddhists took advantage of this conception to construct, with money from the emperor, the vast and famous cave-temple of Yün Kang, in northern Shansi. If we come from the bare plains into the green river valley, we may see to this day hundreds of caves cut out of the steep cliffs of the river bank. Here monks lived in their cells, worshipping the deities, of whom they had thousands of busts and reliefs sculptured in stone, some of more than life-size, some diminutive. The majestic impression made to-day by the figures does not correspond to their original effect, for they were covered with a layer of coloured stucco.

We do not know the names of the artists and craftsmen who made these objects. Probably some at least were foreigners from Turkestan, for in spite of the predominantly Chinese character of these sculptures, some of them are reminiscent of works in Turkestan and even in the Near East. In the past the influences of the Near East on the Far East—influences traced back in the last resort to Greece—were greatly exaggerated; it was believed that Greek art, carried through Alexander's campaign as far as the present Afghanistan, degenerated there in the hands of Indian imitators (the so-called Gandhara art), and ultimately passed on in more and more distorted forms through Turkestan to China. Actually, however, some eight hundred years lay between Alexander's campaign and the Toba period sculptures at Yün Kang, and, owing to the different cultural development, the contents of the Greek and the Toba-period art were entirely different. We may say, therefore, that suggestions came from the centre of the Greco-Bactrian culture (in the present Afghanistan) and were worked out by the Toba artists; old forms were filled with a new content, and the elements in the reliefs of Yün Kang that seem to us to be non-Chinese were the result of this synthesis of Western inspiration and Turkish initiative. It is interesting to observe that all Turkish peoples showed special interest in sculpture, and as a rule in architecture; after the Toba period, sculpture flourished in China in the T'ang period, the period of strong cultural influence from Turkish peoples, and there was a further advance of sculpture and of the cave-dwellers' worship in the period of the "Five Dynasties" (906–960; three of these dynasties were Turkish) and the Mongol period.

But not all Buddhists joined the "Church", just as not all Taoists had joined the Church of popular Taoism. Some Buddhists remained in the small towns and villages and suffered oppression from the central Church. These village Buddhist monks soon became instigators of a considerable series of attempts at revolution. Their Buddhism was of the so-called "Maitreya school", which promised the appearance on earth of a new Buddha who would do away with all suffering and introduce a Golden Age. The Chinese peasantry, exploited by the gentry, came to the support of these monks, whose Messianism gave the poor a hope in this world. The nomad tribes also, abandoned by their nobles in the capital and wandering in poverty with their now worthless herds, joined these monks. We know of many revolts of Hun and Toba tribes in this period, revolts that had a religious appearance but in reality were simply the result of the extreme impoverishment of these remaining tribes.

With the growing influence of the Chinese gentry, however, Confucianism gained ground again, until with the transfer of the capital to Loyang it gained a complete victory, taking the place of Buddhism and becoming once more as in the past the official religion of the State. This process shows us once more how closely the social order of the gentry was associated with Confucianism.

(E) Succession States of the Toba (A.D. 550–580): Northern Ch'i dynasty, Northern Chou dynasty

1 *Reasons for the splitting of the Toba empire*

Events now pursued their logical course. The opposition between the central power, now become entirely Chinese, and the remains of the tribes, who were with their herds mainly in Shansi and the Ordos region and were hopelessly impoverished, grew more and more acute. From 530 onward the risings became more and more formidable. A few Toba who still remained with their old tribes placed themselves at the head of the rebels and conquered not only the whole of Shansi but also the capital, where there was a great massacre of Chinese and pro-Chinese Toba. The rebels were driven back; in this a man of the Kao family distinguished himself, and all the Chinese and pro-Chinese gathered round him. The Kao family, which may have been originally a Hsien Pi family or possibly Chinese, had its ancestral estates in eastern China, and so was closely associated with the gentry of eastern China, who were the actual rulers of the Toba State. In 534 this group took the impotent emperor of their own creation to the city of Yeh in the east, where he reigned *de jure* for a further sixteen years. Then he was deposed, and Kao Yang made himself the first emperor of the Northern Ch'i dynasty (550–577).

The national Toba group, on the other hand, found another man of the imperial family and established him in the west. After a short time this puppet was removed from the throne and a man of the Yü Wen family made himself emperor, founding the "Northern Chou dynasty" (557–580). The Hsien Pi family of Yü Wen was a branch of the Hsien Pi, but was closely connected with the Huns and probably of Turkish origin. All the still existing remains of Toba tribes who had eluded sinification moved into this western empire.

The splitting of the Toba empire into these two separate realms was the result of the policy embarked on at the foundation of the empire. Once the tribal chieftains and nobles had been separated from their tribes and organized militarily, it was inevitable that the two elements should have different social destinies. The nobles could not hold their own against the Chinese; if they were not actually eliminated in one way or another, they disappeared into Chinese families. The rest, the people of the tribe, became destitute and were driven to revolt. The northern peoples had been unable to perpetuate either their tribal or their military organization, and the Toba had been equally unsuccessful in their attempt to perpetuate the two forms of organization alongside each other.

These sociological processes are of particular importance because the ethnical disappearance of the northern peoples in China had nothing to do with any racial inferiority or with any particular power of assimilation; it was a natural process resulting from the different economic, social, and cultural organizations of the northern peoples and the Chinese.

2 *Appearance of the (Gök) Turks*

The Toba had liberated themselves early in the fifth century from the Turco-Mongolian Yüan Yüan peril. None of the fighting that followed was of any great importance. The Toba resorted to the old means of defence against nomads —they built great walls. Apart from that, after their move southward to Loyang, their new capital, they were no longer greatly interested in their northern territories. When the Toba empire split into the Ch'i and the Northern

Chou, the remaining Yüan Yüan entered into treaties first with one realm and then with the other: each realm wanted to secure the help of the Yüan Yüan against the other.

Meanwhile there came unexpectedly to the fore in the north a people grouped round a nucleus tribe of Huns, the tribal union of the "T'u Chüeh", that is to say the Gök Turks, who began to pursue a policy of their own under their khan. In 546 they sent a mission to the western empire, then in the making, of the Northern Chou, and created the first bonds with it, following which the Northern Chou became allies of the Turks. The eastern empire, Ch'i, accordingly made terms with the Yüan Yüan, but in 552 the latter suffered a crushing defeat at the hands of the Turks, their former vassals. The remains of the Yüan Yüan either fled to the Ch'i State or went reluctantly into the land of the Chou. Soon there was friction between the Yüan Yüan and the Ch'i, and in 555 the Yüan Yüan in that State were annihilated. In response to pressure from the Turks, the Yüan Yüan in the western empire of the Northern Chou were delivered up to them and killed in the same year. The Yüan Yüan then disappeared from the history of the Far East. It was supposed in the past that the "Avars" who appeared in the Middle East in 558 were identical with the Yüan Yüan, but the general view now is that they were not, and that after 555 the vestiges of the Yüan Yüan broke up into their several tribes, some of which were admitted into the Turks' tribal league. A few years later the Turks also annihilated the Ephthalites, who had been allied with the Yüan Yüan; this made the Turks the dominant power in Central Asia. One menace to the northern States of China had disappeared—that of the Yüan Yüan. Their place was taken by a much more dangerous power, the Turks.

3 *The Northern Ch'i dynasty; the Northern Chou dynasty*

In consequence of this the main task of the Northern Chou State consisted in the attempt to come to some settlement with its powerful Turkish neighbours, and meanwhile to gain what it could from shrewd negotiations with its other neighbours. By means of intrigues and diplomacy it intervened with some success in the struggles in South China. One of the pretenders to the throne was given protection; he was installed in the present Hankow as a feudal lord depending on Chou, and there he founded the "Later Liang dynasty" (555-587). In this way Chou had brought the bulk of South China under its control without itself making any real contribution to that result.

Unlike the Chinese State of Ch'i, Chou followed the old Toba tradition; here, however, dissolution had proceeded far. Old customs were revived, such as the old sacrifice to Heaven and the lifting of the emperor on to a carpet at his accession to the throne; family names that had been sinified were turned into Toba names again, and even Chinese were given Toba names; but in spite of this the inner cohesion had been destroyed. After two centuries it was no longer possible to go back to the old nomad, tribal life. There were also too many Chinese in the country, with whom close bonds had been forged which, in spite of all attempts, could not be broken. Consequently there was little left but a State essentially similar to the great Toba empire.

There is just as little of importance that can be said of the internal politics of the Ch'i dynasty. The rulers of that dynasty were thoroughly repulsive figures, with no positive achievements of any sort to their credit. Confucianism had been restored in accordance with the Chinese character of the State. It was a bad time for Buddhists, and especially for the followers of the popularized Taoism. In spite of this, about A.D. 555 great new Buddhist cave-temples were created, in imitation of the famous temples of Yün Kang.

The fighting with the western empire, the Northern Chou State, still continued, and Ch'i was seldom successful. In 563 Chou made preparations for a decisive blow against Ch'i, but suffered defeat because the Turks, who had promised aid, gave none and shortly afterwards began campaigns of their own against Ch'i. In 571 Ch'i had some success in the west against Chou, but then it lost parts of its territory to the South Chinese empire, and finally in 576–7 it was defeated by Chou in a great counter-offensive. Thus for some three years all North China was once more under a single rule, though of nothing approaching the strength of the Toba at the height of their power. For in all these campaigns the Turks had played an important part, and at the end they annexed further territory in the north of Ch'i, so that their power extended far into the east.

Meanwhile intrigue followed intrigue at the court of Chou; the mutual assassinations within the ruling group were as incessant as in the last years of the great Toba empire, until the real power passed from the emperor and his Toba entourage to a Chinese family, the Yang. Yang Chien's daughter was the wife of a Chou emperor; his son was married to a girl of the Hun family Tu Ku; her sister was the wife of the father of the Chou emperor. Amid this tangled relationship in the imperial house it is not surprising that Yang Chien should attain great power. The Tu Ku were a very old family of the Hun nobility; originally the name belonged to the Hun house from which the *shan-yü* had to be descended. This family still observed the traditions of the Hun rulers, and relationship with it was regarded as an honour even by the Chinese. Through their centuries of association with aristocratically organized foreign peoples, some of the notions of nobility had taken root among the Chinese gentry; to be related with old ruling houses was a welcome means of evidencing or securing a position of special distinction among the gentry. Yang Chien gained useful prestige from his family connexions. After the leading Chinese cliques had regained predominance in the Chou empire, much as had happened before in the Toba empire, Yang Chien's position was strong enough to enable him to massacre the members of the imperial family and then, in 581, to declare himself emperor. Thus began the Sui dynasty, the first dynasty that was once more to rule all China.

But what had happened to the Toba? With the ending of the Chou empire they disappeared for all time, just as the Yüan Yüan had done a little earlier. So far as the tribes did not entirely disintegrate, the people of the tribes seem during the last years of Toba and Chou to have joined Turkish and other tribes. In any case, nothing more is heard of them as a people, and they themselves lived on under the name of the tribe that led the new tribal league.

Most of the Toba nobility, on the other hand, became Chinese. This process can be closely followed in the Chinese annals. The tribes that had disintegrated in the time of the Toba empire broke up into families of which some adopted the name of the tribe as their family name, while others chose Chinese family names. During the centuries that followed, in some cases, indeed, down to modern times, these families continue to appear, often playing an important part in Chinese history.

(F) The Southern Empires

1 *Economic and social situation in the south*

During the 260 years of alien rule in North China, the picture of South China also is full of change. When in 317 the Huns had destroyed the Chinese Chin dynasty in the north, a Chin prince who normally would not have become heir to the throne declared himself, under the name Yüan Ti, the first emperor of the "Eastern Chin dynasty" (317–419). The capital of this new southern empire adjoined the present Nanking. Countless members of the Chinese gentry had fled from the Huns at that time and had come into the southern empire. They had not done so out of loyalty to the Chinese dynasty, or out of national feeling, but because they saw little prospect of attaining rank and influence at the courts of the alien rulers, and because it was to be feared that the aliens would turn the fields into pasturage, and also that they would make an end of the economic and monetary system which the gentry had evolved for their own benefit.

But the south was not uninhabited. There were already two groups living there—the old autochthonous population, consisting of Yao, Tai, and Yüeh, and the earlier Chinese immigrants from the north, who had mainly arrived in the time of the Three Kingdoms, at the beginning of the third century A.D. The countless new immigrants now came into sharp conflict with the old-established population. Each group looked down on the other and abused it. The two populations not only spoke different languages but differed widely in manners and customs.

The two groups also differed socially: the old immigrants were firmly established on the large properties they had acquired, and dominated their tenants, who were largely autochthones; or they had engaged in large-scale commerce. In any case, they possessed capital, and more capital than was usually possessed by the gentry of the north. Some of the new immigrants, on the other hand, were military people. They came with empty hands, and they had no land. They hoped that the government would give them positions in the military administration, and so provide them with means; they tried to gain possession of the government and to exclude the old settlers as far as possible. The tension was increased by the effect of the influx of Chinese in bringing more land into cultivation, thus producing a boom period such as is produced by the opening up of colonial land. Everyone was in a hurry to grab as much land as possible. There was yet a further difference between the two groups of Chinese: the old settlers had long lost touch with the remainder of their families in the north. They had become South Chinese, and all their interests lay in the south. The new immigrants had left part of their families in the north under alien rule. Their interests still lay to some extent in the north. They were working for the reconquest of the north by military means; at times individuals or groups returned to the north, while others persuaded the rest of their relatives to come south. It would be wrong to suppose that there was no intercommunication between the two parts into which China had fallen. As soon as the Chinese gentry were able to regain any footing in the territories under alien rule, the official relations, often those of belligerency, proceeded alongside unofficial intercourse between individual families and family groupings, and these latter were, as a rule, in no way belligerent.

The lower stratum in the south consisted mainly of the remains of the original non-Chinese population, particularly in border and southern territories which had been newly annexed from time to time. In the centre of the southern State the way of life of the non-Chinese was very quickly assimilated to that of the Chinese, so that the aborigines were soon indistinguishable from Chinese. Their class was increased by impoverished Chinese peasants. This section of the population rarely took any active and visible part in politics, except at times in the form of great popular risings.

Until the third century, the south had been of no great economic importance, in spite of the good climate and the extraordinary fertility of the Yangtze valley. The country had been too thinly settled, and the indigenous population had not become adapted to organized trade. After the move southward of the Chin dynasty the many immigrants had made the country more thickly populated, but not over-populated. Thus the enormous estates of the southern gentry yielded more than before, and naturally much more than the small properties of the gentry in the north, where, moreover, the climate is far less favourable. Thus the southern landowners were able to acquire great wealth, which ultimately made itself felt in the capital.

2 *Struggles between cliques under the Eastern Chin dynasty* (A.D. 317–419)

The gentry immigrating from the north regarded the south as colonial country, and so as more or less uncivilized. They went into its provinces in order to get rich as quickly as possible, and they had no desire to live there for long: they had the same dislike of a provincial existence as had the families of the big landowners. Thus as a rule the bulk of the families remained in the capital, close to the court. Thither the products accumulated in the provinces were sent, and they found a ready sale, as the capital was also a great and long-established trading centre with a rich merchant class. Thus in the capital there was every conceivable luxury and every refinement of civilization. The people of the gentry class, who were maintained in the capital by relatives serving in the provinces as governors or senior officers, themselves held offices at court, though these gave them little to do. They had time at their disposal, and made use of it—in much worse intrigues than ever before, but also in music and poetry and in the social life of the harems. There is no question at all that the highest refinement of the civilization of the Far East between the fourth and the sixth century was to be found in South China, but the accompaniments of this over-refinement were terrible.

We cannot enter into all the intrigues recorded at this time. The details are, indeed, historically unimportant. They were concerned only with the affairs of the court and its entourage. Not a single ruler of the Eastern Chin dynasty possessed personal or political qualities of any importance. The rulers' power was extremely limited, because, with the exception of the founder of the State, Yüan Ti, who had come rather earlier, they belonged to the group of the new immigrants, and so had no firm footing and were therefore caught at once in the net of the newly forming gentry class.

The emperor Yüan Ti lived to see the first great rising. This rising (under Wang Tun) started in the region of the present Hankow, a region that to-day is one of the most important in China; it was already a centre of special activity. To it lead all the trade routes from the western provinces of Szechwan and Kweichow and from the central provinces of Hupei, Hunan, and Kiangsi. Normally the traffic from those provinces comes down the Yangtze, and thus in practice this region is united with that of the lower Yangtze, the environment of Nanking, so that Hankow might just as well have been the capital as Nanking. For this reason, in the period with which we are now concerned the region of the present Hankow was several times the place of origin of great risings whose aim was to gain control of the whole of the southern empire.

Wang Tun had grown rich and powerful in this region; he also had near relatives at the imperial court. So he was able to march against the capital. The emperor, in his weakness, was ready to abdicate, but died before that stage was reached. His son, however, defeated Wang Tun, with the aid of General Yü Liang (A.D. 323). Yü Liang was the empress's brother; he, too, came from a northern family. Yüan Ti's successor also died early, and the young son of Yü Liang's sister came to the throne as Emperor Ch'eng (326–342); his mother ruled as regent, but Yü Liang carried on the actual business of government. Against this clique rose Su Chün, another member of the northern gentry, who had made himself a leader of a band in A.D. 300 but had then been given a military command by the dynasty. In 328 he captured the capital and kidnapped the emperor, but then fell before the counterthrust of the Yü Liang party. The domination of Yü Liang's clique continued after the death of the emperor at the age of twenty-one. His twenty-year-old brother was set in his place; he, too, died two years later, and his two-year-old son became emperor (Mu Ti, 345–361).

Meanwhile this clique was reinforced by the very important Huan family. This family came from the same city as the imperial house, and was a very old gentry family of that city. One of the family attained a high post through personal friendship with Yü Liang: on his death his son Huan Wen came into special prominence, again as a soldier.

Huan Wen, like Wang Tun and others before him, tried to secure a firm foundation for his power, once more in the west. In 347 he reconquered Szechwan and deposed the local dynasty. Following this, Huan Wen and the Yü family undertook several joint campaigns against northern States—the first reaction of the south against the north, which in the past had always been the aggressor. The first fighting took place directly to the north, where the collapse of the "Later Chao" seemed to make intervention easy. The main objective was the regaining of the regions of eastern Honan, northern Anhwei and Kiangsu, in which were the family seats of Huan's and the emperor's families, as well as that of the Hsieh family, which also formed an important group in the court clique. The purpose of the northern campaigns was not, of course, merely to defend private interests of court cliques: the northern frontier was the weak spot of the southern empire, for its plains could easily be overrun. It was then observed that the new "Earlier Ch'in" State was trying to spread from the north-west eastwards into this plain, and Ch'in was attacked in an attempt to gain a more favourable frontier territory. These expeditions brought no important practical benefit to the south; and they were not embarked on with full force, because there was only the one court clique at the back of them, and that not whole-heartedly, since it was too much taken up with the politics of the court.

Huan Wen's power steadily grew in the period that followed. He sent his brothers and relatives to administer the regions along the upper Yangtze; those fertile regions were the basis of his power. In 371 he deposed the reigning emperor, and appointed in his place a frail old prince, who died a year later, as required, and was replaced by a child. The time had now come when Huan Wen might have ascended the throne himself, but he died. None of his family could assemble as much power as Huan Wen had done. The equality of strength of the Huan and the Hsieh saved the dynasty for a time.

In 383 came the great assault of the Tibetan Fu Chien against the south. As we know, it was carried out more by the methods of diplomacy and intrigue than by military means, and it led to the disaster in the north already described. The successes of the southern State especially strengthened the Hsieh family, whose generals had come to the fore. The emperor (Hsiao Wu Ti, 373–396), who had come to the throne as a child, played no part in events at any time during his reign. He occupied himself occasionally with Buddhism, and otherwise only with women and wine. He was followed by his five-year-old son. At this time there were some changes in the court clique. In the Huan family Huan Hsüan, a son of Huan Wen, came especially into prominence. He parted from the Hsieh family, which had been closest to the emperor, and united with the Wang (the empress's) and Yin families. The Wang, an old Shansi family, had already provided two empresses, and was therefore strongly represented at court. The Yin had worked at first with the Hsieh, especially as the two families came from the same region, but afterwards the Yin went over to Huan Hsüan. At first this new clique had success, but later one of its generals, Liu Lao-chih, went over to the Hsieh clique, and its power declined. Wang Kung was killed, and Yin Chung-k'an fell away from Huan Hsüan and was killed by him in 399. Huan Hsüan himself, however, held his own in the regions loyal to him. Liu Lao-chih had originally belonged to the Hsieh clique, and his family came from a region not far from that of the Hsieh. He was very ambitious, however, and always took the side which seemed most to his own interest. For a time he joined Huan Hsüan; then he went over to the Hsieh, and finally returned to Huan Hsüan in 402 when the latter reached the height of his power. At that moment Liu Lao-chih was responsible for the defence of the capital from Huan Hsüan, but instead he passed over to him. Thus Huan Hsüan conquered the capital, deposed the emperor, and began a dynasty of his own. Then came the reaction, led by an earlier subordinate of Liu Lao-chih, Liu Yü. It may be assumed that these two army commanders were in some way related, though the two branches of their family must have been long separated. Liu Yü had distinguished himself especially in the suppression of a great popular rising which about 400 had brought wide stretches of Chinese territory under the rebels' power, beginning with the southern coast. This rising was the first in the south. It was led by members of a secret society which was a direct continuation of the "Yellow Turbans" of the latter part of the second century A.D. The whole course of this rising of the exploited and ill-treated lower classes was very similar to that of the popular rising of the "Yellow Turbans". The movement spread as far as the neighbourhood of Canton, but in the end it was suppressed, mainly by Liu Yü.

Through these achievements Liu Yü's military power and political influence steadily increased; he became the exponent of all the cliques working against the Huan clique. He arranged for his supporters to dispose of Huan Hsüan's chief collaborators; and then, in 404, he himself marched on the capital. Huan Hsüan had to flee, and in his flight he was killed in the upper Yangtze region. The emperor was restored to his throne, but he had as little to say as ever, for the real power was Liu Yü's.

Before making himself emperor, Liu Yü began his great northern campaign, aimed at the conquest of the whole of western China. The Toba had promised to remain neutral, and in 415 he was able to conquer the "Later Ch'in" in Shansi. The first aim of this campaign was to make the trade routes to Central Asia, which had led through the difficult country of Szechwan, more accessible; to this end treaties of alliance had been concluded with the States in Kansu against the "Later Ch'in". In the second place, this war was intended to increase Liu Yü's military strength to such an extent that the imperial crown would be assured to him; and finally he hoped to cut the claws of the pro-Huan Hsüan elements in the "Later Ch'in" kingdom, who, for the sake of the link with Turkestan, had designs on Szechwan.

3 *The Liu-Sung dynasty* (A.D. 420–478) *and the Southern Ch'i dynasty* (479–501)

After his successes in 416–7 in Shensi, Liu Yü returned to the capital, and shortly after this he lost the chief fruits of his victory to Ho-lien P'o-p'o, the Hun ruler in the north, while Liu Yü himself was occupied with the killing of the emperor (419) and the installation of a puppet. In 420 the puppet had to abdicate and Liu Yü became emperor. He called his dynasty the Sung dynasty, but to distinguish it from another and more famous Sung dynasty of later times this is also called the Liu-Sung dynasty.

The struggles and intrigues of cliques against each other continued as before. We shall pass quickly over this period after a glance at the nature of these internal struggles.

Part of the old imperial family and its following fled northwards from Liu Yü and surrendered to the Toba. There they agitated for a campaign of vengeance against South China, and in this they were supported at the court of the Toba by many families of the gentry with landed interests in the south. Thus long-continued fighting started between Sung and Toba, concerned mainly with the domains of the deposed imperial family and its following. This fighting brought little success to South China, and about 450 it produced among the Toba an economic and social crisis that brought the wars to a temporary close. In this pause the Sung turned to the extreme south, and tried to gain influence there and in Annam. The merchant class and the gentry families of the capital who were allied with it were those chiefly interested in this expansion.

About 450 began the Toba policy of shifting the central government to the region of the river Hwang-ho, to Loyang; for this purpose the frontier had to be pushed further south. Their great campaign brought the Toba in 450 down to the Yangtze. The Sung suffered a heavy defeat; they had to pay tribute, and the Toba annexed parts of their northern territory.

The Sung emperors who followed were as impotent as their predecessors, and personally much more repulsive. Nothing happened at court but drinking, licentiousness, and continual murders.

From 460 onward there were a number of important risings of princes; in some of them the Toba had a hand. They hoped by supporting one or another of the pretenders to gain overlordship over the whole of the southern empire. In these struggles in the south the Hsiao family, thanks mainly to General Hsiao Tao-ch'eng, steadily gained in power, especially as the family was united by marriage with the imperial house. In 477 Hsiao Tao-ch'eng finally had the emperor killed by an accomplice, the son of a shamaness; he set a boy on the throne, and made himself regent. Very soon after this the boy emperor and all the members of the imperial family were murdered, and Hsiao Tao-ch'eng created the "Southern Ch'i" dynasty (479–501). Once more the remaining followers of the deposed dynasty fled northward to the Toba, and at once fighting between Toba and the south began again.

This fighting ended with a victory for the Toba, and with the final establishment of the Toba in the new capital of Loyang. South China was heavily defeated again and again, but never finally conquered. There were intervals of peace. In the years between 480 and 490 there was less disorder in the south, at all events in internal affairs. Princes were more often appointed to governorships, and the influence of the cliques was thus weakened. In spite of this, a stable régime was not built up, and in 494 a prince rose against the youthful emperor. This prince, with the help of his clique, including the Ch'en family, which later attained importance, won the day, murdered the emperor, and became emperor himself. All that is recorded about him is that he fought unsuccessfully against the Toba, and that he had the whole of his own family killed out of fear that one of its members might act exactly as he had done. After his death there were conflicts between the emperor's few remaining relatives; in these the Toba again had a hand. The victor was a person named Hsiao Yen; he removed the reigning emperor in the usual way, and made himself emperor. Although he belonged to the imperial family, he altered the name of the dynasty, and reigned from 502 as the first emperor of the "Liang dynasty".

4 *The Liang dynasty* (A.D. 502–556)

The fighting with the Toba continued until 515. As a rule the Toba were the more successful, not least through the aid of princes of the deposed "Southern Ch'i dynasty" and their followers. Wars began also in the west, where the Toba tried to cut off the access of the Liang to the caravan routes to Turkestan. In 507, however, the Toba suffered an important defeat. The southern States had tried at all times to work with the Kansu States against the northern States; the Toba now followed suit and allied themselves with a large group of native chieftains of the south, whom they incited to move against the Liang. This produced great native unrest, especially in the provinces by the upper Yangtze. The natives, who were steadily pushed back by the Chinese peasants, were reduced to migrating into the mountain country or to working for the Chinese in semi-servile conditions; and they were ready for revolt and very glad to work with the Toba. The result of this unrest was not decisive, but it greatly reduced the strength of the regions along the upper Yangtze. Thus the main strength of the southern State was more than ever confined to the Nanking region.

The first emperor of the Liang dynasty, who assumed the name Wu Ti (502–549), became well known in the European world owing to his love of literature and of Buddhism. After he had come to the throne with the aid of his followers, he took no further interest in politics; he left that to his court clique. From now on, however, the political initiative really belonged to the north. At this time there began in the Toba empire the risings of tribal leaders against the government which we have fully described above. One of these leaders, Hou Ching, who had become powerful as a military leader in the north, tried in 547 to conclude a private alliance with the Liang, to strengthen his own position. At the same time the ruler of the northern State of the "Northern Ch'i", then in process of formation, himself wanted to negotiate an alliance with the Liang, in order to be able to get rid of Hou Ching. There was indecision in Liang. Hou Ching, who had been getting into difficulties, now negotiated with a dissatisfied prince in Liang, invaded the country in 548 with the prince's aid, captured the capital in 549, and killed Emperor Wu. Hou Ching now staged the usual spectacle: he put a puppet on the imperial throne, deposed him eighteen months later, and made himself emperor.

This man of the Toba on the throne of South China was

unable, however, to maintain his position; he had not sufficient backing. He was at war with the new rulers in the northern empire, and his own army, which was not very large, melted away; above all, he proceeded with excessive harshness against the helpers who had gained access for him to the Liang, and thereafter he failed to secure a following from among the leading cliques at court. In 552 he was driven out by a Chinese army led by one of the princes, and killed.

The new emperor had been a prince in the upper Yangtze region, and his closest associates were engaged there. They did not want to move to the distant capital, Nanking, because their private financial interests would have suffered. The emperor therefore remained in the city now called Hankow. He left the eastern territory in the hands of two powerful generals, one of whom belonged to the Ch'en family, which he no longer had the strength to remove. In this situation the generals in the east made themselves independent, and this naturally produced tension at once between the east and the west of the Liang empire; this tension was now exploited by the leaders of the Chou State then in the making in the north. On the invitation of a clique in the south, and with its support, the Chou invaded the present province of Hupei, and in 555 captured the Liang emperor's capital. They were now able to achieve their old ambition: a prince of the Chou dynasty was installed as a feudatory of the north, reigning until 587 in the present Hankow. He was permitted to call his feudal territory a kingdom and his dynasty, as we know already, the "Later Liang dynasty".

5 *The Ch'en dynasty* (A.D. 557–588) *and its ending by the Sui*

The more important of the independent generals in the east, Ch'en Pa-hsien, installed a shadow emperor, forced him to abdicate, and made himself emperor. The Ch'en dynasty which thus began was even feebler than the preceding dynasties. Its territory was confined to the lower Yangtze valley. Once more cliques and rival pretenders were at work, and prevented any sort of constructive home policy. Abroad, certain advantages were gained in north China over the Northern Ch'i dynasty, but none of any great importance.

Meanwhile in the north Yang Chien had brought into power the Chinese Sui dynasty. It began by liquidating the feudal State of the "Later Liang". Then followed, in 588–9, the conquest of the Ch'en empire, almost without any serious resistance. This brought all China once more under united rule, and a period of 360 years of division was ended.

6 *Cultural achievements of the south*

For nearly three hundred years the southern empire had witnessed unceasing struggles between important cliques, making impossible any peaceful development within the country. Culturally, however, the period was rich in achievement. The court and the palaces of wealthy members of the gentry attracted scholars and poets, and the gentry themselves had time for artistic occupations. A large number of the best-known Chinese poets appeared in this period, and their works plainly reflect the conditions of that time: they are poems for the small circle of scholars among the gentry and for cultured patrons, spiced with quotations and allusions, elaborate in metre and construction, masterpieces of aesthetic sensitivity—but unintelligible except to highly educated members of the aristocracy. The works were of the most artificial type, far removed from all natural feeling.

Music, too, was never so assiduously cultivated as at this time. But the old Chinese music disappeared in the south as in the north, where dancing troupes and women musicians in the Sogdian commercial colonies of the province of Kansu established the music of western Turkestan. Here in the south, native courtesans brought the aboriginal, non-Chinese music to the court; Chinese poets wrote songs in Chinese for this music, and so the old Chinese music became unfashionable and was forgotten. The upper class, the gentry, bought these girls, often in large numbers, and organized them in troupes of singers and dancers, who had to appear on festal occasions and even at the court. For merchants and other people who lacked full social recognition there were brothels, a quite compulsory feature wherever there were considerable commercial colonies or collections of merchants, including the capital of the southern empire.

In their ideology, as will be remembered, the Chinese gentry were always in favour of Confucianism. Here in the south, however, the association with Confucianism was less serious, the southern gentry, with their relations with the merchant class, having acquired the character of "colonial" gentry. They were brought up as Confucians, but were interested in all sorts of different religious movements, and especially in Buddhism. A different type of Buddhism from that in the north had spread over most of the south, a meditative Buddhism that was very close ideologically to the original Taoism, and so fulfilled the same sociological functions as Taoism. Those who found the official life with its intrigues repulsive, occupied themselves with meditative Buddhism. The monks told of the sad fate of the wicked in the life to come, and industriously filled the gentry with apprehension, so that they tried to make up for their evil deeds by rich gifts to the monasteries. Many emperors in this period, especially Wu Ti, of the Liang dynasty, inclined to Buddhism. Wu Ti turned to it especially in his old age, when he was shut out entirely from the tasks of a ruler and was no longer satisfied with the usual pleasures of the court. Several times he instituted Buddhist ceremonies of purification on a large scale, in the hope of so securing forgiveness for the many murders he had committed.

Genuine Taoism also came to the fore again, and with it the popular religion with its magic, now amplified with the many local deities that had been taken over from the indigenous population of the south. For a time it became the fashion at court to pass the time in learned discussions between Confucians, Buddhists, and Taoists, just as had been done centuries earlier at the wealthy little Indian courts. For the court clique this was more a matter of pastime than of religious controversy. It seems thoroughly in harmony with the political events that here, for the first time in the history of Chinese philosophy, materialist currents made their appearance, running parallel with Machiavellian theories of power for the benefit of the wealthiest of the gentry.

8 Detail from the Buddhist cave-reliefs of Lungmen.
From a print in the author's possession.

9 Statue of Mi-lo (Maitreya, the next future Buddha), in the 'Great Buddha Temple' at Chengting (Hopei).
Photo H. Hammer-Morrisson.

Principal dynasties of North and South China

North and South

Western Chin dynasty (A.D. 265-317)

North		*South*	
1. Earlier Chao (Hsiung Nu)	304–329	1. Eastern Chin (Chinese)	317–419
2. Later Chao (Hsiung Nu)	328–352		
3. Earlier Ch'in (Tibetans)	351–394		
4. Later Ch'in (Tibetans)	384–417		
5. Western Ch'in (Hsiung Nu)	385–431		
6. Earlier Yen (Hsien Pi)	352–370		
7. Later Yen (Hsien Pi)	384–409		
8. Western Yen (Hsien Pi)	384–395		
9. Southern Yen (Hsien Pi)	398–410		
10. Northern Yen (Hsien Pi)	409–436		
11. Tai (Toba),	338–376		
12. Earlier Liang (Chinese)	313–376		
13. Northern Liang (Hsiung Nu)	397–439		
14. Western Liang (Chinese?)	400–421		
15. Later Liang (Tibetans)	386–403		
16. Southern Liang (Hsien Pi)	379–414		
17. Hsia (Hsiung Nu)	407–431		
18. Toba (Turks)	385–550		
		2. Liu-Sung	420–478
		3. Southern Ch'i	479–501
19. Northern Ch'i (Chinese?)	550–576	4. Liang	502–556
20. Northern Chou (Toba)	557–579	5. Ch'en	557–588
21. Sui (Chinese)	580–618	6. Sui	580–618

Chapter VIII

THE EMPIRES OF THE SUI AND THE T'ANG

(A) The Sui dynasty (A.D. 580–618)

1 *Internal situation in the newly unified empire*

THE last of the northern dynasties, the Northern Chou, had been brought to an end by Yang Chien, and the Sui dynasty had come into power; rapid campaigns had made an end of the remaining petty States, and China was united once more, after 360 years, and brought under Chinese rule. This began a new epoch in the history of the Far East. But the events of 360 years could not be wiped out by a change of dynasty. The short Sui period can only be described as a period of transition to unified forms. In the last resort the union of the various parts of China proceeded from the north. The north had always, beyond question, been militarily superior, because its ruling class had consisted of warlike peoples. Yet it was not a northerner who had united China, but a Chinese, though, owing to mixed marriages, he was certainly not entirely unrelated to the northern peoples. The rule, however, of the actual northern peoples was at an end. The start of the Sui dynasty, while the Chou still held the north, was evidence, just like the emergence in the north-east, some thirty years earlier, of the Northern Ch'i dynasty, that the Chinese gentry, with their landowning basis, had gained the upper hand over the warrior nomads.

The Chinese gentry had not come unchanged out of that struggle. Culturally they had taken over many things from the foreigners, beginning with music and the style of their clothing, in which they had entirely adopted the northern pattern, and including other elements of daily life. Among the gentry were now many formerly alien families who had gradually become entirely Chinese. On the other hand, the foreigners' feudal outlook had influenced the gentry, so that a sense of distinctions of rank had developed among them. There were Chinese families who regarded themselves as superior to the rest, just as had been the case among the northern peoples, and who married only among themselves or with the ruling house and not with ordinary families of the gentry. At the same time the contempt of the military underwent modification; the gentry were even ready to take over high military posts, and also to profit by them.

The new Sui empire found itself faced with many difficulties. During the three and a half centuries of division, north and south had grown different from each other. They no longer spoke the same language in everyday life (we distinguish to this day between a Nanking and Peking "High Chinese", to say nothing of dialects). The social and economic structure was very different in the two parts of the country. How could unity be restored in these things?

Then there was the problem of population. The north-eastern plain had always been thickly populated; it had early come under Toba rule, and had been able to develop further. The region round the old northern capital, on the other hand, had suffered greatly from the struggles before the Toba period, and had never entirely recovered. The country had become thinly populated, and has remained so to this day, except in the towns. Meanwhile, in the south the population had greatly increased in the region north of Nanking, while the regions south of the Yangtze and the upper Yangtze valley were more thinly peopled. In the matter of population, however, the north unquestionably led.

The founder of the Sui dynasty, known by his reign name of Wen Ti (589–604), came from the west, close to Ch'ang-an. There he and his following had their extensive domains. Owing to the scanty population there, and the resulting shortage of agricultural labourers, these properties were very much less productive than the small properties in the north-east. This state of things was well known in the south, and it was expected, with good reason, that the government would try to transfer parts of the population to the north-west, in order to settle a peasantry round the capital for the support of its greatly increasing staff of officials, and to satisfy the gentry of the region. This produced several revolts in the south.

As an old soldier who had long been a subject of the Toba, Wen Ti had no great understanding of theory: he was a practical man. He opposed Confucianist education, because it gave him no serviceable officials of the sort he wanted. He demanded from his officials the same obedience and sense of duty as from his soldiers; and he was above all thrifty, almost miserly, because he realized that the finances of his State could only be brought into order by the greatest exertions. The budget had to be drawn up for the vast territory of the empire without any possibility of saying in advance whether the revenues would come in and whether the transport of dues to the capital would function.

This cautious calculation was entirely justified, but it aroused great opposition. Both east and south were used to a much better style of living; yet the gentry of both regions were now required to cut down their consumption. On top of this they were excluded from the conduct of political affairs. In the past, under the Northern Ch'i empire in the north-east and under the Ch'en empire in the south, there had been thousands of positions at court in which the whole of the gentry could find support of some kind. Now the central government was far in the west, and other people were its administrators. In the past the gentry had had a profitable and easily accessible market for their produce in the neighbouring capital; now the capital was far away, entailing long-distance transport at heavy risk with little profit.

The dissatisfied circles of the gentry in the north-east and in the south placed themselves under Prince Kuang. The prince and his followers murdered the emperor and set aside the heir-apparent; and Kuang came to the throne, assuming the name of Yang Ti. His first act was to transfer the capital back to the east, to Loyang, close to the grain-producing regions. His second achievement was to order the construction of great canals, to facilitate the transport of grain to the capital and to provide a valuable new market for the producers in the north-east and the south. It was at this time that the first forerunner of the famous "Imperial Canal" was constructed, the canal that unites the Yangtze with the Yellow River. Small canals had long been in existence, connecting streams together, so that it was possible to travel from north to south by water, but these canals were not deep enough or broad enough to take large freight barges. There are records of lighters of 500 and even 800 tons capacity! These are dimensions unheard of in the West in those times. In addition to a serviceable canal to the south, Yang Ti made another that went north almost to the present Peking.

Hand in hand with these successes of the north-eastern and southern gentry went strong support for Confucianism, and a reorganization of the Confucian examination system. As a rule, however, the examinations were circumvented as an unimportant formality; the various governors were ordered each to send annually to the capital three men with the required education, for whose quality they were held personally responsible: merchants and artisans were expressly excluded.

2 *Relations with Turks and with Korea*

In foreign affairs an extraordinarily fortunate situation for the Sui dynasty had come into existence. The T'u-chüeh, the Turks, much the strongest people of the north, had given support now to one and now to another of the northern kingdoms, and this, together with their many armed incursions, had made them the dominant political factor in the north. But in the first year of the Sui period (581) they split into two sections, so that the Sui had hopes of gaining influence over them. At first both sections of the Turks had entered into alliance with China, but this was not a sufficient safeguard for the Sui, for one of the

Turkish khans was surrounded by Toba who had fled from the vanished State of the Northern Chou, and who now tried to induce the Turks to undertake a campaign for the reconquest of North China. The leader of this agitation was a princess of the Yü Wen family, the ruling family of the Northern Chou. The Chinese fought the Turks several times; but much more effective results were gained by their diplomatic missions, which incited the eastern against the western Turks and vice versa, and also incited the Turks against the Toba clique. In the end one of the sections of Turks accepted Chinese overlordship, and some tribes of the other section were brought over to the Chinese side; fresh disunion was also sown among the Turks.

Under the emperor Yang Ti, P'ei Chü carried this policy further. He induced the Tölös tribes to attack the T'u-yü-hun, and then himself attacked the latter, so destroying their power. The T'u-yü-hun were a people living in the extreme north of Tibet, under a ruling class apparently of Hsien Pi; the people were largely Tibetan. The purpose of the conquest of the T'u-yü-hun was to safeguard access to Central Asia. An effective Turkestan policy was, however, impossible so long as the Turks were still a formidable power. Accordingly, the intrigues that aimed at keeping the two sections of Turks apart were continued. In 615 came a decisive counter-attack from the Turks. Their khan, Shih Pi, made a surprise assault on the emperor himself, with all his following, in the Ordos region, and succeeded in surrounding them. They were in just the same desperate situation as when, eight centuries earlier, the Chinese emperor had been beleaguered by Mao Tun. But the Chinese again saved themselves by a trick. The young Chinese commander, Li Shih-min, succeeded in giving the Turks the impression that large reinforcements were on the way; a Chinese princess who was with the Turks spread the rumour that the Turks were to be attacked by another tribe—and Shih Pi raised the siege, although the Chinese had been entirely defeated.

In the Sui period the Chinese were faced with a further

problem. Korea, or, rather, the chief of the three States in Korea, had generally been on friendly terms with the southern State during the period of China's division, and for this reason had been more or less protected from its North Chinese neighbours. After the unification of China, Korea had reason for seeking an alliance with the Turks, in order to secure a new counterweight against China.

A Turco-Korean alliance would have meant for China a sort of encirclement that might have grave consequences. The alliance might be extended to Japan, who had certain interests in Korea. Accordingly the Chinese determined to attack Korea, though at the same time negotiations were set on foot. The fighting, which lasted throughout the Sui period, involved technical difficulties, as it called for combined land and sea attacks; in general it brought little success.

3 *Reasons for collapse*

The continual warfare entailed great expense, and so did the intrigues, because they depended for their success on bribery. Still more expensive were the great canal works. In addition to this, the emperor Yang Ti, unlike his father, was very extravagant. He built enormous palaces, and undertook long journeys throughout the empire with an immense following. All this wrecked the prosperity which his father had built up and had tried to safeguard. The only productive expenditure was that on the canals, and they could not begin to pay in so short a period. The emperor's continual journeys were due, no doubt, in part simply to the pursuit of pleasure, though they were probably intended at the same time to hinder risings and to give the emperor direct control over every part of the country. But the empire was too large and too complex for its administration to be possible in the midst of journeying. The whole of the chancellery had to accompany the emperor, and all the transport necessary for the feeding of the emperor and his government had continually to be diverted to wherever he happened to be staying. All this produced disorder and unrest. The gentry, who at first had so strongly supported the emperor and had been able to obtain anything they wanted from him, now began to desert him and set up pretenders. From 615 onward, after the defeat at the hands of the Turks, risings broke out everywhere. The emperor had to establish his government in the south, where he felt safer. There, however, in 618, he was assassinated by conspirators led by Toba of the Yü Wen family. Everywhere now independent governments sprang up, and for five years China was split up into countless petty States.

(B) The T'ang dynasty (A.D. 618–906)

1 *Reforms and decentralization*

The hero of the Turkish siege, Li Shih-min, had allied himself with the Turks in 615–6. There were special reasons for his ability to do this. In his family it had been a regular custom to marry women belonging to Toba families, so that he naturally enjoyed the confidence of the Toba party among the Turks. There are various theories as to the origin of his family, the Li. The family itself claimed to be descended from the ruling family of the Western Liang. It is doubtful whether that family was purely Chinese, and in any case Li Shih-min's descent from it is a matter of doubt. It is possible that his family was a sinified Toba family, or at least came from a Toba region. However this may be, Li Shih-min continued the policy which had been pursued since the beginning of the Sui dynasty by the members of the deposed Toba ruling family of the Northern Chou—the policy of collaboration with the Turks in the effort to remove the Sui.

The nominal leadership in the rising that now began lay in the hands of Li Shih-min's father, Li Yüan; in practice Li Shih-min saw to everything. At the end of 617 he was outside the first capital of the Sui, Ch'ang-an, with a Turkish army that had come to his aid on the strength of the treaty of alliance. After capturing Ch'ang-an he installed

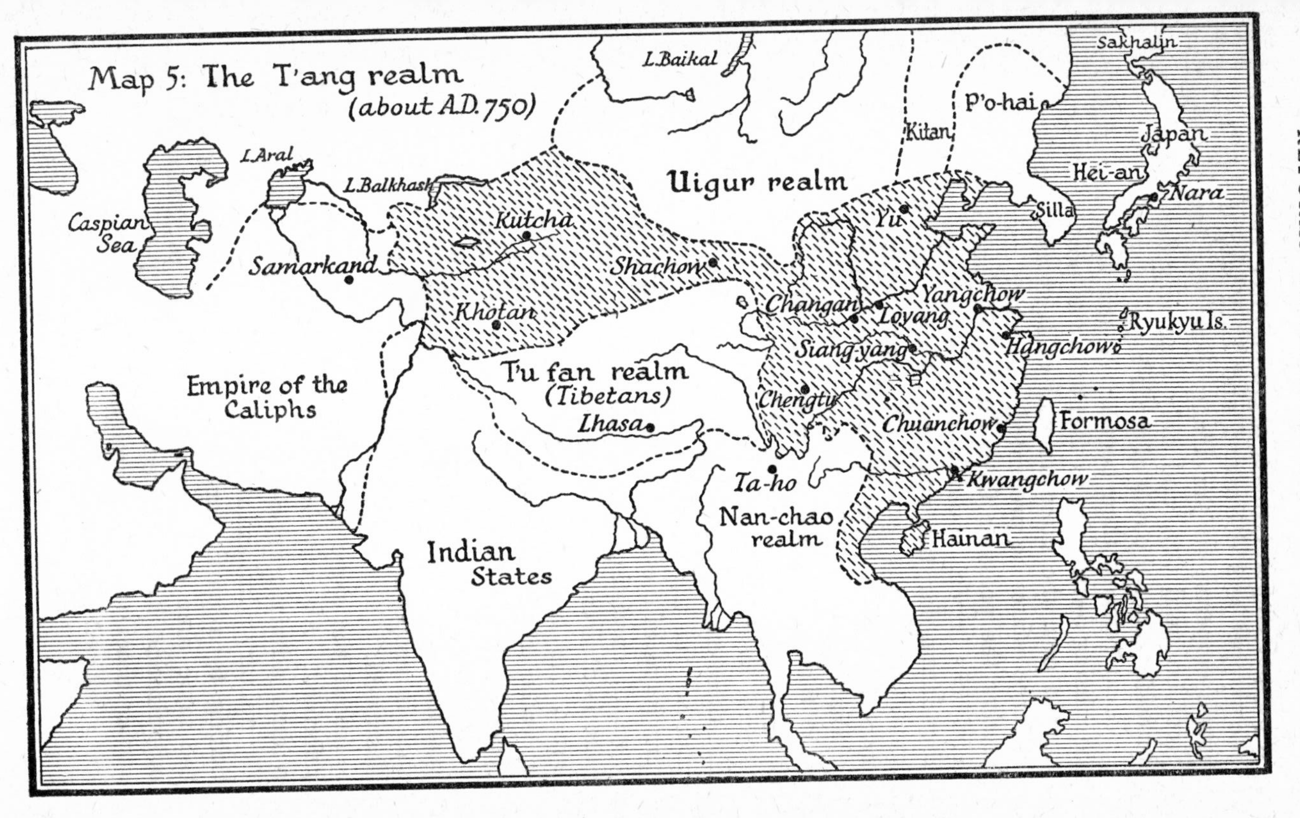

Map 5: The T'ang realm (about A.D. 750)

a puppet emperor there, a grandson of Yang Ti. In 618 the puppet was dethroned and Li Yüan, the father, was made emperor, in the T'ang dynasty. Internal fighting went on until 623, and only then was the whole empire brought under the rule of the T'ang.

Great reforms then began. A new land law aimed at equalizing ownership, so that as far as possible all peasants should own the same amount of land and the formation of large estates be prevented. The law aimed also at protecting the peasants from the loss of their land. This, it had been hoped, would provide a sound and solid economic foundation for the empire. From the first, however, members of the gentry who were connected with the imperial house were given a privileged position; then officials were excluded from the prohibition of leasing, so that there continued to be tenant farmers in addition to the independent peasants. Moreover, the temples enjoyed special treatment, and were also exempted from taxation. All these exceptions brought grist to the mills of the gentry, and so did the failure to carry into effect many of the provisions of the law. Before long a new gentry had been formed, consisting of the old gentry together with those who had directly aided the emperor's ascent to the throne. From the beginning of the eighth century there were repeated complaints that peasants were "disappearing". They were entering the service of the gentry as tenant farmers or farm workers, and owing to the privileged position of the gentry in regard to taxation, the revenue sank in proportion as the number of independent peasants decreased.

About the same time, in 624, the administration was reformed. As early as in the Han period there had been a dual administration—the civil and, independent of it, the military administration. One and the same area would belong to a particular administrative prefecture and at the same time to a particular military prefecture. This organization had persisted during the Toba period. In earlier times the civil administration had always been of more importance than the military; now the latter gained the upper hand. New military governors-general were appointed, no longer to a small prefecture like the usual military governors, but to command a number of districts making up a whole province. This assured a better functioning of the military machine, but put the governors-general in a position to pursue a policy of their own, even against the central government. In addition to this, the financial administration of their commands was put under them, whereas in the past it had been in the hands of the civil administration of the various provinces. The civil administration was also reorganized (see the table on pages 83–4).

Toward the end of the T'ang period the State secretariat was set up in two parts: it was in possession of all information about the economic and political affairs of the empire, and it made the actual decisions. Moreover, a number of technical departments had been created—in all, a system that might compare favourably with European systems of the eighteenth century! At the end of the T'ang period there was added to this system a section for economic affairs, working quite independently of it and directly under the emperor; it was staffed entirely with economic or financial experts, while for the staffing of the other departments no special qualification was demanded, only the passing of the State examinations. In addition to these, at the end of the T'ang period a new department was in preparation, a sort of Privy Council, a mainly military organization, probably intended to control the generals (section 3 of the table on page 83), as the State secretariat controlled the civil officials. The Privy Council became more and more important in the tenth century, and especially in the Mongol epoch. Its absence in the early T'ang period gave the military governors much too great freedom, ultimately with baneful results.

At first, however, the reform of A.D. 624 worked well. The administration showed energy, and taxes flowed in. In the middle of the eighth century the annual budget of the State included the following items: over a million tons of corn for the consumption of the capital and the palace and for salaries of civil and military officials; 27 million pieces of textiles, also for the consumption of capital and palace and army, and for supplementary purchases of corn; two million strings of money (a string nominally held a thousand copper coins) for salaries and for the army. This was much more than the State budget of the Han period. The population of the empire had also increased; it seems to have amounted to some fifty millions. In the capital a large staff of officials had been created to meet all administrative needs. The capital grew enormously, sometimes containing two million people. Great numbers of young members of the gentry streamed into the capital for the examinations held under the Confucian system.

The crowding of people into the capital and the accumulation of resources there promoted a rich cultural life. We know of many poets of that period whose poems were real masterpieces; and artists whose works were admired centuries later. These poets and artists were the pioneers of the flourishing culture of the later T'ang period. Hand in hand with this went luxury and refinement of manners. For those who retired from the bustle of the capital to work on their estates and to enjoy the society of their friends, there was time to occupy themselves with Taoism and Buddhism, especially meditative Buddhism. Everyone, of course, was Confucian, as was fitting for a member of the gentry, but Confucianism was so taken for granted that it was not discussed. It was the basis of morality for the gentry, but held no problems. It no longer contained anything of interest.

Conditions had been much the same once before, at the court of the Han emperors, but with one great difference: at that time everything of importance took place in the capital; now, in addition to the actual capital, Ch'ang-an, there was the second capital, Loyang, in no way inferior to the other in importance; and the great towns in the south also played their part as commercial and cultural centres that had developed in the 360 years of division between north and south. There the local gentry gathered to lead a cultivated life, though not quite in the grand style of the capital. If an official was transferred to the

Yangtze, it no longer amounted to a punishment as in the past; he would not meet only uneducated people, but a society resembling that of the capital. The institution of governors-general further promoted this decentralization: the governor-general surrounded himself with a little court of his own, drawn from the local gentry and the local intelligentsia. This placed the whole edifice of the empire on a much broader foundation, with lasting results.

2 *Turkish policy*

The foreign policy of this first period of the T'ang, lasting until about 690, was mainly concerned with the Turks and Turkestan. There were still two Turkish realms in the Far East, both of considerable strength but in keen rivalry with each other. The T'ang had come into power with the aid of the eastern Turks, but they admitted the leader of the western Turks to their court; he had been at Ch'ang-an in the time of the Sui. He was murdered, however, by Chinese at the instigation of the eastern Turks. The next khan of the eastern Turks nevertheless turned against the T'ang, and gave his support to a still surviving pretender to the throne representing the Sui dynasty; the khan contended that the old alliance of the eastern Turks had been with the Sui and not with the T'ang. The T'ang therefore tried to come to terms once more with the western Turks, who had been affronted by the assassination; but the negotiations came to nothing in face of an approach made by the eastern Turks to the western, and of the distrust of the Chinese with which all the Turks were filled. About 624 there were strong Turkish invasions, carried right up to the capital. Suddenly, however, for reasons not disclosed by the Chinese sources, the Turks withdrew, and the T'ang were able to conclude a fairly honourable peace. This was the time of the maximum power of the eastern Turks. Shortly afterwards disturbances broke out (627), under the leadership of Turkish Uighurs and their allies. The Chinese took advantage of these disturbances, and in a great campaign in 629–30 succeeded in overthrowing the eastern Turks; the khan was taken to the imperial court in Ch'ang-an, and the Chinese emperor made himself "Heavenly Khan" of the Turks. In spite of the protest of many of the Ministers, who pointed to the result of the settlement policy of the Later Han dynasty, the eastern Turks were settled in the bend of the upper Hwang-ho and placed more or less under the protectorate of two governors-general. Their leaders were admitted into the Chinese army, and the sons of their nobles lived at the imperial court. No doubt it was hoped in this way to turn the Turks into Chinese, as had been done with the Toba, though for entirely different reasons. More than a million Turks were settled in this way, and some of them did actually become Chinese later, and gained important posts.

In general, however, this in no way broke the power of the Turks. The great Turkish empire, which extended as far as Byzantium, continued to exist. The Chinese success had done no more than safeguard the frontier from a direct menace and frustrate the efforts of the supporters of the Sui dynasty and the Toba dynasty, who had been living among the eastern Turks and had built on them. The power of the western Turks remained a lasting menace to China, especially if they should succeed in co-operating with the Tibetans. After the annihilation of the T'u-yü-hun by the Sui at the very beginning of the seventh century, a new political unit had formed in northern Tibet, the T'u-fan, who also seem to have had an upper class of Turks and Mongols and a Tibetan lower class. Just as in the Han period, Chinese policy was bound to be directed to preventing a union between Turks and Tibetans. This, together with commercial interests, seems to have been the political motive of the Chinese Turkestan policy under the T'ang.

3 *Conquest of Turkestan and Korea. Summit of power*

The Turkestan wars began in 639 with an attack on the city-State of Kao-ch'ang (Khocho). This State had been on more or less friendly terms with North China since the Toba period, and it had succeeded again and again in preserving a certain independence from the Turks. Now, however, Kao-ch'ang had to submit to the western Turks, whose power was constantly increasing. China made that submission a pretext for war. By 640 the whole basin of Turkestan was brought under Chinese dominance. The whole campaign was really directed against the western Turks, to whom Turkestan had become subject. The western Turks had been crippled by two internal events, to the advantage of the Chinese: there had been a tribal rising, and then came the rebellion and the rise of the Uighurs (640–650). These events belong to Turkish history, and we shall confine ourselves here to their effects on Chinese history. The Chinese were able to rely on the Uighurs; above all, they were furnished by the Tölös Turks with a large army, with which they turned once more against Turkestan in 647–48, and now definitely established their rule there.

The active spirit at the beginning of the T'ang rule had not been the emperor but his son Li Shih-min, who was not, however, named as heir to the throne because he was not the eldest son. The result of this was tension between Li Shih-min and his father and brothers, especially the heir to the throne. When the brothers learned that Li Shih-min was claiming the succession, they conspired against him, and in 626, at the very moment when the western Turks had made a rapid incursion and were once more threatening the Chinese capital, there came an armed collision between the brothers, in which Li Shih-min was the victor. The brothers and their families were exterminated, the father compelled to abdicate, and Li Shih-min became emperor, assuming the name T'ai Tsung (627–649). His reign marked the zenith of the power of China and of the T'ang dynasty. Their inner struggles and the Chinese penetration of Turkestan had weakened the position of the Turks; the reorganization of the administration and of the system of taxation, the improved transport resulting from the canals constructed under the Sui, and the useful results of the creation of great administrative areas under rigid military control, had brought China inner stability and in consequence external power and prestige. The reputation which she then obtained as the most powerful State of the Far East endured when her inner stability had begun to deteriorate. Thus in 638 the Sassanid ruler Yedzgerd sent a mission to China asking for her help against the Arabs. Three further missions came at intervals of a good many years. The Chinese declined, however, to send a military expedition to such a distance; they merely conferred on the ruler the title of a Chinese governor; this was of little help against the Arabs, and in 675 he fled to the Chinese court.

The last years of T'ai Tsung's reign were filled with a great war against Korea, which represented a continuation of the plans of the Sui emperor Yang Ti. This time Korea came firmly into Chinese possession. In 661, under T'ai Tsung's son, the Korean fighting was resumed, this time against Japanese who were defending their interests in Korea. This was the period of great Japanese enthusiasm for China. The Chinese Constitution was copied, and Buddhism was adopted, together with every possible element of Chinese culture. This meant that China's commercial relations with Japan were bringing in large profits, and so the Korean middleman must be eliminated.

T'ai Tsung's son, Kao Tsung (650–683), merely carried to a conclusion what had been begun. Externally China's prestige continued at its zenith. The caravans streamed into China from western and central Asia, bringing great quantities of luxury goods. At this time, however, the foreign colonies were not confined to the capital but were installed in all the important trading ports and inland trade centres. The whole country was covered by a commercial network; foreign merchants who had come overland to China met others who had come by sea. The foreigners set up their own counting-houses and warehouses; whole quarters of the capital were inhabited entirely by foreigners, who lived as if they were in their own country. They brought with them their own religions, Manichaeism, Mazdaism, and Nestorian Christianity. The first Jews came into China, apparently as dealers in fabrics, and the first Arabian Mohammedans made their appearance. In China the foreigners bought silkstuffs and collected everything of value that they could find, especially precious metals. Culturally this influx of foreigners enriched China; economically, as in earlier periods, it did not; its disadvantages were only compensated for a time by the very beneficial results of the trade with Japan, and this benefit did not last long.

4 *The reign of the empress Wu: Buddhism and capitalism*

The pressure of the western Turks had been greatly weakened in this period, especially as their attention had been diverted to the west, where the advance of Islam and of the Arabs was a new menace for them. On the other hand, from 650 onward the Tibetans gained immensely in power, and pushed from the south into the Tarim basin. In 678 they inflicted a heavy defeat on the Chinese, and it cost the T'ang decades of diplomatic effort before they attained, in 699, their aim of breaking up the Tibetans' realm and destroying their power. In the last year of Kao Tsung's reign, 683, came the first of the wars of liberation of the northern Turks, known until then as the western Turks, against the Chinese. And with the end of Kao Tsung's reign began the decline of the T'ang régime. Most of the historians attribute it to a woman, the later empress Wu. She had been a concubine of T'ai Tsung, and after his death had become a Buddhist nun—a frequent custom of the time—until Kao Tsung fell in love with her and made her a concubine of his own. In the end he actually divorced the empress and made the concubine empress (655). She gained more and more influence, being placed on a par with the emperor and soon entirely eliminating him in practice; in 680 she removed the rightful heir to the throne and put her own son in his place; after Kao Tsung's death in 683 she became regent for her son. Soon afterward she dethroned him in favour of his twenty-two-year-old brother; in 690 she deposed him too and made herself empress in the "Chou dynasty" (690–705). This officially ended the T'ang dynasty.

Matters, however, were not so simple as this might suggest. For otherwise on the empress's deposition there would not have been a mass of supporters moving heaven and earth to treat the new empress Wei (705–712) in the same fashion. There is every reason to suppose that behind the empress Wu there was a group opposing the ruling clique. In spite of everything, the T'ang government clique was very pro-Turkish, and many Turks and members of Toba families had government posts and, above all, important military commands. No campaign of that period was undertaken without Turkish auxiliaries. The fear seems to have been felt in some quarters that this T'ang group might pursue a military policy hostile to the gentry. The T'ang group had its roots mainly in western China; thus the eastern Chinese gentry were inclined to be hostile to it. The first act of the empress Wu had been to transfer the capital to Loyang in the east. On the other hand, the eastern gentry, who supported the empress Wu and later the empress Wei, were closely associated with the foreign merchants of western Asia and the Buddhist Church to which they adhered. In gratitude for help from the Buddhists, the empress Wu endowed them with enormous sums of money, and tried to make Buddhism a sort of State religion.

A similar development had taken place in the Toba and also in the Sui period. Temples to-day are generally dependent on an endowment of land, which is rented to individual farmers; in a few rare cases the endowment is a sum of money, the interest on which is used for the upkeep of the temple and the maintenance of its monks. The same is true of the primary schools founded from time to time by interested officials: they were endowed with grants of public land. If the officials' interest ceased the schools were liable to fall into decay. To this day the amount of land belonging to temples and schools is considerable. In the T'ang period and later, such land was exempt from taxation. Like earlier rulers, the empress Wu seems to have aimed at combining spiritual leadership with her position as ruler of the empire.

In this epoch Buddhism helped to create the first beginnings of large-scale capitalism. In connexion with the growing foreign trade, the monasteries grew in importance as repositories of capital; the temples bought more and more land, became more and more wealthy, and so gained increasing influence over economic affairs. They accumulated large quantities of metal, which they stored in the form of bronze figures of Buddha, and with these stocks they exercised controlling influence over the money market. There is a constant succession of records of the total weight of the bronze figures, as an indication of the money value they represented.

The cultural influence of Buddhism found expression in new and improved translations of countless texts, and in the passage of pilgrims along the caravan routes, helped by the merchants, as far as western Asia and India, like the famous Hsüan Tsang. Translations were made not only from Indian or other languages into Chinese, but also, for instance, from Chinese into the Uighur and other Turkish tongues, and into Tibetan, Korean, and Japanese.

The attitude of the Turks can only be understood when we realize that the background of the events of the time of the empress Wu was formed by the activities of groups of the eastern Chinese gentry. The northern Turks, who since 630 had been under Chinese overlordship, had fought many wars of liberation against the Chinese; and through the conquest of neighbouring Turks they had gradually become once more, in the decade-and-a-half after the death of Kao Tsung, a great Turkish realm. In 698 the Turkish khan, at the height of his power, demanded a Chinese prince for his daughter—not, as had been usual in the past, a princess for his son. His intention, no doubt, was to conquer China with the prince's aid, to remove the empress Wu, and to restore the T'ang dynasty—but under Turkish overlordship! Thus, when the empress Wu sent a member of her own family, the khan rejected him and demanded the restoration of the deposed T'ang emperor. To enforce this demand, he embarked on a great campaign against China. In this the Turks must have been able to rely on the support of a strong group inside China, for before the Turkish attack became dangerous the empress Wu recalled the deposed emperor, at first as "heir to the throne"; thus she yielded to the khan's principal demand.

In spite of this, the Turkish attacks did not cease, and after a series of imbroglios within the country the son of one of the deposed emperors succeeded with his clique in removing and exterminating the supporters of the empress Wu and, after her death, of the empress Wei. There began now a period of forty-five years, which the Chinese describe as the second blossoming of T'ang culture, a period that became famous especially for its painting and literature, particularly during the reign of Hsüan Tsung (713–755).

5 *Second blossoming of T'ang culture*

The T'ang literature shows the co-operation of many favourable factors. The ancient Chinese classical style of official reports and decrees led to the clear prose style of the essayists, of whom Han Yü (*c.* 800) and Liu Tsung-yüan (747–796) call for special mention. But entirely new forms of sentences make their appearance in prose writing, with new pictures and similes brought from India through the medium of the Buddhist translations. Poetry was also enriched by the simple songs that spread in the north under Turkish influence, and also by southern influences. The great poets of the T'ang period adopted the rules of form laid down by the poetic art of the south in the fifth century; but while at that time the writing of poetry was a learned pastime, precious and formalistic, the T'ang poets brought to it genuine feeling. Widespread fame came to Li T'ai-po (701–762) and Tu Fu (712–770); in China two poets almost equal to these two in popularity were Po Chü-i and Yüan Chên, who in their works kept as close as possible to the vernacular.

New forms of poetry rarely made their appearance in the T'ang period, but the existing forms were brought to the highest perfection. Not until the end of the T'ang period did there appear the form of a "free" versification, with lines of no fixed length. This form came from the indigenous folk-songs of south-western China, and was spread through the agency of the *filles de joie* in the tea-houses. Before long it became the custom to string such songs together in a continuous series—the first step towards opera. For these song sequences were sung by way of accompaniment to the theatrical productions. The Chinese theatre had developed from two sources—from religious games, bullfights and wrestling, among Turkish and Mongol peoples, which developed into dancing displays; and from sacrificial games of South Chinese origin. Thus the Chinese theatre, with its union with music, should rather be called opera, although it offers a sort of pantomimic show. What amounted to a court conservatoire trained actors and musicians as early as in the T'ang period for this court opera.

In plastic art there are fine sculptures in stone and bronze, and we have also technically excellent fabrics, the finest of lacquer, and remains of artistic buildings; but the principal achievement of the T'ang period lies undoubtedly in the field of painting. As in poetry, in painting there are strong traces of Western influences; even before the T'ang period, the painter Hsieh Ho laid down the six fundamental laws of painting, in all probability drawn from Indian practice. Foreigners were continually brought into China as decorators of Buddhist temples, since the Chinese could not know at first how the new gods had to be presented. The Chinese regarded these painters as craftsmen, but admired their skill and their technique and learned from them.

The most famous Chinese painter of the T'ang period is Wu Tao-tzŭ, who was also the painter most strongly influenced by Central Asian works. As a pious Buddhist he painted pictures for temples among others. Among the landscape painters, Wang Wei ranks first; he was also a famous poet, and aimed at uniting poem and painting into an integral whole. With him begins the great tradition of Chinese landscape painting, which attained its zenith later, in the Sung epoch.

Porcelain had been invented in China more than a

hundred years earlier. There was as yet none of the white porcelain that is preferred to-day; the inside was a brownish-yellow; but on the whole it was already technically and artistically of a very high quality. Since porcelain was at first produced only for the requirements of the court and of high dignitaries—mostly in State workshops—a few centuries later the T'ang porcelain had become a great rarity. But in the centuries that followed, porcelain became an important new article of Chinese export. The Chinese prisoners taken by the Arabs in the great battle of Samarkand (751), the first clash between the world of Islam and China, brought to the West the knowledge of Chinese culture, of several Chinese crafts, of the art of papermaking, and also of porcelain.

The emperor Hsüan Tsung gave active encouragement to all things artistic. Poets and painters contributed to the elegance of his magnificent court ceremonial. As time went on he showed less and less interest in public affairs, and grew increasingly inclined to Taoism and mysticism in general—an outcome of the fact that the conduct of matters of State was taken out of his hands. On the whole, however, Buddhism was pushed into the background in favour of Confucianism, as a reaction from the unusual privileges that had been accorded to the Buddhists in the past fifteen years under the empress Wu.

6 *Revolt of a military governor*

At the beginning of Hsüan Tsung's reign the capital had been in the east at Loyang; then it was transferred once more to Ch'ang-an in the west. The emperor came gradually under the influence of his court clique and its unscrupulous leader Li Lin-fu. The mother of the heir to the throne belonged to the Li clique; when she died, Li Lin-fu and his associates procured for the emperor a concubine named Yang, This woman, usually called "Concubine Yang" (Yang Kui-fei), became the heroine of countless stage-plays and stories; all the misfortunes that marked the end of Hsüan Tsung's reign were attributed solely to her. This is incorrect, as she was but a link in the chain of influences that played upon the emperor. Naturally she found important official posts for her brothers and all her relatives; but more important than these was a military governor named An Lu-shan. His mother was a Turkish shamaness, his father, a foreigner of unknown origin from the region of Jehol. An Lu-shan succeeded in gaining favour with the Li clique, which hoped to make use of him for its own ends. Chinese sources describe him as a prodigy of evil, and it will be very difficult to-day to gain a true picture of his personality. In any case, he was certainly a very capable officer. His rise started from a victory over the Kitan in 744. He spent some time establishing relations with the court, and then went back to resume operations against the Kitan. He made so much of the Kitan peril that he was permitted a larger army than usual, and he had command of 150,000 troops in the neighbourhood of Peking. Meanwhile Li Lin-fu died, and within the Li clique the Yang family tried to seize power. They turned, therefore, against An Lu-shan. But he marched against the capital, Ch'ang-an, with 200,000 men; on his way he conquered Loyang and made himself emperor (756: Yen dynasty). T'ang troops were sent against him under the leadership of the Chinese Kuo Tzu-i, a Kitan commander, and a Turk, Ko-shu Han.

The first two generals had considerable success, but Ko-shu Han, whose task was to prevent access to the western capital, was quickly defeated and taken prisoner. The emperor fled betimes, and An Lu-shan captured Ch'ang-an. The emperor now abdicated; his son, emperor Su Tsung (756–762), also fled, though not with him into Szechwan, but into north-western Shensi. There he defended himself against An Lu-shan and his capable general Shih Ssu-ming (himself a Turk), and sought aid in Central Asia. A small Arab troop came from the caliph Abu-Cafar, and also small bands from Turkestan; of more importance was the arrival of Uighur cavalry in substantial strength. At the end of 757 there was a great battle in the neighbourhood of the capital, in which An Lu-shan was defeated by the Uighurs; shortly afterwards he was murdered by one of his eunuchs. His followers fled; Loyang was captured and looted by the Uighurs. The victors further received in payment from the T'ang government 10,000 rolls of silk with a promise of 20,000 rolls a year; the Uighur khan was given a daughter of the emperor as his wife. An Lu-shan's general, the Turk Shih Ssu-ming, entered into An Lu-shan's heritage, and dominated so large a part of eastern China that the Chinese once more made use of the Uighurs to bring him down. The commanders in the fighting against Shih Ssu-ming this time were once more Kuo Tzu-i and the Kitan general, together with Pu-ku Huai-en, a member of a Tölös family that had long been living in China. At first Shih Ssu-ming was victorious, and he won back Lo-yang, but then he was murdered by his own son, and only by taking advantage of the disturbances that now arose were the government troops able to quell the dangerous rising.

In all this, two things seem interesting and important. To begin with, An Lu-shan had been a military governor. His rising showed that while this new office, with its great command of power, was of value in attacking external enemies, it became dangerous, especially if the central power was weak, the moment there were no external enemies of any importance. An Lu-shan's rising was the first of many similar ones in the later T'ang period. The gentry of eastern China had shown themselves entirely ready to support An Lu-shan against the government, because they had hoped to gain advantage as in the past from a realm with its centre once more in the east. In the second place, the important part played by aliens in events within China calls for notice: not only were the rebels An Lu-shan and Shih Ssu-ming non-Chinese, but so also were most of the generals opposed to them. They showed not a trace of national feeling: they regarded themselves as Chinese, not as members of another national group. The Turkish Uighurs brought in to help against them were fighting actually against Turks, though they regarded those Turks as Chinese. We must not bring to the circumstances of those times the present-day notions with regard to national feeling.

7 *The rôle of the Uighurs. Confiscation of the capital of the monasteries*

This rising and its sequels broke the power of the dynasty, and also of the empire. The extremely sanguinary wars had brought fearful suffering upon the population. During the years of the rising, no taxes came in from the greater part of the empire, but great sums had to be paid to the peoples who had lent aid to the empire. And the looting by government troops and by the auxiliaries injured the population as much as the war itself did.

When the emperor Su Tsung died, in 762, Tengri, the khan of the Uighurs, decided to make himself ruler over China. The events of the preceding years had shown him that China alone was entirely defenceless. Part of the court clique supported him, and only by the intervention of P'u-ku Huai-en, who was related to Tengri by marriage, was his plan frustrated. Naturally there were countless intrigues against P'u-ku Huai-en. He entered into alliance with the Tibetan T'u-fan, and in this way the union of Turks and Tibetans, always feared by the Chinese, had come into existence. In 763 the Tibetans captured and burned down the western capital, while P'u-ku Huai-en with the Uighurs advanced from the north. Undoubtedly this campaign would have been successful, giving an entirely different turn to China's destiny, if P'u-ku Huai-en had not died in 765 and the Chinese under Kuo Tzŭ-i had not succeeded in breaking up the alliance. The Uighurs now came over into an alliance with the Chinese, and the two allies fell upon the Tibetans and robbed them of their booty. China was saved once more.

Friendship with the Uighurs had to be paid for this time even more dearly. They crowded into the capital and compelled the Chinese to buy horses, in payment for which they demanded enormous quantities of silkstuffs. They behaved in the capital like lords, and expected to be maintained at the expense of the government. The system of military governors was adhered to in spite of the country's experience of them, while the difficult situation throughout the empire, and especially along the western and northern frontiers, facing the Tibetans and the more and more powerful Kitan, made it necessary to keep considerable numbers of soldiers permanently with the colours. This made the military governors stronger and stronger; ultimately they no longer remitted any taxes to the central government, but spent them mainly on their armies. Thus from 750 onward the empire consisted of an impotent central government and powerful military governors, who handed on their positions to their sons as a further proof of their independence. When in 781 the government proposed to interfere with the inheriting of the posts, there was a great new rising, which in 783 again extended as far as the capital; in 784 the T'ang government at last succeeded in overcoming it. A compromise was arrived at between the government and the governors, but it in no way improved the situation. Life became more and more difficult for the central government. At court, eunuchs ruled in the interests of the various cliques. Several emperors fell victim to them or to the drinking of the "elixir of long life". Abroad, the Chinese lost their dominion over Turkestan, for which Uighurs and Tibetans competed. There is nothing to gain from any full description of events at court. The struggle between cliques soon became a struggle between eunuchs and literati, in much the same way as at the end of the second Han dynasty. Trade steadily diminished, and the State became impoverished because no taxes were coming in and great armies had to be maintained, though they did not even obey the government.

Events that exerted on the internal situation an influence not to be belittled were the break-up of the Uighurs (from 832 onward), the appearance of the Turkish Sha-t'o, and, almost at the same time, the dissolution of the Tibetan empire (from 842). Many other foreigners had placed themselves under the Uighurs living in China, in order to be able to do business under the political protection of the Uighur embassy, but the Uighurs no longer counted, and the T'ang government decided to seize the capital sums which these foreigners had accumulated. It was hoped in this way especially to remedy the financial troubles of the moment, which were partly due to a shortage of metal for minting. As the trading capital was still placed with the temples as banks, the government attacked the religion of the Uighurs, Manichaeism, and also the religions of the other foreigners, Mazdaism, Nestorianism, and apparently also Islam. In 843 alien religions were prohibited; aliens were also ordered to dress like Chinese. This gave them the status of Chinese citizens and no longer of foreigners, so that Chinese justice had a hold over them. That this law abolishing foreign religions was aimed solely at the foreigners' capital is shown by the proceedings at the same time against Buddhism, which had long become a completely Chinese Church. Several thousand Buddhist temples and monasteries were secularized, and all statues were required to be melted down and delivered to the government, even those in private possession. The monks were to become ordinary citizens once more. Until then monks had been free of taxation, as had the land belonging to the temples and leased to tenants.

Thus the edict of 843 must not be described as concerned with religion: it was a measure of compulsion aimed at filling the government coffers. All the property of foreigners and a large part of the property of the Buddhist Church came into the hands of the government. The law was not applied to Taoism, because the ruling gentry of the time were, as so often before, Confucianist and at the same time Taoist. As early as 846 there came a reaction: with the new emperor, Confucians came into power who were at the same time Buddhists and who now evicted some of the Taoists. From this time one may observe closer co-operation between Confucianism and Buddhism; not only with meditative Buddhism as at the beginning of the T'ang epoch and earlier, but with the main branch of Buddhism, monastery Buddhism. From now onward the Buddhist doctrines of transmigration and retribution, which had been really directed against the gentry and in favour of the common people, were turned into an instrument serving the gentry: everyone who was unfortunate in this life must show such amenability to the government and the gentry that he would have a chance of a better existence at least in the next life. Thus the revolutionary Buddhist doctrine of retribution became a reactionary doctrine that was of great service to the gentry. One of the Buddhist Confucians in whose works this revised version makes its appearance most clearly was Niu Seng-yu, who was at once summoned back to court in 846 by the new emperor.

8 *First successful peasant revolt. Collapse of the empire*

The chief sufferers from the continual warfare of the military governors, the sanguinary struggles between the cliques, and the universal impoverishment which all this fighting produced, were, of course, the common people. The Chinese annals are filled with records of popular risings, but not one of these had attained any wide extent, for want of organization. In 860 began the first great popular rising, a revolt caused by famine in the province of Chekiang. Government troops suppressed it with bloodshed. Further popular risings followed. In 874 began a great rising in the south of the present province of Hopei, the chief agrarian region. The rising was led by a peasant, Wang Hsien-chih, together with an unsuccessful scholar, Huang Ch'ao, who had fallen into poverty, had joined the hungry peasants, and had formed a fighting group of his own. Wang and Huang both proved good organizers of the peasant masses, and in a short time they had captured the whole of eastern China, without the military governors being able to do anything against them, for the provincial troops were more inclined to show sympathy to the peasant armies than to fight them. The terrified government issued an order to arm the people of the other parts of the country against the rebels; naturally this helped the rebels more than the government, since the peasants thus armed went over to the rebels. Finally Wang was offered a high office. But Huang urged him not to betray his own people, and Wang declined the offer. In the end the government, with the aid of the troops of the Turkish Sha-t'o, defeated

Wang and beheaded him (878). Huang Ch'ao now moved into the south-east and the south, where in 879 he captured and burned down Canton; according to an Arab source, over 120,000 foreigners lost their lives in addition to the Chinese. From Canton Huang Ch'ao returned to the north, laden with loot from that wealthy commercial city. His advance was held up again by the Sha-t'o troops; he turned away to the lower Yangtze, and from there marched north again. At the end of 880 he captured the eastern capital. The emperor fled from the western capital, Ch'ang-an, into Szechwan, and Huang Ch'ao now captured with ease the western capital as well, and removed every member of the ruling family on whom he could lay hands. He then made himself emperor, in a Ch'i dynasty. It was the first time that a peasant rising had succeeded against the gentry.

There was still, however, the greatest disorder in the empire. There were other peasant armies on the move, armies that had deserted their governors and were fighting for themselves; finally, there were still a few supporters of the imperial house and, above all, the Turkish Sha-t'o, who had a competent commander with the sinified name of Li K'o-yung. The Sha-t'o, who had remained loyal to the government, revolted the moment the government had been overthrown. They ran the risk, however, of defeat at the hands of an alien army of the Chinese government's, commanded by an Uighur, and they therefore fled to the Tatars. In spite of this, the Chinese entered again into relations with the Sha-t'o, as without them there could be no possibility of getting rid of Huang Ch'ao. At the end of 881 Li K'o-yung fell upon the capital; there was a fearful battle. Huang Ch'ao was able to hold out, but a further attack was made in 883 and he was defeated and forced to flee; in 884 he was killed by the Sha-t'o.

This popular rising, which had only been overcome with the aid of the Turks, brought the end of the T'ang dynasty. In 885 the T'ang emperor was able to return to the capital, but the only question now was whether China should be ruled by the Sha-t'o under Li K'o-yung or by some other military commander. In a short time Chu Ch'üan-chung, a former follower of Huang Ch'ao, proved to be the strongest of the commanders. In 890 open war began between the two leaders. Li K'o-yung was based on Shansi; Chu Ch'üan-chung had control of the plains in the east. Meanwhile the governors of Szechwan in the west and Chekiang in the south-east made themselves independent. Both declared themselves kings or emperors and set up dynasties of their own (from 895).

Within the capital, the emperor was threatened several times by revolts, so that he had to flee and place himself in the hands of Li K'o-yung as the only leader on whose loyalty he could count. Soon after this, however, the emperor fell into the hands of Chu Ch'üan-chung, who killed the whole entourage of the emperor, particularly the eunuchs; after a time he had the emperor himself killed, set a puppet—as had become customary—on the throne, and at the beginning of 907 took over the rule from him, becoming emperor in the "Later Liang dynasty".

That was the end of the T'ang dynasty, at the beginning of which China had risen to unprecedented power. Its downfall had been brought about by the military governors, who had built up their power and had become independent hereditary satraps, exploiting the people for their own purposes, and by their continual mutual struggles undermining the economic structure of the empire. In addition to this, the empire had been weakened first by its foreign trade and then by the dependence on foreigners, especially Turks, into which it had fallen owing to internal conditions. A large part of the national income had gone abroad. Such is the explanation of the great popular risings which ultimately brought the dynasty to its end.

Chapter IX

THE EPOCH OF THE SECOND DIVISION OF CHINA

(A) The period of the Five Dynasties (A.D. 906–960)

1 *Political situation in the tenth century*

THE Chinese call the period from 906 to 960 the "period of the Five Dynasties" (*Wu Tai*). This is not quite accurate. It is true that there were five dynasties in rapid succession in North China; but at the same time there were ten other dynasties in South China. The ten southern dynasties, however, are regarded as not legal; for that matter, not much is known about them. In any case, the south was much better off with its illegal dynasties than the north with the legal ones. The dynasties in the south (we may dispense with giving their names) were the realms of some of the military governors so often mentioned above. These governors had already become independent at the end of the T'ang epoch; they declared themselves kings or emperors and ruled particular provinces in the south, the chief of which covered the territory of the present provinces of Szechwan and Chekiang. In both these territories there was comparative peace, and both enjoyed economic prosperity, since they were able to control their own affairs and were no longer dependent on a corrupt central government. They also made great cultural progress, and they did not lose their importance later when they were annexed in the period of the Sung dynasty. This fact was connected with some very important new developments.

2 *Monopolistic trade in South China. Printing and paper money in the north*

The prosperity of the small States of South China was largely due to the growth of trade, especially the tea trade. The habit of drinking tea seems to have been an ancient Tibetan custom, which spread to south-eastern China in the third century A.D. Since then there had been two centres of production, Szechwan and south-eastern China. Until the eleventh century Szechwan had remained the leading producer, and tea had been drunk in the Tibetan fashion, mixed with flour, salt, and ginger. It then began to be drunk without admixture. In the T'ang epoch tea drinking spread all over China, and there sprang up a class of wholesalers who bought the tea from the peasants, accumulated stocks, and distributed them. From 783 date the first attempts of the State to monopolize the tea trade and to make it a source of revenue; but it failed in an attempt to make the cultivation a State monopoly. A tea commissariat was accordingly set up to buy the tea from the producers and supply it to traders in possession of a State licence. There naturally developed then a pernicious collaboration between State officials and the wholesalers. The latter soon eliminated the small traders, so that they themselves secured all the profit; official support was secured by bribery. The State and the wholesalers alike were keenly interested in the prevention of tea-smuggling, which was strictly prohibited.

The position was much the same with regard to salt. We have here for the first time the association of officials with wholesalers or even with a monopoly trade. This was of the utmost importance in all later times. Monopoly progressed most rapidly in Szechwan, where there had always been a numerous commercial community. In the period of political fragmentation Szechwan, as the principal tea-producing region and at the same time an important producer of salt, was much better off than any other part of China.

10 Ladies of the Court: clay models which accompanied the dead person to the grave. T'ang period.
In the collection of the Museum für Völkerkunde, Berlin.

11 Distinguished founder: a temple banner found at Khotcho, Turkestan.

Museum für Völkerkunde, Berlin. No. 1B 4524, illustration B 408.

South-eastern China was also the chief centre of porcelain production, although china clay is found also in North China. The use of porcelain spread more and more widely. The first translucent porcelain made its appearance, and porcelain became an important article of commerce both within the country and for export. Porcelain goods were sent to farthest India and to Indonesia as well as to the Middle East and to Japan. Porcelain manufacture calls for considerable fixed and working capital; the small manufacturers produce far too much seconds; thus we have here the first beginnings of an industry that developed, not, indeed, as in Europe, but, like the tea trade, into a wholesale and even a monopolistic system.

The third important new development to be mentioned was that of printing, which at the end of the T'ang epoch was known in the form of wood-block printing. In the Far East, just as in Europe, this invention had far-reaching consequences. Books, which until then had been very dear, because they had had to be produced by copyists, could now be produced cheaply and in quantity. It became possible for a scholar to accumulate a library of his own and to work in a wide field, where earlier he had been confined to a few books or even a single text. The results were the spread of education, beginning with reading and writing, among wider groups, and the broadening of education: a large number of texts were read and compared, and no longer only a few. Private libraries came into existence, so that the imperial libraries were no longer the only ones. Publishing soon grew in extent, and in private enterprise works were printed that were not so serious and politically important as the classic books of the past. Thus a new type of literature, the literature of entertainment, could come into existence. Not all these consequences showed themselves at once; some made their first appearance later, in the Sung period.

A fourth important innovation, this time in North China, was the introduction of prototypes of paper money. The Chinese copper "cash" was difficult or expensive to transport, simply because of its weight. It thus presented great obstacles to trade. Occasionally a region with an adverse balance of trade would lose all its copper money, with the result of a local deflation. So long as there was an orderly administration, the government could send it money, though at considerable cost; but if the administration was not functioning well, the deflation continued. For this reason some provinces prohibited the export of copper money from their territory at the end of the eighth century. As the provinces were in the hands of military governors, the central government could do next to nothing to prevent this. On the other hand, the prohibition automatically made an end of all external trade. The merchants accordingly began to prepare deposit certificates, and in this way to set up a sort of transfer system. Soon these deposit certificates entered into circulation as a sort of medium of payment, and gradually this led to a banking system and the linking of wholesale trade with it. This made possible a much greater volume of trade. Toward the end of the T'ang period the government began to issue deposit certificates of its own: the merchant deposited his copper money with a government agency, receiving in exchange a certificate which he could put into circulation like money. Meanwhile the government could put out the deposited money at interest, or throw it into general circulation. The government's deposit certificates were now printed. They were the predecessors of the paper money used from the time of the Sung.

3 *Political history of the Five Dynasties*

The southern States were a factor not to be ignored in the calculations of the northern dynasties. Although the southern kingdoms were involved in a confusion of mutual hostilities, any one of them might come to the fore as the ally of Turks or other northern Powers. The capital of the first of the five northern dynasties (once more a Liang dynasty, but not to be confused with the Liang dynasty of the south in the sixth century) was, moreover, quite close to the territories of the southern dynasties, close to the site of the present Kaifeng, in the fertile plain of eastern

China with its good means of transport. Militarily the town could not be held, for its one and only defence was the Yellow River. The founder of this Later Liang dynasty, Chu Ch'üan-chung (906), was himself an eastern Chinese and, as will be remembered, a past supporter of the revolutionary Huang Ch'ao, but he had then gone over to the T'ang and had gained high military rank.

His northern frontier remained still more insecure than the south, for Chu Ch'üan-chung did not succeed in destroying the Turkish general Li K'o-yung; on the contrary, the latter continually widened the range of his power. Fortunately he, too, had an enemy at his back—the Kitan or Khitan, whose ruler had made himself emperor in 916, and so staked a claim to reign over all China. The first Kitan emperor held a middle course between Chu and Li, and so was able to establish and expand his empire in peace. The striking power of his empire, which from 937 onward was officially called the Liao empire, grew steadily, because the old tribal league of the Kitan was transformed into a centrally commanded military organization.

To these dangers from abroad threatening the Later Liang State were added internal troubles. Chu Ch'üan-chung's dynasty was one of the three that had come to power through a popular rising. He himself was of peasant origin, and so were a large part of his subordinates and helpers. Many of them had originally been independent peasant leaders; others had been under Huang Ch'ao. All of them were opposed to the gentry, and the great slaughter of the gentry of the capital shortly before the beginning of Chu's rule had been welcomed by Chu and his followers. The gentry therefore would not co-operate with Chu, and preferred to join the Turk Li K'o-yung. But Chu could not confidently rely on his old comrades. They were jealous of his success in gaining the place they all coveted, and were ready to join in any independent enterprise as opportunity offered. All of them, moreover, as soon as they were given any administrative post, busied themselves with the acquisition of money and wealth as quickly as possible. These abuses not only ate into the revenues of the State but actually produced a common front between the peasantry and the remnants of the gentry against the upstarts.

In 917, after Li K'o-yung's death, the Sha-t'o Turks beat off an attack from the Kitan, and so were safe for a time from the northern menace. They then marched against the Liang State, where a crisis had been produced in 912 after the murder of Chu Ch'üan-chung by one of his sons. The Liang generals saw no reason why they should fight for the dynasty, and all of them went over to the enemy. Thus the "Later T'ang dynasty" (923–936) came into power in North China, under the son of Li K'o-yung.

The dominant element at this time was quite clearly the Chinese gentry, especially in western and central China. The Sha-t'o themselves must have been extraordinarily few in number, probably little more than 100,000 men. Most of them, moreover, were politically passive, being simple tribesmen, Only the ruling family and its following played any active part, together with a few families related to it by marriage. The whole State was regarded by the Sha-t'o rulers as a sort of family enterprise, members of the family being placed in the most important positions. As there were not enough of them, they adopted into the family large numbers of aliens of all nationalities. Military posts were given to faithful members of Li K'o-yung's or his successor's bodyguard, and also to domestic servants and other clients of the family. Thus, while in the Later Liang State elements from the peasantry had risen in the world, some of these neo-gentry reaching the top of the social pyramid in the centuries that followed, in the Sha-t'o State some of its warriors, drawn from the most various peoples, entered the gentry class through their personal relations with the ruler. But in spite of all this the bulk of the officials came once more from the Chinese gentry. These educated Chinese not only succeeded in winning over the rulers themselves to the Chinese cultural ideal, but persuaded them to adopt laws that substantially restricted the privileges

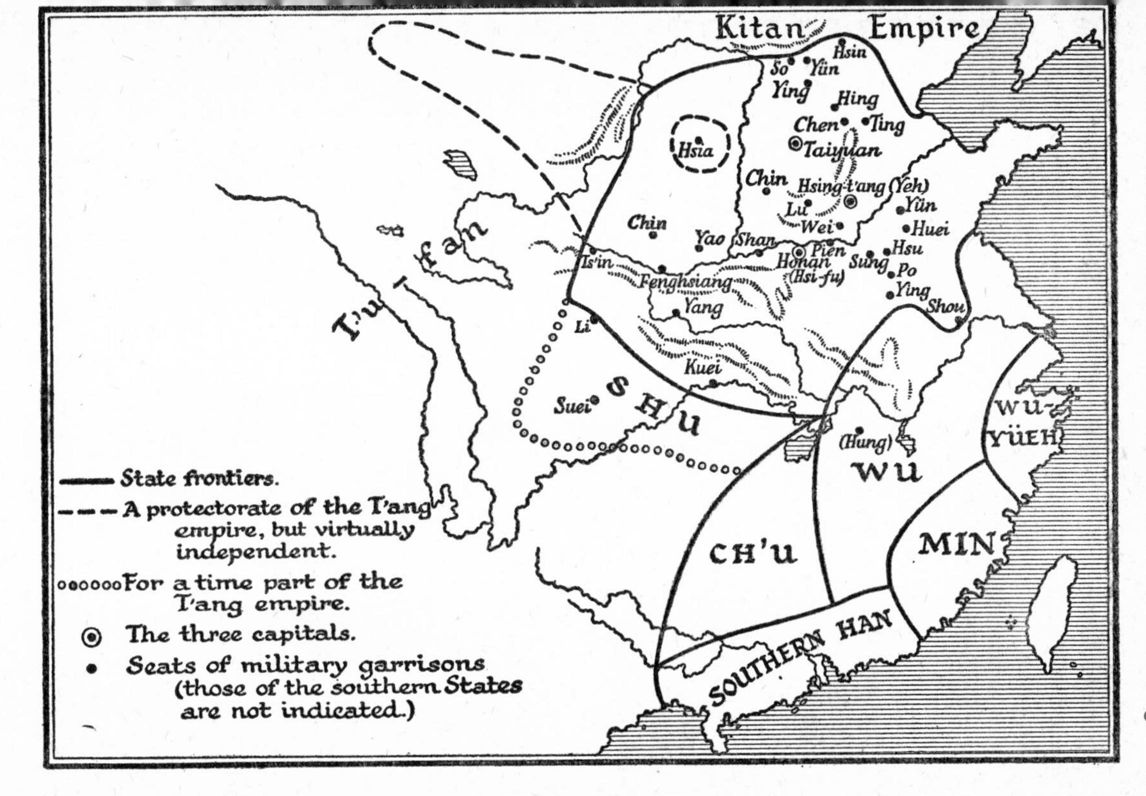
Kitan Empire
Hsin
So
Yün
Ying
Hing
Chen
Ting
Taiyüan
Hsia
Chin
Hsing-t'ang (Yeh)
Lu
Wei
Yün
Huei
Chin
Yao
Shan
Pien
Honan
(Hsi-fu)
Sung
Hsu
Po
Ying
Shou
Ts'in
Fenghsiang
Yang
Li
Kuei
Suei
SHU
T'u-fan
(Hung)
WU
WU-YÜEH
CH'U
MIN
SOUTHERN HAN
State frontiers.
A protectorate of the T'ang empire, but virtually independent.
For a time part of the T'ang empire.
The three capitals.
Seats of military garrisons (those of the southern States are not indicated.)

of the Sha-t'o and brought advantages only to the Chinese gentry. Consequently all the Chinese historians are enthusiastic about the "Later T'ang", and especially about the emperor Ming Ti, who reigned from 927 onward, after the assassination of his predecessor. They also abused the Liang because they were against the gentry.

In 936 the Later T'ang dynasty gave place to the Later Chin dynasty (936–946), but this involved no change in the structure of the empire. The change of dynasty meant no more than that instead of the son following the father the son-in-law had ascended the throne. It is of more importance that the son-in-law, the Sha-t'o Turk Shih Ching-t'ang, succeeded in doing this by allying himself with the Kitan and ceding to them some of the northern provinces. The youthful successor, however, of the first ruler of this dynasty was soon made to realize that the Kitan regarded the founding of his dynasty as no more than a transition stage on the way to their annexation of the whole of North China. The old Sha-t'o nobles, who had not been sinified in the slightest, suggested a preventive war; the actual court group, strongly sinified, hesitated, but ultimately were unable to avoid war. The war was very quickly decided by several governors in eastern China going over to the Kitan, who had promised them the imperial title. In the course of 946–7 the Kitan occupied the capital and almost the whole of the country. In 947 the Kitan ruler proclaimed himself emperor of the Kitan and the Chinese.

The Chinese gentry seem to have accepted this situation because a Kitan emperor was just as acceptable to them as a Sha-t'o emperor; but the Sha-t'o were not prepared to submit to the Kitan régime, because under it they would have lost their position of privilege. At the head of this opposition group stood the Sha-t'o general Liu Chih-yüan, who founded the "Later Han dynasty" (947–950). He was only able to hold out against the Kitan because in 947 the Kitan emperor died and his son had to leave China and retreat to the north; fighting had broken out between the empress dowager, who had some Chinese support, and the young heir to the throne. The new Turkish dynasty, however, was unable to withstand the internal Chinese resistance. Its founder died in 948, and his son, owing to his youth, was entirely in the hands of a court clique. In his effort to free himself from the tutelage of this group he made a miscalculation, for the men on whom he thought he could depend were largely supporters of the clique. So he lost his throne and his life, and a Chinese general, Kuo Wei, took his place, founding the "Later Chou dynasty" (951–959).

A feature of importance was that in the years of the short-lived "Later Han dynasty" a tendency showed itself among the Chinese military leaders to work with the States in the south. The increase in the political influence of the south was due to its economic advance while the north was reduced to economic chaos by the continual heavy fighting, and by the complete irresponsibility of the Sha-t'o ruler in financial matters: several times in this period the whole of the money in the coffers of the State was handed out to soldiers to prevent them from going over to some enemy or other. On the other hand, there was a tendency in the south for the many neighbouring States to amalgamate, and as this process took place close to the frontier of North China the northern States could not passively look on. During the "Later Han" period there were wars and risings, which continued in the time of the "Later Chou".

On the whole, the few years of the rule of the second emperor of the "Later Chou" (954–958) form a bright spot in those dismal 55 years. Sociologically regarded, that dynasty formed merely a transition stage on the way to the Sung dynasty that now followed: the Chinese gentry ruled under the leadership of an upstart who had risen from the ranks, and they ruled in accordance with the old principles of gentry rule. The Sha-t'o, who had formed the three preceding dynasties, had been so reduced that they were now a tiny minority and no longer counted. This minority had only been able to maintain its position through the special sociological conditions created by the "Later Liang" dynasty: the Liang, who had come from the lower classes of the population, had driven the gentry into the arms of the Sha-t'o Turks. As soon as the upstarts, in so far as they had not fallen again or been exterminated, had more or less assimilated themselves to the old gentry, and on the other hand the leaders of the Sha-t'o had become numerically too weak, there was a possibility of resuming the old form of rule.

There had been certain changes in this period. The north-west of China, the region of the old capital Ch'ang-an, had been so ruined by the fighting that had gone on mainly there and farther north, that it was eliminated as a centre of power for a hundred years to come; it had been largely depopulated. The north was under the rule of the Kitan: its trade, which in the past had been with the Hwang-ho basin, was now perforce diverted to Peking, which soon became the main centre of the power of the Kitan. The south, particularly the lower Yangtze region and the province of Szechwan, had made economic progress, at least in comparison with the north; consequently it had gained in political importance.

(B) The Northern Sung dynasty

1 *Southward expansion*

The founder of the Sung dynasty, Chao K'uang-yin, came of a Chinese military family living to the south of Peking. He advanced from general to emperor, and so differed in no way from the emperors who had preceded him. But his dynasty did not disappear as quickly as the others; for this there were several reasons. To begin with, there was the simple fact that he remained alive longer than the other founders of dynasties, and so was able to place his rule on a firmer foundation. But in addition to this he followed a new course, which in certain ways smoothed matters for him and for his successors, in foreign policy.

This Sung dynasty, as Chao K'uang-yin named it, no longer turned against the northern peoples, particularly the Kitan, but against the south. This was not exactly an heroic policy: the north of China remained in the hands of the Kitan. There were frequent clashes, but no real effort was made to destroy the Kitan, whose dynasty was now called "Liao". The second emperor of the Sung was actually heavily defeated several times by the Kitan. But they, for their part, made no attempt to conquer the whole of China, especially since the task would have become more and more burdensome the farther south the Sung expanded. And very soon there were other reasons why the Kitan should refrain from turning their whole strength against the Chinese.

As we said, the Sung turned at once against the States in the south. Some of the many small southern States had made substantial economic and cultural advance, but militarily they were not strong. Chao K'uang-yin (named as emperor T'ai Tsu) attacked them in succession. Most of them fell very quickly and without any heavy fighting, especially since the Sung dealt mildly with the defeated rulers and their following. The gentry and the merchants in these small States could not but realize the advantages of a widened and well-ordered economic field, and they were therefore entirely in favour of the annexation of their country so soon as it proved to be tolerable. And the Sung empire could only endure and gain strength if it had control of the regions along the Yangtze and around Canton, with their great economic resources. The process of absorbing the small States in the south continued until 980. Before it was ended, the Sung tried to extend their influence in the south beyond the Chinese border, and secured a sort of protectorate over parts of Annam (973). This sphere of influence was politically insignificant and not directly of any economic importance; but it fulfilled for the Sung the same functions which colonial territories fulfilled for Europeans, serving as a field of operation for the commercial class, who imported raw materials from it —mainly, it is true, luxury articles such as special sorts of wood, perfumes, ivory, and so on—and exported Chinese manufactures. As the power of the empire grew, this zone of influence extended as far as Indonesia: the process had begun in the T'ang period. The trade with the south had not the deleterious effects of the trade with Central Asia. There was no sale of refined metals, and none of fabrics, as the natives produced their own textiles, which sufficed for their needs. And the export of porcelain brought no economic injury to China, but the reverse.

This Sung policy was entirely in the interest of the gentry and of the trading community which was now closely connected with them. Undoubtedly it strengthened China. The policy of non-intervention in the north was endurable even when peace with the Kitan had to be bought by the payment of an annual tribute. From 1004 onwards, 100,000 ounces of silver and 200,000 bales of silk were paid annually to the Kitan, amounting in value to about 270,000 strings of cash, each of 1,000 coins. The State budget amounted to some 20,000,000 strings of cash. In 1038 the payments amounted to 500,000 strings, but the Budget was by then much larger. One is liable to get a false impression when reading of these big payments if one does nor take into account what percentage they formed of the total revenues of the State. The tribute to the Kitan amounted to less than 2 per cent. of the revenue, while the expenditure on the army accounted for 25 per cent. of the Budget. It cost much less to pay tribute than to maintain large armies and go to war. Financial considerations played a great part during the Sung epoch. The taxation revenue of the empire rose rapidly after the pacification of the south; soon after the beginning of the dynasty the State Budget was double that of the T'ang. If the State expenditure in the eleventh century had not continually grown through the increase in military expenditure—in spite of everything!—there would have come a period of great prosperity in the empire.

2 *Administration and army. Inflation*

One of the first acts of the new Sung emperor, in 963, was a fundamental reorganization of the administration of the country. The old system of a civil administration and a military administration independent of it was brought to an end and the whole administration of the country placed in the hands of civil officials. The gentry welcomed this measure and gave it full support, because it enabled the influence of the gentry to grow and removed the fear of competition from the military, some of whom did not belong by birth to the gentry. The generals by whose aid the empire had been created were put on pension, or transferred to civil employment, as quickly as possible. The army was demobilized, and this measure was bound up with the settlement of peasants in the regions which war had depopulated, or on new land. Soon after this the revenue noticeably increased. Above all, the army was placed directly under the central administration, and the system of military governors was thus brought to an end. The soldiers became mercenaries of the State, whereas in the past there had been conscription. In 975 the army had numbered only 378,000, and its cost had not been insupportable. Although the numbers increased greatly, reaching 912,000 in 1017 and 1,259,000 in 1045, this implied no increase in military strength; for men who had once been soldiers remained with the army even when they were too old for service. Moreover, the soldiers grew more and more exacting; when detachments were transferred to another region, for instance, the soldiers would not carry their baggage; an army of porters had to be assembled. The soldiers also refused to go to regions remote from their homes until they were given extra pay. Such allowances gradually became customary, and so the military expenditure grew by leaps and bounds without any corresponding increase in the striking power of the army.

The government was unable to meet the whole cost of the army out of taxation revenue. The attempt was made to cover the expenditure by coining fresh money. In connexion with the increase in commercial capital described above, and the consequent beginning of an industry, China's metal production had greatly increased. In 1050 thirteen times as much silver, eight times as much copper, and fourteen times as much iron was produced as in 800.

Thus the circulation of the copper currency was increased. The cost of minting, however, amounted in China to about 75 per cent. of the value of the money coined. In addition to this, the metal was produced in the south, while the capital was in the north. The coin had therefore to be carried a long distance to reach the capital and to be sent on to the soldiers in the north.

To meet the increasing expenditure, an unexampled quantity of new money was put into circulation. The State Budget increased from 22,200,000 in A.D. 1000 to 150,800,000 in 1021. The Kitan State coined a great deal of silver, and some of the tribute was paid to it in silver. The greatly increased production of silver led to its being put into circulation in China itself. And this provided a new field of speculation, through the variations in the rates for silver and for copper. Speculation was also possible with the deposit certificates, which were issued in quantities by the State from the beginning of the eleventh century, and to which the first true paper money was soon added. The paper money and the certificates were redeemable at a definite date, but at a reduction of at least 3 per cent. of their value; this, too, yielded a certain revenue to the State.

The inflation that resulted from all these measures brought profit to the big merchants. With the social structure of medieval Europe, a similar situation led to industrialization and so to a modern State. In China, however, the gentry, in their capacity of officials, hindered the growth of independent trade, and permitted its existence only in association with themselves. As they also represented landed property, it was in that that the newly-formed capital was invested. Thus we see in the Sung period, and especially in the eleventh century, the greatest accumulation of estates that there had ever been up to then in China. Under the Chinese economic system, large-scale landowning always proved socially and politically injurious. To this day the peasant who rents his land pays 40-50 per cent. of the produce to the landowner, who is responsible for payment of the normal land tax. The landlord, however, has always found means of evading payment. As each district had to yield a definite amount of taxation, the more the big landowners succeeded in evading payment the more had to be paid by the independent small farmers. These independent peasants could then either "give" their land to the big landowner and pay rent to him, thus escaping from the attentions of the tax-officer, or simply leave the district and secretly enter another one where they were not registered. In either case the government lost taxes.

Large-scale landowning proved especially injurious in the Sung period, for two reasons. To begin with, the official salaries, which had always been small in China, were now totally inadequate, and so the officials were given a fixed quantity of land, the yield of which was regarded as an addition to salary. This land was free from part of the taxes. Before long the officials had secured the liberation of the whole of their land from the chief taxes. In the second place, the taxation system was simplified by making the amount of tax proportional to the amount of land owned. The lowest class, however, in this new system of taxation comprised more land than a poor peasant would actually own, and this was a heavy blow to the small peasant-owners, who in the past had paid a proportion of their produce. Most of them had so little land that they could barely live on its yield. Their liability to taxation was at all times a very heavy burden to them while the big landowners got off lightly. Thus this measure, though administratively a saving of expense, proved unsocial.

All this made itself felt especially in the south with its great estates of tax-evading landowners. Here the remaining small peasant-owners had to pay the new taxes or to become tenants of the landowners and lose their property. The north was still suffering from the war-devastation of the tenth century. As the landlords were always the first sufferers from popular uprisings as well as from war, they had disappeared, leaving their former tenants as free peasants. This had the grotesque result that the thinly populated province of Shensi in the north-west yielded about a quarter of the total revenues of the State: it had no large landowners, no wealthy gentry, with their evasion of taxation, only a mass of newly-settled small peasants' holdings. For this reason the government was particularly interested in that province, and closely watched the political changes in its neighbourhood. In 990 a man belonging to a sinified Toba family, living on the border of Shensi, had made himself king with the support of the Toba. In 1034 came severe fighting, and in 1038 the king proclaimed himself emperor, in the Hsia dynasty, and threatened the whole of north-western China. Tribute was also paid to this State (250,000 strings), but the fight against it continued, to save that important province.

These were the main events in internal and external affairs during the Sung period until 1068. It will be seen that foreign affairs were of much less importance than home.

3 *Reaction: retail (Wang An-shih) versus wholesale trade*

The situation just described was bound to produce a reaction. In spite of the inflationary measures the revenue fell, partly in consequence of the tax evasions of the great landowners. It fell from 150,000,000 in 1021 to 116,000,000 in 1065. Expenditure did not fall, and there was a constant succession of Budget deficits. The young emperor Shen Tsung (1068–1085) became convinced that the policy followed by the ruling clique of officials and gentry was bad, and he gave his adhesion to a small group led by Wang An-shih. The ruling gentry clique represented especially the interests of the merchants in Szechwan and Kiangsi. It advocated a policy of *laisser-faire* in trade: it held that everything would adjust itself. Wang An-shih himself came from Kiangsi, and was therefore supported at first by the government clique, within which the Kiangsi group was trying to gain predominance over the Szechwan group. But Wang An-shih came from a poor family, as did his supporters, for whom he quickly secured posts. They represented the interests of the smaller landholders and the small dealers. This group succeeded in gaining power, and in carrying out a number of reforms, all directed against the monopolist merchants. Credits for small peasants were introduced, and officials were given bigger salaries, in order to make them independent and to recruit officials who were not big landowners. The army was greatly reduced, and in addition to the paid soldiery a national militia was created. Special attention was paid to the province of Shensi, whose conditions were taken more or less as a model.

As soon as the first decrees were issued against the monopolist merchants (that is to say, merchants who monopolized the trade of a particular region and had squeezed out all the smaller traders), furious opposition was offered to them. Even some of Wang An-shih's former adherents came out against him. After a few years the emperor was no longer able to retain Wang An-shih, and had to abandon the new policy. How really economic interests were here at issue may be seen from the fact that for many of the new decrees which were not directly concerned with economic affairs, such, for instance, as the reform of the examination system, Wang An-shih was furiously attacked though his opponents had themselves advocated them in the past and had no practical objection to offer to them. The contest, however, between the two groups of traders was not over. The monopolists had the upper hand from 1086 to 1102, but then the advocates of the policy represented by Wang again came into power for a short time. They had but little success to show, as they did not remain in power long enough and, owing to wrecking tactics on the part of the monopolists, they were never able to make their control really effective.

4 *Cultural situation (philosophy, literature, painting)*

Culturally the eleventh century was the most active period China had so far experienced, apart from the fourth century B.C. As a consequence of the immensely increased number of educated people resulting from the invention of printing, circles of scholars and private schools set up by scholars were scattered all over the country. The various philosophical schools differed in their political attitude and in the choice of literary models with which they were politically in sympathy. Thus Wang An-shih and his followers preferred the rigid classic style of Han Yü, who lived in the T'ang period and had also been an opponent of the monopolistic tendencies of capitalism. For the Wang An-shih group formed itself into a school with a philosophy of its own and with its own commentaries on the classics. As the representative of the small merchants and the small landholders, this school advocated policies of State control and sometimes almost socialistic solutions.

But the Wang An-shih school was unable to hold its own against the school that stood for monopolist capitalism, the new philosophy described as Neoconfucianism or the Sung school. Here Confucianism and Buddhism were for the first time united. We saw how the main current of Buddhism had changed from a revolutionary to a reactionionary doctrine. The new greater gentry of the eleventh century adopted a number of elements of this reactionary Buddhism and incorporated them in the Confucianist system. This brought into Confucianism a metaphysic which it had lacked in the past, greatly extending its influence on the people and at the same time taking the wind out of the sails of Buddhism. The greater gentry never again placed themselves on the side of the Buddhist Church as they had done in the T'ang period. When they got tired of Confucianism, they interested themselves in Taoism or the politically innocent meditative Buddhism.

The Neoconfucianists compiled the great analytical works of history and encyclopaedias whose authority continues to this day, interpreting all history in accordance with their outlook; they issued new commentaries on all the classics, to spread interpretations that served their purposes. In the field of commentary this school of thought was given perfect expression by the famous scholar Chu Hsi (*c.* 1200), who also wrote one of the chief historical works.

Among the encyclopaedias is one that gives summary accounts of the achievements of Chinese medicine. In this period medicine made substantial progress. About 1145 the first autopsy was made, on the body of a South Chinese captive.

The Wang An-shih school of political philosophy had opponents also in the field of literary style, the so-called Shu Group (Shu means the present province of Szechwan), whose leaders were the famous Three Sus. The greatest of the three was Su Tung-p'o (1036–1101); the others were his father, Su Shih, and his brother, Su Che. It is characteristic of these Shu poets, and also of the Kiangsi school associated with them, that they made as much use as they could of the vernacular. It had not been usual to introduce the phrases of everyday life into poetry, but Su Tung-p'o made use of the most everyday expressions, without diminishing his artistic effectiveness by so doing; on the contrary, the result is to give his poems much more genuine feeling than those of other poets. These two tendencies were supported, like Neoconfucianism, by representatives of monopolist capitalism, and so were in harmony with the writings of the T'ang period poet Po Chü-i. Politically, in their conservatism they were sharply opposed to the Wang An-shih group. Midway between the two stood the so-called Loyang School, whose greatest leaders were the historian and poet Ssu-ma Kuang and the poet Shao Yung (1011–1077). These two played no part in politics, but lived in retirement, disgusted with everyday life. Their poems are Taoist in inspiration; their thinking is deeper than that of the other schools, and their philosophy more individualistic. In addition to its poems, the Sung literature was famous for the so-called *pi-chi* or miscellaneous notes. These consist of short notes of the most various sort, notes on literature, art, politics, archaeology, all mixed together. The *pi-chi* are a treasure-house for the history of the culture of the time; they contain many details, often of importance, about China's neighbouring peoples. They were intended to serve as suggestions for learned conversation when scholars came together; they aimed at showing how wide was a scholar's knowledge. To this group we must add the accounts of travel, of which some of great value dating from the Sung period are still extant; they contain information of the greatest importance about the early Mongols and also about Turkestan and South China. While the Sung period was one of the highest art in general, painting more and more assumed the first place. In this field, too, we talk of "schools", a northern and a southern school, though the painters themselves did not always come from the north or the south. With the founding of the Academy of Painting in the north there was formed the so-called "academic style", which attached special value to colour and to delicacy of execution of details; the southern style, on the contary, dispensed both with colour effect, preferring black china ink, and with the painting of details, preferring to convey impressions. The most extreme pictures in this style show nothing but a line or two to indicate, for instance, a landscape; all else must be supplied by the observer's imagination: he must try to feel it, sunk in contemplation of the picture. Famous in this style was Li Lung-mien, who was born in 1106. Ma Yüan, and his brother and son, Hsia Kui and Mu Hai, dispensed with colour effects and painted only in black-and-white. This style was connected with the tendency of that time to flee from the world, with the absorption in meditative Buddhism, and implies a turning to intuitive and at the same time individualistic thought.

Finally, art craft has left us famous porcelains of the Sung period. The most characteristic production of that time is the green porcelain known as "Celadon". It consists usually of a rather solid paste, less like porcelain than stoneware, covered with a green glaze; decoration is incised, not painted, under the glaze. In the Sung period, however, came the first pure white porcelain with incised ornamentation under the glaze, and also with painting on the glaze. Not until near the end of the Sung period did the blue and white porcelain begin (blue painting on a white ground). The cobalt needed for this came from Asia Minor. In exchange for the colour, Chinese porcelain went to Asia Minor. This trade did not, however, grow greatly until the Mongol epoch; later really substantial orders were placed in China, the Chinese executing the patterns wanted in the West.

5 *Military collapse*

In foreign affairs the whole eleventh century was a period of diplomatic manoeuvring, with every possible effort to avoid war. There was long-continued fighting with the Kitan, and at times also with the Turco-Tibetan Hsia, but diplomacy carried the day: tribute was paid to both enemies, and the effort was made to stir up the Kitan against the Hsia and vice versa; the other parties also intrigued in like fashion. In 1110 the situation seemed to improve for the Sung in this game, as a new enemy appeared in the rear of the Liao (Kitan), the Tungusic Juchên, who in the past had been more or less subject to the Kitan. In 1114 the Juchên made themselves independent and became a political factor. The Kitan were crippled, and it became an easy matter to attack them. But this pleasant situation did not last long. The Juchên conquered Peking, and in 1125 the Kitan empire was destroyed; but in the same year the Juchên marched against the Sung. In 1126 they captured the Sung capital; the emperor and his father, who had retired a little earlier, were taken prisoner, and the Northern Sung dynasty was at an end.

The collapse came so quickly because the whole edifice of security between the Kitan and the Sung was based on a policy of balance and of diplomacy. Neither State was armed in any way, and so both collapsed at the first assault from a military power.

(C) The Liao (Kitan) dynasty in the north (937–1125)

1 *Sociological structure. Claim to the Chinese imperial throne*

The Kitan, a league of tribes under the leadership of an apparently Mongol tribe, had grown steadily stronger in north-eastern Mongolia during the T'ang epoch. They had gained the allegiance of many tribes in the west and also in Korea and Manchuria, and in the end, about A.D. 900, had become the dominant power in the north. The process of growth of this nomad power was just the same as that of other nomad States, such as the Toba State, and therefore need not be described again in any detail here. When the T'ang dynasty was deposed, the Kitan were among the claimants to the Chinese throne, feeling fully justified in their claim as the strongest power in the Far East. Owing to the strength of the Sha-t'o Turks, who themselves claimed leadership in China, the expansion of the Kitan empire slowed down. In the many battles the Kitan suffered several setbacks. They also had enemies in the rear, a State named Po-hai, ruled by Tunguses, in northern Korea, and the new Korean State of Kao-li, which liberated itself from Chinese overlordship in 919.

In 927 the Kitan finally destroyed Po-hai. This brought many Tungus tribes, including the Djurdjen (Juchên), under Kitan dominance. Then, in 936, the Kitan gained the allegiance of the Turkish general Shih Ching-t'ang, and he was set on the Chinese throne as a feudatory of the Kitan. It was hoped now to secure dominance over China, and accordingly the Mongol name of the dynasty was altered to "Liao dynasty" in 937, indicating the claim to the Chinese throne. Considerable regions of North China came at once under the direct rule of the Liao. As a whole, however, the plan failed: the feudatory Shih Ching-t'ang tried to make himself independent; Chinese fought the Liao; and the Chinese sceptre soon came back into the hands of a Sha-t'o dynasty (947). This ended the plans of the Liao to conquer the whole of China.

For this there were several reasons. A nomad people was again ruling the agrarian regions of North China. This time the representatives of the ruling class remained military commanders, and at the same time retained their herds of horses. As early as 1100 they had well over 10,000 herds, each of more than a thousand animals. The army commanders had been awarded large regions which they themselves had conquered. They collected the taxes in these regions, and passed on to the State only the yield of the wine tax. On the other hand, in order to feed the armies, in which there were now many Chinese soldiers, the frontier regions were settled, the soldiers working as peasants in times of peace, and peasants being required to contribute to the support of the army. Both processes increased the interest of the Kitan ruling class in the maintenance of peace. That class was growing rich, and preferred living on the income from its properties or settlements to going to war, which had become a more and more serious matter after the founding of the great Sung empire, and was bound to be less remunerative. The herds of horses were a further excellent source of income, for they could be sold to the Sung, who had no horses. Then, from 1004 onward, came the tribute payments from China, strengthening the interest in the maintenance of peace. Thus great wealth accumulated in Peking, the capital of the Liao; in this wealth the whole Kitan ruling class participated, but the tribes in the north, owing to their remoteness, had no share in it. In 988 the Chinese began negotiations, as a move in their diplomacy, with the Turkish ruler of the later realm of the Hsia; in 990 the Kitan also negotiated with him, and they soon became a third partner in the diplomatic game. Delegations were continually going from one to another of the three realms, and they were joined by trade missions. Agreement was soon reached on frontier questions, on armament, on questions of demobilization, on the demilitarization of particular regions, and so on, for the last thing anyone wanted was to fight.

Then came the rising of the tribes of the north. They had remained military tribes; of all the wealth nothing reached them, and they were given no military employment, so that they had no hope of improving their position. The leadership was assumed by the tribe of the Juchên (1114). In a campaign of unprecedented rapidity they captured Peking, and the Liao dynasty was ended (1125), a year earlier, as we know, than the end of the Sung.

2 *The State of the Kara-Kitai*

A small troop of Liao, under the command of a member of the ruling family, fled into the west. They were pursued without cessation, but they succeeded in fighting their way through. After a few years of nomad life in the mountains of northern Turkestan, they were able to gain the collaboration of a few more tribes, and with them they then invaded western Turkestan. There they founded the "Western Liao" State, or, as the western sources call it, the "Kara-Kitai" State, with its capital at Balasagun. This State must not be regarded as a purely Kitan State. The Kitan formed only a very thin stratum, and the real power was in the hands of autochthonous Turkish tribes, to whom the Kitan soon became entirely assimilated in culture. Thus the history of this State belongs to that of western Asia, especially as the relations of the Kara-Kitai with the Far East were entirely broken off. In 1211 the State was finally destroyed.

(D) The Hsi-Hsia State in the north (1038–1227)

1 *Continuation of Turkish traditions*

After the end of the Toba State in North China in 550, some tribes of the Toba, including members of the ruling tribe with the tribal name Toba, withdrew to the borderland between Tibet and China, where they ruled over Tibetan and Tangut tribes. At the beginning of the T'ang dynasty this tribe of Toba joined the T'ang. The tribal leader received in return, as a distinction, the family name of the T'ang dynasty, Li. His dependence on China was, however, only nominal, and soon came entirely to an end. In the tenth century the tribe gained in strength. It is typical of the long continuance of old tribal traditions that a leader of the tribe in the tenth century married a woman belonging to the family to which the khans of the Hsiung Nu and all Turkish ruling houses had belonged since 200 B.C. With the rise of the Kitan in the north and of the Tibetan State in the south, the tribe decided to seek the friendship of China. Its first mission, in 982, was well received. Presents were sent to the chieftain of the tribe, he was helped against his enemies, and he was given the status of a feudatory of the Sung; in 988 the family name of the Sung, Chao, was conferred on him. Then the Kitan took a hand. They over-trumped the Sung by proclaiming the tribal chieftain king of Hsia (990). Now the small State became interesting. It was pampered by Liao and Sung in the effort to win it over or to keep its friendship. The State grew; in 1031 its ruler resumed the old family name of the Toba, thus proclaiming his intention to continue the Toba empire; in 1034 he definitely parted from the Sung, and in 1038 he proclaimed himself emperor in the Hsia dynasty, or, as the Chinese generally called it, the "Hsi-Hsia", which means the Western Hsia. This name, too, had associations with the old Hun tradition; it recalled the State of Ho-lien P'o-p'o in the early fifth century. The State soon covered the present province of Kansu, small parts of the adjoining Tibetan territory, and parts of the Ordos region. It attacked the province of Shensi, but the Chinese and the Liao attached the greatest importance to that territory. Thus that was the scene of most of the fighting.

The Hsia State had a ruling group of Toba, but these Toba had become entirely Tibetanized. The language of the country was Tibetan; the customs were those of the Tanguts. A script was devised, in imitation of the Chinese script. Only in recent years has it begun to be studied.

In 1125, when the Tungusic Juchên destroyed the Liao, the Hsia also lost large territories in the east of their country, especially the province of Shensi, which they had conquered; but they were still able to hold their own. Their political importance to China, however, vanished, since they were now divided from southern China and as partners were no longer of the same value to it. Not until the Mongols became a power did the Hsia recover some of their importance; but they were among the first victims of the Mongols: in 1209 they had to submit to them, and in 1227, the year of the death of Jenghiz Khan, they were annihilated.

(E) The empire of the Southern Sung dynasty (1127–1279)

1 *Foundation*

In the disaster of 1126, when the Juchên captured the Sung capital and destroyed the Sung empire, a brother of the captive emperor escaped. He made himself emperor in Nanking and founded the "Southern Sung" dynasty, whose capital was soon shifted to the present Hangchow. The foundation of the new dynasty was a relatively easy matter, and the new State was much more solid than the southern kingdoms of 800 years earlier, for the south had long been economically supreme, and the great families that had ruled the State were virtually all from the south. The loss of the north was of no importance at all to this governing group, and meant no loss of estates to it. Thus the transition from the Northern to the Southern Sung was not of fundamental importance. Consequently the Juchên had no chance of success when they arranged for Liu Yü, who came of a northern Chinese family of small peasants and had become an official, to be proclaimed emperor in the "Ch'i" dynasty in 1130. They hoped that this puppet might attract the southern Chinese, but seven years later they dropped him.

2 *Internal situation*

As the social structure of the Southern Sung empire had not been changed, the country was not affected by the dynastic development. Only the policy of diplomacy could not be pursued at once, as the Juchên were bellicose at first and would not negotiate. There were therefore several battles at the outset (in 1131 and 1134), in which the Chinese were actually the more successful, but not decisively. The Sung military group was faced as early as in 1131 with furious opposition from the greater gentry, led by Ch'in K'ui, one of the largest landowners of all. His estates were around Nanking, and so in the deployment region and the region from which most of the soldiers had to be drawn for the defensive struggle. Ch'in K'ui secured the assassination of the leader of the military party, General Yo Fei, in 1141, and was able to conclude peace with the Juchên. The Sung had to accept the status of vassals and to pay annual tribute to the Juchên. This was the situation that best pleased the greater gentry. They paid hardly any taxes (in many districts the greater gentry directly owned more than 30 per cent. of the land, in addition to which they had indirect interests in the soil), and they were now free from the war peril that ate into their revenues. The tribute amounted only to 500,000 strings of cash. Popular literature, however, to this day represents Ch'in K'ui as a traitor and Yo Fei as a national hero.

In 1165 it was agreed between the Sung and the Juchên to regard each other as States with equal rights. In spite of this, fighting continued, but it was mainly of the character of frontier engagements. Not until 1204 did the military party, led by Han T'o-wei, regain power; it resolved upon an active policy against the north. In preparation for this a military reform was carried out. The campaign proved a disastrous failure, as a result of which large territories in the north were lost. The Sung sued for peace; Han T'o-wei's head was cut off and sent to the Juchên. In this way was peace restored in 1208. The old treaty relationship was now resumed, but the relations between the two States remained tense. Meanwhile the Sung observed with malicious pleasure how the Mongols were growing steadily stronger, first destroying the Hsia State and then aiming the first heavy blows against the Juchên. In the end the Sung entered into alliance with the Mongols (1233) and joined them in attacking the Juchên, thus hastening the end of the Juchên State.

The Sung now faced the Mongols, and were defenceless against them. All the buffer States had gone. The Sung were quite without adequate military defence. They hoped to stave off the Mongols in the same way as they had met the Kitan and the Juchên. This time, however, they misjudged the situation. In the great operations begun by the Mongols in 1273 the Sung were defeated over and over again. In 1276 their capital was taken by the Mongols and the emperor was made prisoner. For three years longer there was a Sung emperor, in flight from the Mongols, until the last emperor in South China threw himself into the sea.

3 *Cultural situation; reasons for the collapse*

The Southern Sung period was again one of flourishing culture. The imperial court was entirely in the power of the greater gentry; several times the emperors, who personally do not deserve individual mention, were compelled to abdicate. They then lived on with a court of their own, devoting themselves to pleasure in much the same way as the "reigning" emperor. Round them was a countless swarm of poets and artists. Never was there a time so rich in poets, though hardly one of them was in any way outstanding. The poets, unlike those of earlier times, belonged to the lesser gentry, who were suffering from the prevailing inflation. Salaries bore no relation to prices. Food was not dear, but the things which a man of the upper class ought to have were far out of reach: a big house cost 2,000 strings of cash, a concubine 800 strings. Thus the lesser gentry and the intelligentsia all lived on their patrons among the greater gentry—with the result that they were entirely shut out of politics. This explains why the literature of the time is so unpolitical, and also why scarcely any philosophical works appeared. The writers took refuge more and more in romanticism and flight from realities.

The greater gentry, on the other hand, led a very elegant life, building themselves magnificent palaces in the capital. They also speculated in every direction. They speculated in land, in money, and above all in the paper money that was coming more and more into use. In 1166 the paper circulation exceeded the value of 10,000,000 strings!

In this period members of the gentry had a new and additional field for speculation. They married their daughters to rich merchants, even foreign traders, thus entering into association with the merchants and sharing the profits of the flourishing international commerce of the time. The organizing of such enterprise at this time was mainly in the hands of Indian capitalists, who owned one or more ships and financed their voyages. They were also ready to ship other people's goods and sell them on commission.

These foreign merchants and shipowners lived in special quarters of the ports, and exercised governmental rights in these quarters, sometimes, indeed, ruling whole cities. The Chinese government was represented only by port commissioners who supervised imports and exports and collected Customs duties. We do not know the amount of duty collected, but in the year 1160, apart from land tax, 36 per cent. of the revenues of the government came from taxes on alcoholic liquor, 50 per cent. from salt taxes, 7 per cent. from tea taxes, and 7 per cent. from Customs duties.

To increase the revenue the government opened wine-shops, restaurants, and public-houses. In the city of Hang-chow alone, in the latter part of the twelfth century, the government owned 23 establishments that were probably houses of ill-fame.

The growth of State activity and State control that marked the Sung period in economic affairs may also be observed in the field of social welfare and education. Both of these, before and after the Sung period, relied mainly on endowments. Under a law of 1098 State funds were allocated to a "Bureau for Housing and Care", a sort of rest-home for poor old people, a "Bureau of Medical Care" to give free treatment to the inmates of the homes and to other persons, and a "Burial Office" for burials of poor people; in 1144 twelve cemeteries were assigned to this office. In 1130 the first home for old people was opened, and after an abortive effort the first government hospitals were opened in 1143. The first orphanage is said to have been opened in 1247, and the first government drug store in 1248. About the same time a school for higher education. a sort of university, with 700 students, was opened at Hang-chow with government funds.

Another social institution of this period that should be mentioned was the fire-guard. In the city of Hangchow in 1264 the fire department had fourteen fire stations in the city and nine outside it, with specially trained firemen.

About the middle of the thirteenth century the contrasts grew more and more extreme. The state of the peasants who had been reduced to tenants was appalling. The lesser gentry were poverty-stricken, but the greater gentry continued to live in luxury. The defensive strength of the country had fallen in proportion.

At this stage, Chia Ssu-tao drafted a reform law. Chia had come to the court through his sister becoming the emperor's concubine, but he himself belonged to the lesser gentry. His proposal was that State funds should be applied to the purchase of land in the possession of the greater gentry over and above a fixed maximum. Peasants were to be settled on this land, and its yield was to belong to the State, which would be able to use it to meet military expenditure. In this way the country's military strength was to be restored. Chia's influence lasted just ten years, until 1275. He began putting the law into effect in the region south of Nanking, where the principal estates of the greater gentry were then situated. He brought upon himself, of course, the mortal hatred of the greater gentry, and paid for his action with his life. The emperor, in entering upon this policy, had, no doubt, hoped to recover some of his power, but the greater gentry brought him down. The gentry now openly played into the hands of the approaching Mongols, so hastening the final collapse of the Sung. The peasants and the lesser gentry would have fought the Mongols if it had been possible; but the greater gentry enthusiastically went over to the Mongols, hoping to save their property and so their influence by quickly joining the enemy. On a long view they had not judged badly. The Mongols removed the members of the gentry from all political posts, but left them their estates; and before long the greater gentry reappeared in political life. And when, later, the Mongol empire in China was brought down by a popular rising, the greater gentry showed themselves to be the most faithful allies of the Mongols!

(F) The empire of the Juchên in the north (1115–1234)

1 *Rapid expansion from northern Korea to the Yangtze*

The Juchên had in the past been only a small league of Tungus tribes, whose name is preserved in that of the present Tungus tribe of the Djurdjen, which came under the domination of the Kitan after the collapse of the State of Po-hai in northern Korea. We have already briefly mentioned the reasons for their rise. After their first successes against the Kitan (1114), their chieftain at once proclaimed himself emperor (1115), giving his dynasty the name "Chin". The Chin quickly continued their victorious progress. In 1125 the Kitan empire was destroyed. It will be remembered that the Sung were at once attacked, although they had recently been allied with the Chin against the Kitan. In 1126 the Sung capital was taken. The Chin invasions were pushed further south, and in 1130 the Yangtze was crossed. But the Chin did not hold the whole of these conquests, until their empire was consolidated. Their partial withdrawal closed the first phase of the Chin empire.

2 *United front of all Chinese*

But a few years after this maximum expansion, a withdrawal began which went on much more quickly than usual in such cases. The reasons were to be found both in external and in internal politics. The Juchên had gained great agrarian regions in a rapid march of conquest. Once more great cities with a huge urban population and immense wealth had fallen to alien conquerors. Now the Juchên wanted to enjoy this wealth as the Kitan had done before them. All the Juchên people counted as citizens of the highest class; they were free from taxation and only liable to military service. They were entitled to take possession of as much cultivable land as they wanted; this they did, and they took not only the "State domains" actually granted to them but also peasant properties, so that Chinese free peasants had nothing left but the worst fields, unless they became tenants on Juchên estates. A united front was therefore formed between all Chinese, both peasants and landowning gentry, against the Chin, such as it had not been possible to form against the Kitan. This made an important contribution later to the rapid collapse of the Chin empire.

The Chin who had thus come into possession of the cultivable land, and at the same time of the wealth of the towns, began a sort of competition with each other for the best winnings, especially after the government had returned to the old Sung capital, Pien-liang (now Kaifeng, in eastern Honan). Serious crises developed in their own ranks. In 1149 the ruler was assassinated by his chancellor (a member of the imperial family), who in turn was murdered in 1161. The Chin thus failed to attain what had been secured by all earlier conquerors, a reconciliation of the various elements of the population and the collaboration of at least one group of the defeated Chinese.

3 *Start of the Mongol empire*

The cessation of fighting against the Sung brought no real advantage in external affairs, though the tribute payments appealed to the greed of the rulers and were therefore welcomed. There could be no question of further campaigns against the south, for the Hsia empire in the west had not been destroyed, though some of its territory had been annexed; and a new peril soon made its appearance in the rear of the Chin. When in the tenth century the Sha-t'o Turks had had to withdraw from their dominating position in China, because of their great loss of numbers and consequently of strength, they went back into Mongolia and there united with the Tatars, among whom a new small league of tribes had formed toward the end of the eleventh century, consisting mainly of Mongols (Tatars) and Turks. In 1139 one of the chieftains of the Juchên rebelled and entered into negotiations with the South Chinese. He was killed, but his sons and his whole tribe then rebelled and went into Mongolia, where they made common cause with the Mongols. The Chin pursued them, and fought against them and against the Mongols, but without success. Accordingly negotiations were begun, and a promise was given to deliver meat and corn every year and to cede twenty-seven military strongholds. A high title was conferred on the tribal leader of the Mongols, in the hope of gaining his favour. He declined it, however, and in 1147 assumed the title of emperor of the "greater Mongol empire". This was the beginning of the power of the Mongols, who remained thereafter a dangerous enemy of the Chin in the north, until in 1189 Jenghiz Khan became their leader and made the Mongols the greatest power of central Asia. In any case, the Chin had reason to fear the Mongols from 1147 onward, and therefore were the more inclined to leave the Sung in peace.

In 1210 the Mongols began the first great assault against the Chin, the moment they had conquered the Hsia. In the years 1215–7 the Mongols took the military key-positions from the Chin. After that there could be no serious defence of the Chin empire. There came a respite only because the Mongols had turned against the West. But in 1234 the empire finally fell to the Mongols.

Many of the Chin entered the service of the Mongols, and with their permission returned to Manchuria; there they fell back to the cultural level of a warlike nomad people. Not until the sixteenth century did these Tunguses recover, reorganize, and appear again in history this time under the name of Manchus.

The North Chinese under Chin rule did not regard the Mongols as enemies of their country, but were ready at once to collaborate with them. The Mongols were even more friendly to them than to the South Chinese, and treated them rather better, until under Mongol rule the relations to the two parts of China grew uniform.

12 Ancient tiled pagoda at Chengting (Hopei).
Photo H. Hammer-Morrisson.

13 Horse-training. Painting by Li Kung-lin. Late Sung period.
Manchu Royal House Collection.

MODERN TIMES

Chapter X

THE MONGOL EPOCH (1280-1368)

1 *Beginning of the new epoch*

WE have already used the terms "antiquity" and "Middle Ages", in common use in Western history, to indicate the corresponding ages in China. There is, indeed, a clear distinction between the two ages. Antiquity was the age of feudalism, and the Middle Ages were the age of the gentry. But is there a "modern" age, and when did it begin? If we want a perfectly clear distinction, we should have to set the beginning of modern times as late as 1911, after the old form of society had been finally brought to an end, the State system built upon it abolished, and the new Western civilization accepted in full. For the old gentry, the class first formed centuries before the Christian era, continued to exist until 1911. Nevertheless, there is a difference between the ages before and after 1280. I am not referring to the fact that between 1280 and 1911 China had two experiences of foreign dynasties, but to the fact that a new class, ranking below the gentry, came into existence, which in all the centuries down to 1911 was denied full political activity, and was, indeed, entirely disfranchised, a class greatly resembling our European middle class. As the appearance of the middle class was one of the most distinctive features of modern times in Europe, we date modern times in China from the appearance of this similar class.

Just as, however, in China the transition from antiquity to the Middle Ages cannot be given an exact date, so the transition from the Middle Ages to modern times cannot be precisely indicated; it belongs to the period of Mongol rule, which must therefore be regarded as a period of transition.

Politically regarded, modern times in China have been

mainly an age of alien rule. Of the 631 years from 1280 to 1911, China was under national rulers for 276 years and under alien rule for 355. The alien rulers were first the Mongols, and later the Tungus Manchus. It is interesting to note that the alien rulers in the earlier period came mainly from the north-west, and only in modern times did peoples from the north-east rule over China. This is due in part to the fact that only peoples who have attained a certain level of civilization are capable of dominance. In antiquity and the Middle Ages, eastern Mongolia and Manchuria were at a relatively low level of civilization, from which they emerged only gradually through permanent contact with other nomad peoples, especially Turks. We are dealing here, of course, only with the Mongol epoch in China and not with the great Mongol empire, so that we need not enter further into these questions.

Yet another point is characteristic of modern times: the Mongols were the first alien people to rule the whole of China; the Manchus, who appeared in the seventeenth century, were the second and last. All alien peoples before these two ruled only parts of China. Why was it that the Mongols were able to be so much more successful than their predecessors? In the first place the Mongol political league was numerically stronger than those of the earlier alien peoples; secondly, the military organization and technical equipment of the Mongols were exceptionally advanced for their day. It must be borne in mind, for instance, that during their many years of war against the Sung dynasty in South China the Mongols already made use of small cannon in laying siege to towns. We have no exact knowledge of the number of Mongols who invaded and occupied China, but it is estimated that there were more than a million Mongols living in China. Not all of them, of course, were really Mongols! The name covered Turks, Tunguses, and others; among the auxiliaries of the Mongols were Uighurs, men from Central Asia and the Middle East, and even Europeans. When the Mongols attacked China they had the advantage of all the arts and crafts and all the new technical advances of western and central Asia and of Europe. Thus they had attained a high degree of technical progress, and at the same time their number was very great.

2 "*Nationality legislation*"

It was only after the Hsia empire in North China, and then the empire of the Juchên, had been destroyed by the Mongols, and only after long and remarkably modern tactical preparation, that the Mongols conquered South China, the empire of the Sung dynasty. They were now faced with the problem of ruling their great new empire. The conqueror of that empire, Kublai, himself recognized that China could not be treated in quite the same way as the Mongols' previous conquests; he therefore separated the empire in China from the rest of the Mongol empire. Mongol China became an independent realm within the Mongol empire, a sort of Dominion. The Mongol rulers were well aware that in spite of their numerical strength they were still only a minority in China, and this implied certain dangers. They therefore elaborated a "nationality legislation", the first of its kind in the Far East. The purpose of this legislation was, of course, to be the protection of the Mongols. The population of conquered China was divided into four groups—(1) Mongols, themselves falling into four sub-groups (the oldest Mongol tribes, the White Tatars, the Black Tatars, the Wild Tatars); (2) Central Asian auxiliaries (Maimans, Uighurs, and various other Turkish peoples, Tanguts, and so on); (3) North Chinese; (4) South Chinese. The Mongols formed the privileged ruling class. They remained militarily organized, and were distributed in garrisons over all the big towns of China as soldiers, maintained by the State. All the higher government posts were reserved for them, so that they also formed the head of the official staffs. The auxiliary peoples were also admitted into the government service; they, too, had privileges, but were not all soldiers but in many cases merchants, who used their privileged position to promote business. Not a few of these merchants were Uighurs and Mohammedans; many Uighurs were also employed as clerks, as the Mongols were very often unable to read and write Chinese, and the government offices were bilingual, working in Mongolian and Chinese.

The clever Uighurs quickly learned enough of both languages for official purposes, and made themselves indispensable assistants to the Mongols. In the Mongol legislation the South Chinese had the lowest status, and virtually no rights. Intermarriage with them was prohibited. The Chinese were not allowed to carry arms. For a time they were forbidden even to learn the Mongol or other foreign languages. In this way they were to be prevented from gaining official positions and playing any political part. Their ignorance of the languages of northern, central, and western Asia also prevented them from engaging in commerce like the foreign merchants, and every possible difficulty was put in the way of their travelling for commercial purposes. On the other hand, foreigners were, of course, able to learn Chinese, and so to gain a footing in Chinese internal trade.

Through legislation of this type the Mongols tried to build up and to safeguard their domination over China. Yet their success did not last a hundred years.

3 *Military position*

In foreign affairs the Mongol epoch was for China something of a breathing space, for the great wars of the Mongols took place at a remote distance from China and without any Chinese participation. Only a few concluding wars were fought under Kublai in the Far East. The first was his war against Japan (1281): it ended in complete failure, the fleet being destroyed by a storm. In this campaign the Chinese furnished ships and also soldiers. The subjection of Japan would have been in the interest of the Chinese, as it would have opened a market which had been almost closed against them in the Sung period. Mongol wars followed in the south. In 1282 began the war against Burma; in 1284 Annam and Cambodia were conquered; in 1292 a campaign was started against Java. It proved impossible to hold Java, but almost the whole of Indo-

China came under Mongol rule, to the satisfaction of the Chinese, for Indo-China had already been one of the principal export markets in the Sung period. After that, however, there was virtually no more warfare, apart from small campaigns against rebellious tribes. The Mongol soldiers now lived on their pay in their garrisons, with nothing to do. The old campaigners died, and were followed by their sons, brought up also as soldiers; but these young Mongols were born in China, had seen nothing of war, and learned of the soldiers' trade either nothing or very little; so that after about 1320 serious things happened. An army nominally 1,000 strong was sent against a group of barely fifty bandits and failed to defeat them. Most of the 1,000 soldiers no longer knew how to use their weapons, and many did not even join the force. Such incidents occurred again and again.

4 *Sociological position*

The results, however, of conditions within the country were of much more importance than events abroad. The Mongols made Peking their capital, as was entirely natural, for Peking was near their homeland, Mongolia. The emperor and his entourage could return to Mongolia in the summer, when China became too hot or too humid for them; and from Peking they were able to maintain contact with the rest of the Mongol empire. But as the city had become the capital of a vast empire, an enormous staff of officials had to be housed there, consisting of persons of many different nationalities. The emperor naturally wanted to have a magnificent capital, a city really worthy of so vast an empire. As the many wars had brought in vast booty, there was money for the building of great palaces, of a size and magnificence never before seen in China. They were built by Chinese forced labour, and to this end men had to be brought from all over the empire—poor peasants, whose fields went out of cultivation while they were held in bondage far away. If they ever returned home, they were destitute and had lost their land. The rich gentry, on the other hand, were able to buy immunity from forced labour. The immense increase in the population of Peking (the huge court with its enormous expenditure, the mass of officials, the great merchant community, largely foreigners, and the many servile labourers), necessitated vast supplies of food. Now, as mentioned in earlier chapters, since the time of the Later T'ang the region round Nanking had become the main centre of production in China, and the Chinese population had gone over more and more to the consumption of rice instead of pulse or wheat. As rice could not be grown in the north, practically the whole of the food supplies for the capital had to be brought from the south. The transport system taken over by the Mongols had not been created for long-distance traffic of this sort. The capital of the Sung had lain in the main centre of production. Consequently, a great fleet had suddenly to be built, canals and rivers had to be regulated, and some new canals excavated. This again called for a vast quantity of forced labour, often brought from afar to the points at which it was needed. The Chinese peasants had suffered in the Sung period. They had been exploited by the large landowners. The Mongols had not removed these landowners, as the Chinese gentry had at once gone over to their side. The Mongols had deprived them of their political power, but had left them their estates, the basis of their power. In past changes of dynasty the gentry had either maintained their position or been replaced by a new gentry: the total number of their class had remained virtually unchanged. Now, however, in addition to the original gentry there were about a million Mongols, for whose maintenance the peasants had also to provide, and their standard of maintenance was high. This was an enormous increase in the burdens of the peasantry.

Two other elements further pressed on the peasants in the Mongol epoch—the Church and the traders. The upper classes among the Chinese had in general little interest in religion, but the Mongols, owing to their historical development, were very religious. Some of them, and some of their allies, were Buddhists, some were still shamanists. The Chinese Buddhists and representatives of the popular Taoism approached the Mongols and the foreign Buddhist monks, and tried to enlist the interest of the Mongols and their allies. The old shamanism was unable to compete with the higher religions, and the Mongols in China became Buddhist or interested themselves in the popular Taoism. They showed their interest especially by the endowment of temples and monasteries. The temples were given great estates, and the peasants on those estates became temple servants. The land belonging to the temples was free from taxation.

We have as yet no exact statistics of the Mongol epoch, only approximations. These set the total area under cultivation at some six million *ch'ing* (a *ch'ing* is the ideal size of the farm worked by a peasant family, but it was rarely held in practice); the population amounted to fourteen or fifteen million families. Of this total tillage some 170,000 *ch'ing* were allotted to the temples; that is to say, the farms for some 400,000 peasant families were taken from the peasants and no longer paid taxes to the State. The peasants, however, had to make payments to the temples. Some 200,000 *ch'ing* with some 450,000 peasant families were turned into military settlements; that is to say, these peasants had to work for the needs of the army. Their taxes went not to the State but to the army. Moreover, in the event of war they had to render service to the army. In addition to this, all higher officials received official properties, the yield of which represented part payment of their salaries. Then, Mongol nobles and dignitaries received considerable grants of land, which was taken away from the free peasants; the peasants had then to work their farms as tenants and to pay dues to their landlords, no longer to the State. Finally, especially in North China, many peasants were entirely dispossessed, and their land was turned into pasturage for the Mongols' horses; the peasants themselves were put to forced labour. On top of this came the exploitation of the peasants by the great landowners of the past. All this meant an enormous diminution in the number of free peasants and thus of taxpayers. As the State was involved in more expenditure than in the past owing to the large number of Mongols who were its virtual pensioners, the taxes had to be continually increased. Meanwhile the many peasants working as tenants of the great landlords, the temples, and the Mongol nobles were entirely at their mercy. The many merchants from abroad, especially those belonging to the peoples allied to the Mongols, also had in every respect a privileged position in China. They were free of taxation, free to travel all over the country, and received privileged treatment in the use of means of transport. They were thus able to accumulate great wealth, most of which went out of China to their own country. This produced a general impoverishment of China. Chinese merchants fell more and more into dependence on the foreign merchants; the only field of action really remaining to them was the local trade within China and the trade with Indo-China, where the Chinese had the advantage of knowing the language.

The impoverishment of China began with the flow abroad of her metallic currency. To make up for this loss, the government was compelled to issue great quantities of paper money, which very quickly depreciated, because after a few years the government would no longer accept the money at its face value, so that the population could place no faith in it. The depreciation further impoverished the people.

Thus we have in the Mongol epoch in China the imposing picture of a commerce made possible with every country from Europe to the Pacific; this, however, led to the impoverishment of China. We also see the rising of mighty temples and monumental buildings, but this again only contributed to the denudation of the country. The Mongol epoch was thus one of continual and rapid impoverishment in China, simultaneously with a great display of magnificence. The enthusiastic descriptions of the Mongol empire in China offered by travellers from the Near East or from Europe, such as Marco Polo, give an entirely false picture: as foreigners they had a privileged position, living in the cities and seeing nothing of the situation of the general population.

5 *Popular risings: National rising*

It took time for the effects of all these factors to become evident. The first popular rising came in 1325. Statistics of 1329 show that there were then some 7,600,000 persons in the empire who were starving; as this was only the figure of the officially admitted sufferers, the true figure must have been much higher. In any case, seven-and-a-half millions were a substantial percentage of the total population, estimated at 45,000,000. The risings that now came incessantly were led by men of the lower orders—a cloth-seller, a fisherman, a peasant, a salt smuggler, the son of a soldier serving a sentence, an office messenger, and so on. They never attacked the Mongols as aliens, but always the rich in general, whether Chinese or foreign. Wherever they came, they killed all the rich and distributed their money and possessions.

As already mentioned, the Mongol garrisons were unable to cope with these risings. But how was it that the Mongol rule did not collapse until some forty years later? The Mongols parried the risings by raising loans from the rich and using the money to recruit volunteers to fight the rebels. The State revenues would not have sufficed for these payments, and the item was not one that could be included in the military budget. What was of much more importance was that the gentry themselves recruited volunteers and fought the rebels on their own account, without the authority or the support of the government. Thus it was the Chinese gentry, in their fear of being killed by the insurgents, who fought them and so bolstered up the Mongol rule.

In 1351 the dykes along the Yellow River burst. The dykes had to be reconstructed and further measures of conservancy undertaken. To this end the government impressed 170,000 men. Following this action, great new revolts broke out. Everywhere in Honan, Kiangsu, and Shantung, the regions from which the labourers were summoned, revolutionary groups were formed, some of them amounting to 100,000 men. Some groups had a religious tinge; others declared their intention to restore the emperors of the Sung dynasty. Before long great parts of central China were wrested from the hands of the government. The government recognized the menace to its existence, but resorted to contradictory measures. In 1352 southern Chinese were permitted to take over certain official positions. In this way it was hoped to gain the full support of the gentry, who had a certain interest in combating the rebel movements. On the other hand, the government tightened up its racial laws. All the old racial laws were brought back into force, with the result that in a few years the aim of the rebels became no longer merely the expulsion of the rich but also the expulsion of the Mongols: a social movement thus became a national one. A second element contributed to the change in the character of the popular rising. The rebels captured many towns. Some of these towns refused to fight and negotiated terms of submission. In these cases the rebels did not murder the whole of the gentry, but took some of them into their service. The gentry did not agree to this out of sympathy with the rebels, but simply in order to save their own lives. Once they had taken the step, however, they could not go back; they had no alternative but to remain on the side of the rebels.

In 1352 Kuo Tzŭ-hsing rose in southern Honan. Kuo was the son of a wandering soothsayer and a blind beggar-woman. He had success; his group gained control of a considerable region round his home. There was no longer any serious resistance from the Mongols, for at this time the whole of eastern China was in full revolt. In 1353 Kuo was joined by a man named Chu Yüan-chang, the son of a small peasant, probably a tenant farmer. Chu's parents and all his relatives had died from a plague, leaving him destitute. He had first entered a monastery and become a monk. This was a favourite resource—and has been almost to the present day—for poor sons of peasants who were threatened with starvation. As a monk he had gone about begging, until in 1353 he returned to his home and collected a group, mostly men from his own village, sons of peasants and young fellows who had already been peasant leaders. At that time monks were often peasant leaders. They were trusted because they promised divine aid, and because they were usually rather better educated than the rest of the peasants. Chu took his small group to Kuo, who received him gladly, entered into alliance with him, and in sign of friendship gave him his daughter in marriage. In 1355 Kuo died, and Chu took over his army, now many thousands strong. In his campaigns against towns in eastern China, Chu succeeded in winning over some capable members of the gentry. One was the chairman of a committee that yielded a town to Chu; another was a scholar whose family had always been opposed to the Mongols, and who had himself suffered injustice several times in his official career, so that he was glad to join Chu out of hatred of the Mongols.

These men gained great influence over Chu, and persuaded him to give up attacking rich individuals, and instead to establish an assured control over large parts of the country. He would then, they pointed out, be permanently enriched, while otherwise he would only be in funds at the moment of the plundering of a town. They set before him strategic plans with that aim. Through their counsel Chu became no longer the leader of a popular rising but a fighter against the dynasty. Of all the peasant leaders he was now the only one pursuing a definite aim. He marched first against Nanking, the great city of central China, and captured it with ease. He then crossed the Yangtze and conquered the rich provinces of the southeast. He was a rebel who no longer slaughtered the rich or plundered the towns, and the whole of the gentry with all their followers came over to him *en masse*. The armies of volunteers went over to Chu, and the whole edifice of the dynasty collapsed.

The years 1355–1368 are full of small battles. After his conquest of the whole of the south, Chu went north. In 1368 his generals captured Peking almost without a blow. The Mongol ruler fled on horseback with his immediate entourage into the north of China, and soon after into Mongolia. The Mongol dynasty had been brought down, almost without resistance. The Mongols in the isolated garrisons marched northward wherever they could. The only resistance offered came from the regions in which other Chinese popular leaders had established themselves, especially the remote provinces in the west and south-west, which had a different social structure and had been relatively little affected by the Mongol régime.

Thus the collapse of the Mongols came for the following reasons: (1) They had not succeeded in maintaining their armed strength or that of their allies during the period of peace that followed Kublai's conquest. The Mongol soldiers had become effeminate through their life of idleness in the towns. (2) The attempt to rule the empire through Mongols or other aliens, and to exclude the Chinese gentry entirely from the administration, failed through insufficient knowledge of the sources of revenue and through the abuses due to the favoured treatment of aliens. The whole country, and especially the peasantry, was completely impoverished and so driven into revolt. There was also a psychological reason for this. In the middle of the fourteenth century it was obvious to the Mongols that their hold over China was growing more and more precarious, and that there was little to be got out of the impoverished country; and they seem in consequence to have lost interest in the troublesome task of maintaining their rule, preferring, in so far as they had not already entirely degenerated, to return to their old home in the north. It is important to bear in mind these reasons for the collapse of the Mongols, so that we may compare them later with the reasons for the collapse of the Manchus.

No mention need be made here of the names of the Mongol rulers in China after Kublai. After his death in 1294, grandsons and great-grandsons of his followed each other in rapid succession on the throne; not one of them was of any personal significance. They had no influence on the government of China. Their life was spent in intriguing against one another. There were seven Mongol emperors after Kublai.

6 *Cultural*

During the Mongol epoch a large number of the Chinese scholars withdrew from official life. They lived in retirement among their friends, and devoted themselves mainly to the pursuit of the art of poetry, which had been elaborated in the Later Sung epoch, without themselves arriving at any important innovations in form. Their poems were built up meticulously on the rules laid down by the various schools; they are routine productions rather than the outcome of any true poetic inspiration. In the realm of prose the best achievements were the "miscellaneous notes" already mentioned, collections of learned essays. The foreigners who wrote in Chinese during this epoch are credited with no better achievements by the Chinese historians of literature. Chief of them were a statesman named Yeh-lü Ch'u-ts'ai, a Kitan in the service of the Mongols; and a Mongol named T'o-t'o (Tokto). The former accompanied Jenghiz Khan in his great campaign against Turkestan, and left a very interesting account of his journeys, together with many poems about Samarkand and Turkestan. His other works are mainly letters and poems addressed to friends. They differ in no way in style from the Chinese literary works of the time, and are neither better nor worse than those works. He shows strong traces of Taoist influence, as do other contemporary writers. We know that Jenghiz Khan was more or less inclined to Taoism, and admitted a Taoist monk to his camp (1221–1224). This man's account of his travels has also been preserved, and with the numerous European accounts of Central Asia written at this time it forms an important source. The Mongol Tokto was the head of an historical commission that issued the annals of the Sung dynasty, the Kitan, and the Juchên dynasty. The annals of the Sung dynasty became the largest of all the historical works, but they were fiercely attacked from the first by Chinese critics on account of their style and their hasty composition, and, together with the annals of the Mongol dynasty, they are regarded as the worst of the annals preserved. Tokto himself is less to blame for this than the circumstance that he was compelled to work in great haste, and had not time to put into order the overwhelming mass of his material.

The greatest literary achievements, however, of the Mongol period belong beyond question to the theatre (or, rather, opera). The emperors were great theatre-goers, and the wealthy private families were also enthusiasts, so that gradually people of education devoted themselves to writing librettos for the operas, where in the past this work had been left to others. Most of the authors of these librettos remained unknown: they used pseudonyms, partly because playwriting was not an occupation that befitted a scholar, and partly because in these works they criticized the conditions of their day. These works are divided in regard to style into two groups, those of the "southern" and the "northern" drama; these are distinguished from each other in musical construction and in their intellectual attitude: in general the northern works are more heroic and the southern more sentimental, though there are exceptions. The most famous northern works of the Mongol epoch are *P'i-p'a-chi* ("The Story of a Lute"), written about 1356, probably by Kao Ming, and *Chao-shih ku-erh-chi* ("The Story of the Orphans of Chao"), a work that enthralled Voltaire, who made a paraphrase of it; its author was the otherwise unknown Chi Chün-hsiang. One of the most famous of the southern dramas is *Hsi-hsiang-chi* ("The Story of the Western Room"), by Wang Shih-fu and Kuan Han-ch'ing. Kuan lived under the Juchên dynasty as a physician, and then among the Mongols. He is said to have written fifty-eight dramas, many of which became famous.

In the plastic arts, foreign influence made itself felt during the Mongol epoch much more than in literature. This was due in part to the Mongol rulers' predilection for the Lamaism that was widespread in their homeland. Lamaism is a special form of Buddhism which developed in Tibet, where remnants of the old national Tibetan cult (*Bhon*) were fused with Buddhism into a distinctive religion. During the rise of the Mongols this religion, which closely resembled the shamanism of the ancient Mongols, spread in Mongolia, and through the Mongols it made great progress in China, where it had been insignificant until their time. Religious sculpture especially came entirely under Tibetan influence (particularly that of the sculptor Aniko, who came from Nepal, where he was born in 1244). This influence was noticeable in the Chinese sculptor Liu Yüan; after him it became stronger and stronger, lasting until the Manchu epoch.

In architecture, too, Indian and Tibetan influence was felt in this period. The Tibetan pagodas came into special prominence alongside the previously known form of pagoda, which has many storeys, growing smaller as they go upward; these towers originally contained relics of Buddha and his disciples. The Tibetan pagoda has not this division into storeys, and its lower part is much larger in circumference, and often round. To this day Peking is rich in pagodas in the Tibetan style.

The Mongols also developed in China the art of carpet-knotting, which to this day is found only in North China in the zone of northern influence. There were carpets before these, but they were mainly of felt. The knotted carpets were produced in imperial workshops—only, of course, for the Mongols, who were used to carpets. A further development probably also due to Western influence was that of cloisonné technique in China in this period.

Painting, on the other hand, remained free from alien influence, with the exception of the craft painting for the temples. The most famous painter of the Mongol epoch, Chao Mêng-fu (also called Chao Chung-mu, 1254–1322), a relative of the deposed imperial family of the Sung dynasty, painted entirely in the style of the Academic School. Another group of painters, of whom Ni Tsan (1301–1374) is the most famous, developed the so-called "Literati style", an offspring of the so-called "southern style". This style was followed particularly in the Ming epoch.

Chapter XI

THE MING EPOCH (1368-1644)

1 *Start. National feeling*

IT was necessary to give special attention to the reasons for the downfall of Mongol rule in China, in order to make clear the cause and the character of the Ming epoch that followed it. It is possible that the erroneous impression might be gained that the Mongol epoch in China was entirely without merits, and that the Mongol rule over China differed entirely from the Mongol rule over other countries of Asia. Chinese historians have no good word to say of the Mongol epoch, and avoid the subject as far as they can. It is true that the union of the national Mongol culture with Chinese culture, as envisaged by the Mongol rulers, was not a sound conception, and consequently did not endure for long. Nevertheless, the Mongol epoch in China left indelible traces, and without it China's further development would certainly have taken a different course.

The many popular risings during the latter half of the period of Mongol rule in China were all of a purely economic and social character, and at first they were not directed at all against the Mongols as representatives of an alien people. The rising under Chu Yüan-chiang, which steadily gained impetus, was at first a purely social movement; indeed, it may fairly be called revolutionary. Chu was of the humblest origin; he became a monk and a peasant leader at one and the same time. Only three times in Chinese history has a man of the peasantry become emperor and founder of a dynasty. The first of these three men founded the Han dynasty; the second founded the first of the so-called "Five Dynasties" in the tenth century; Chu was the third.

Not until the Mongols had answered Chu's rising with

a tightening of the nationality laws did the revolutionary movement become a national movement, directed against the foreigners as such. And only when Chu came under the influence of the first people of the gentry who joined him, whether voluntarily or perforce, did what had been a proletarian revolutionary movement become a struggle for the substitution of one dynasty for another without interfering with the existing social system. Both these points were of the utmost importance to the whole development of the Ming epoch.

The Mongols were driven out fairly quickly and without great difficulty. This was not due to any superiority in the quality of the Chinese armies, but to the military deterioration of the Mongol armies and the consequent desire of the Mongols themselves not to undertake any long campaigns but to retire to their old, untroubled homeland. The Chinese drew from the ease of their success a sense of superiority. And this, together with the first awakening of national feeling as a reaction against the humiliating racial laws of the Mongols, led to a hatred of foreigners, which remained typical of the whole governing class during the Ming epoch. China closed her frontiers against aliens, regarding them as people of lower civilization and as disturbers of the peace. This spirit was kept alive throughout the Ming epoch, though, of course, it did not prevent the continuance of diplomatic intercourse with foreign countries as distant as the Turkish States of western Asia.

2 *Wars against Mongols and Japanese*

It had been easy to drive the Mongols out of China, but they were never really beaten in their own country. On the contrary, they seem to have regained strength after their withdrawal from China: they were soon capable of counter-thrusts, while Chinese offensives had as a rule very little success, and at all events no decisive success. In the course of time, however, the Chinese gained a certain influence over Turkestan, but it was never absolute, always challenged. After the Mongol empire had fallen to pieces, small States came into existence in Turkestan, for a long time with varying fortunes; the most important one during the Ming epoch was that of Hami, until in 1473 it was occupied by the city-State of Turfan. At this time China actively intervened in the policy of Turkestan in a number of combats with the Mongols. As the situation changed from time to time, these city-States united more or less closely with China or fell away from her altogether. In this period, however, Turkestan was of no military or economic importance to China.

In the time of the Ming there also began in the east and south the plague of Japanese piracy. This, too, was an outcome of the Mongol rule, in so far as the Japanese had been roused by the Mongol attacks on Japan to undertake military campaigns against China. As early as 1387 the Chinese had to begin the building of fortifications along the eastern and southern coasts of the country. The Japanese attacks had the character of organized raids: a small, fast-sailing flotilla would land in a bay, as far as possible without attracting notice; the soldiers would march against the nearest town, generally overcoming it, looting, and withdrawing. This inflicted painful injuries on China, as it was the wealthiest regions that suffered from the looting. The defensive measures adopted, however, from time to time during the Ming epoch were of little avail, as it was impossible effectively to garrison the whole coast. Some of the coastal settlements were transferred inland, to prevent Chinese peasants from co-operating with the Japanese, and to give the Japanese so long a march inland as to allow time for defensive measures. The Japanese pirates prevented the creation of a Chinese navy in this period by their continual threats to the coastal cities in which the shipyards lay. Not until much later, at a time of unrest in Japan in 1467, was there any peace from the Japanese pirates.

Toward the end of the Ming epoch the Japanese sea-rovers were replaced by Europeans; at all events, the Chinese placed that interpretation on the appearance and the activities of the Europeans. All this increased the hatred of foreigners and strengthened the national feeling that had been aroused at the beginning of the Ming epoch.

3 *Social legislation within the existing order*

Of still more importance, however, was the conversion of the rising under Chu Yüan-chang from a proletarian revolutionary movement into a conservative and reactionary one; for it prevented a thorough healing and recovery of China. At the time when Chu Yüan-chang conquered Peking, in 1368, becoming the recognized emperor of China (Ming dynasty), it seemed as though he would remain a revolutionary in spite of everything. His first laws were directed against the rich. Many of the rich were compelled to migrate to the capital, Nanking, thus losing their land and the power based on it. The land was redistributed among poor peasants; new land registers were also compiled, in order to prevent the rich from evading taxation. The number of monks living in idleness was cut down and set fixed limits; the possessions of the temples were reduced, land exempted from taxation being thus made taxable—all this, incidentally, although Chu had himself been a monk! These laws might have paved the way to social harmony and removed the worst of the poverty of the Mongol epoch. But all this was frustrated in the very first years of Chu's reign. The laws were only half carried into effect or not at all, especially in the hinterland of the present Shanghai. That region had been conquered by Chu at the very beginning of the Ming epoch; in it lived the wealthy landowners who had already been paying the bulk of the taxes under the Mongols. The emperor depended on this wealthy class for the financing of his great armies, and so could not be too hard on it.

Chu Yüan-chang and his entourage were also unable to free themselves from some of the ideas of the Mongol epoch. Their conception of an emperor was formed by the Mongol emperors with their magnificence and the huge expenditure of their life in Peking; they were oblivious of the fact that Peking had been the capital of a vast empire embracing almost the whole of Asia, and so able to spend much more than a capital only of China. It did not occur to Chu and his supporters that they could have done without imperial state and splendour; on the contrary, they felt compelled to display it. At first Chu personally showed no excessive signs of this tendency, though they emerged later; but he conferred great fiefs on all his relatives, friends, and supporters; he would give to a single person land on which 20,000 peasant families could have lived; he ordered the payment of State pensions to members of the imperial family, just as the Mongols had done, and the total of these pension payments was often higher than the revenue of the region involved. For the capital alone over eight million *shih* of corn had to be provided in payment of pensions—that is to say, more than 160,000 tons! These pension payments were in themselves a heavy burden on the State; not only that, but they formed a difficult transport problem! We have no close figure of the total population at the beginning of the Ming epoch; about 1500 it is estimated to have been 53,280,000, and this population had to provide some 266,000,000 *shih* in taxes. At the beginning of the Ming epoch the population and revenue must, however, have been smaller.

Laws were also issued against the trading community, but not in order to prevent excesses but in subservience to the gentry, who had always been hostile to the commercial community, for reasons which have already been explained. This time the commercial legislation was directed also against foreigners, who were, indeed, the leading merchants. It was just the great merchants, however, who were the most successful in saving themselves and their property. Almost all the foreigners were driven out of the country or murdered, but a number of foreign merchants were able to assume Chinese names and remain in China. Thus the laws against the trading community did not attain the ends they were intended to serve. The injurious effects of commerce on the peasantry remained. The general result of the factors mentioned was that the Ming dynasty had an inauspicious start. And the effect of these factors grew greater as the population grew, as the numbers grew of the new rich with their illegal exploitation of the peasants, and as corruption increased.

4 *Beginning of the "bourgeoisie"*

Corruption in general was one of the chief characteristics of the Ming epoch. There had always been corruption in China, but never on such a scale as under the Ming. The reason is interesting. The fourteenth century was the period in which a new class first gave clear evidence of its presence, a class corresponding in some degree to the European bourgeoisie. After the invention of printing in the Sung epoch there was a gradual increase in the quantity of printed books at prices within reach. The small merchant, who had the main share in trade within the various branches of the Chinese economic system, had in the past been able to write nothing beyond his figures and a few words. He had not been able to buy texts for himself, still less to be accepted as a pupil by a man of learning. Now he could buy books without difficulty. The first people to spread printed books among the population were the Buddhists—for mission purposes. Then other books came into the market. Self-education was possible with their aid, as the main element in education was then learning by heart. Finally the better craftsman or the fairly prosperous farmer often had the opportunity of gaining some education. He was able to learn the required texts, and could ascertain from printed collections of examination papers how the papers were compiled; he could therefore sit at an examination.

Thus a new group entered the class of officials in the Ming epoch, men who did not belong to the landowning gentry, but, though born in poor circumstances or with few possessions, were able to pass the examinations. Attendance, however, at the examinations cost a good deal. The candidate had to travel to the local or provincial capital, and for the higher examinations to the capital of the country; he had to live there for several months, and had as a rule to bribe the examiners or at least to gain the favour of influential people. There were many cases of candidates becoming destitute. Most of them were heavily in debt when at last they gained a position. They naturally set to work at once to pay their debts out of their salary, and to accumulate fresh capital to meet future emergencies. The salaries of officials were, however, so small that it was impossible to make ends meet; and at the same time every official was liable with his own capital for the receipt in full of the taxes for the collection of which he was responsible. Consequently every official began at once to collect more taxes than were really due, so as to be able to cover any deficits, and also to cover his own cost of living—including not only the repayment of his debts but the acquisition of capital or land so as to rise in the social scale. The old gentry had been rich landowners, and had had no need to exploit the peasants on such a scale.

The Chinese empire was greater than it had been before the Mongol epoch, and the population was also greater, so that more officials were needed. Thus in the Ming epoch there began a certain democratization, larger sections of the population having the opportunity of gaining government positions; but this democratization brought no benefit to the general population but resulted in further exploitation of the peasants.

The new middle class did not consist of great families like the gentry. When, therefore, people of that class wanted to play a political part in the central government, or to gain a position there, they had either to get into close touch with one of the families of the gentry, or to try to approach the emperor direct. In the immediate entourage of the emperor, however, were the eunuchs. A good many members of the middle class had themselves castrated after they had passed their State examination. As originally eunuchs were forbidden to acquire education, the new educated eunuchs, when they had once secured a position, were able to gain great influence in the immediate entourage of the emperor; later such educated eunuchs were preferred, especially as many offices were created which were only filled by eunuchs and for which educated eunuchs were needed. Whole departments of eunuchs came into existence at court, and these were soon made use of for confidential business of the emperor's outside the palace.

These eunuchs worked, of course, in the interest of their families. On the other hand, they were very ready to accept large bribes from the gentry for placing the desires of people of the gentry before the emperor and gaining his consent. The emperor himself hoped to use these eunuchs to counteract the power of cliques of the gentry. Thus the eunuchs generally accumulated great wealth, which they shared with their middle-class relatives. The rise of the middle class was therefore connected with the increased influence of the eunuchs at court. During the Ming epoch the eunuchs became a factor of immense importance, but a harmful one. Altogether the social situation at the beginning of the Ming epoch was by no means healthy, and gave promise of coming crises.

5 *Literature, art, art crafts*

The new social element, the middle class, soon made its mark in literature. The classical Chinese novel, for which the way had been paved by the narrative works of the Mongol epoch, was brought to perfection under the Ming. To this day every Chinese knows and reads with enthusiasm *Shui-hu-chuan* ("The Story of the River Bank"), probably written about 1550 by Wang Tao-k'un, in which the ruling class was first described in its decay. Against it are held up as ideals representatives of the middle class in the guise of the gentleman brigand. Every Chinese also knows the great satirical novel *Hsi-yu-chi* ("The Westward Journey"), by Pêng Mêng-lung (end of the sixteenth century), in which ironical treatment is meted out to all religions and sects against a mythological background, with a freedom that would not have been possible earlier. The characters are not presented as individuals but as representatives of human types: the intellectual, the hedonist, the pious man, and the simpleton, are drawn with incomparable skill, with their merits and defects. A third famous novel is *San-kuo yen-i* ("The Tale of the Three Men"), by Lo Kuan-chung. Just as the European middle class read with avidity the romances of chivalry, so the comfortable class in China was enthusiastic over romanticized pictures of the struggle of the gentry in the third century. "The Tale of the Three Rich men" became the model for countless novels of its own and subsequent periods. Toward the end of the Ming epoch the short story began to develop, though its finest period belongs to the last three centuries. The collection of short stories entitled *Chin-ku ch'i-kuan* ("Strange Stories of New Times and Old"), compiled by Pêng Mêng-lung, is world-famous and has been translated into many European languages. The short stories and the novels used an entirely unliterary vernacular, and appealed in their many-sided social criticisms and in their general theme to the middle class.

Little original work was done in the Ming epoch in the fields generally regarded as "literature" by educated Chinese, those of poetry and the essay. There are some admirable essays, but these are only isolated examples out of thousands. So also with poetry: the poets of the gentry, united in "associations", chose the poets of the Sung epoch as their models to emulate.

The Chinese drama made further progress in the Ming epoch. Many of the finest Chinese dramas were written under the Ming; they are still produced again and again to this day. The most famous dramatists of the Ming epoch are Wang Shih-chên (1526–1590) and T'ang Hsien-tsu (1556–1617). T'ang wrote the well-known drama *Mu-tan-t'ing* ("The Peony Flag"), one of the finest love-stories of Chinese literature, full of romance and remote from all reality. This is true also of the other dramas by T'ang, especially his "Four Dreams", a series of four plays. In them a man lives in dream through many years of his future life, with the result that he realizes the worthlessness of life and decides to become a monk.

Together with the development of the drama (or, rather, the opera) in the Ming epoch went an important endeavour in the modernization of music, the attempt to create a "well-adjusted scale" made in 1584 by Chu Tsai-yü. This solved in China a problem which was not tackled till later in Europe. The first Chinese theorists of music who occupied themselves with this problem were Ching Fang (77–37 B.C.) and Ho Ch'êng-t'ien (A.D. 370–447).

In the Mongol epoch, most of the Chinese painters had lived in central China; this remained so in the Ming epoch, and central China has continued down to modern times to be the real cultural centre of China. Of the many painters of the Ming epoch, all held in high esteem in China, mention must be made especially of Ch'iu Ying (*c.* 1525), T'ang Yin (1470–1523), and Tung Ch'i-ch'ang (1555–1639). Ch'iu Ying painted in the Academic Style, indicating every detail, however small, and showing preference for a Turkey-green ground. T'ang Yin is the painter of elegant women; Tung became famous especially as a calligraphist and a theoretician of the art of painting; a textbook of the art was written by him.

But the principal achievement in the art of the Ming epoch lay in its architecture. This included the restoration of the famous Great Wall, which had long been in dilapidation; the great city walls of Peking; and large parts of the palaces of Peking, begun in the Mongol epoch. It was at this time that the official style which we may observe to this day in North China was developed, the style still employed everywhere, although in the age of concrete it has lost its justification.

In the Ming epoch the porcelain with blue decoration on a white ground became general; the first examples, from the famous kilns in Ching-te-chen, in the province of Kiangsi, were relatively coarse, but in the fifteenth century the production was much finer. In the sixteenth century the quality deteriorated, owing to the disuse of the cobalt from the Middle East (perhaps from Persia) in favour of Sumatra cobalt, which did not yield the same brilliant colour. In the Ming epoch there also appeared the first brilliant red colour, a product of iron, and a start was then made with three-colour porcelain (with lead glaze) or five-colour (enamel). The many porcelains exported to western Asia and Europe first influenced European ceramics (Delft), and then were imitated in Europe (Böttger); the early European porcelains long showed Chinese influence (the so-called onion pattern, blue on a white ground). In addition to the porcelain of the Ming epoch, of which the finest specimens are in the serai at Istanbul, especially famous are the lacquers (carved lacquer, lacquer painting, gold lacquer) of the Ming epoch and the cloisonné work of the same period. These are closely associated with the contemporary work in Japan.

6 *Politics at court*

It is a strange thing that the Ming epoch is one of the periods of Chinese history that have been most neglected. Only in recent years have Chinese scholars begun to pay rather more attention to this epoch. The reason is that the historical material is very voluminous, but the political events of the period are of no interest, so that there is little temptation to study them. The contemporary European accounts are mostly based on an out-of-date book that gives excessive space to foreign policy and fails to make the home policy intelligible. If, however, we bear in mind what has been said above, the history of the Ming epoch is easy to understand.

After the founding of the dynasty by Chu Yüan-chang, important questions had to be dealt with apart from the social legislation. What was to be done, for instance, with Chu's helpers? Chu, like many revolutionaries before and after him, recognized that these people had been serviceable in the years of struggle but could no longer remain useful. He got rid of them by the simple device of setting one against another so that they murdered one another. In the first decades of his rule the dangerous cliques of gentry had formed again, and were engaged in mutual struggles. The most formidable clique was led by Hu Wei-yung. Hu was a man of the gentry of Chu's old homeland, and one of his oldest supporters. Hu and his relations controlled the country after 1370, until in 1380 Chu succeeded in beheading Hu and exterminating his clique. New cliques formed before long and were exterminated in turn.

Chu had founded Nanking in the years of revolution, and he made it his capital. In so doing he met the wishes of the rich grain producers of the Yangtze delta. But the north was the most threatened part of his empire, so that troops had to be permanently stationed there in considerable strength. Thus Peking, where Chu placed one of his sons as "king", was a post of exceptional importance.

In Chu Yüan-chang's last years (he was named T'ai-tsu as emperor) difficulties arose in regard to the dynasty. The heir to the throne died in 1391; and when the emperor himself died in 1398, the son of the late heir-apparent was installed as emperor (Hui Ti, 1399–1402). This choice had the support of some of the influential parties, especially of the south. But a protest against his enthronement came from the other son of Chu Yüan-chang, who as king in Peking had hoped to become emperor. With his strong army this prince, Ch'eng Tsu, marched south and captured Nanking, where the palaces were burnt down. There was a great massacre of supporters of the young emperor, and the victor made himself emperor (better known under his reign name, Yung Lo). As he had established himself in Peking, he transferred the capital to Peking, where it remained throughout the Ming epoch. Nanking became a sort of subsidiary capital.

This transfer of the capital to the north, as the result of the victory of the military party, produced a new element of instability: the north was of military importance, but the Yangtze region remained the economic centre of the country. The interests of the gentry of the Yangtze region were injured by the transfer. The new middle class was also a loser, as it also lived mainly in central China. The first Ming emperor had taken care to make his court resemble the court of the Mongol rulers, but on the whole had exercised relative economy. Yung Lo (1403–1424), however, lived in the actual palaces of the Mongol rulers, and all the luxury of the Mongol epoch was revived. This made the reign of Yung Lo the most magnificent period of the Ming epoch, but beneath the surface decay had begun.

7 *Navy. Southward expansion*

After the collapse of Mongol rule in Indo-China, partly through the simple withdrawal of the Mongols, and partly through attacks from various Chinese generals, there were independence movements in south-west China and Indo-China. In 1393 wars broke out in Annam. Yung Lo considered that the time had come to annex these regions to China and so to open a new field for Chinese trade, which was suffering continual disturbance from the Japanese. He sent armies to Yunnan and Indo-China; at the same time he had a fleet built by one of his eunuchs, Cheng Ho. The fleet was successfully protected from attack by the Japanese. Cheng Ho, who had promoted the plan and also carried it out, began in 1405 his famous voyage to Indo-China, which had been envisaged as giving at least moral support to the land operations, but was also intended to renew trade connexions with Indo-China, where they had been interrupted by the collapse of Mongol rule. Cheng Ho sailed past Indo-China and ultimately reached the coast of Arabia. His account of his voyage is an important source of information about conditions in southern Asia early in the fifteenth century. Cheng Ho and his fleet made some further cruises, but they were discontinued. There may have been several reasons. (1) As State enterprises, the expeditions were very costly. Foreign goods could be obtained more cheaply and with less trouble if foreign merchants came themselves to China or Chinese merchants travelled at their own expense. (2) The moral success of the naval enterprises was assured. China was recognized as a power throughout southern Asia, and Annam had been reconquered. (3) After the collapse of the Mongol emperor Timur, who died in 1406, there no longer existed any great power in Central Asia, so that trade missions from the kingdom of the Shahruk in North Persia were able to make their way to China, including the famous mission of 1409–1411. Finally, the fleet did not need to be permanently guarded against the Japanese, as it had been stationed not in South China but in the

Yangtze region. As early as 1411 the canals had been repaired, and from 1415 onward all the traffic of the country went by the canals, so evading the Japanese peril. This ended the short chapter of Chinese naval history.

These travels of Cheng Ho seem to have had one more cultural result: a large number of fairy-tales from the Middle East were brought through them to China, or at all events reached China at that time. The Chinese, being a realistically-minded people, have produced few fairy-tales of their own. The bulk of their finest fairy-tales were brought by Buddhist monks, in the course of the first millennium A.D., from India by way of Central Asia. The Buddhists made use of them to render their sermons more interesting and impressive. As time went on, these stories spread all over China, modified in harmony with the spirit of the people and adapted to the Chinese environment. Only the fables failed to strike root in China: the matter-of-fact Chinaman was not interested in animals that talked and behaved to each other like human beings. In addition, however, to these early fairy-tales, there is another group of stories that did not spread throughout China, but are found only in the south-eastern coastal provinces. These came from the Middle East, especially from Persia. The fairy-tales of Indian origin spread not only to Central Asia but at the same time to Persia, where they found a very congenial soil. The Persians made radical changes in the stories and gave them the form in which they came to Europe by various routes—through North Africa to Spain and France; through Constantinople, Venice, or Genoa to France; through Russian Turkestan to Russia, Finland, and Sweden; through Turkey and the Balkans to Hungary and Germany. Thus the stories found a European home. And this same Persian form was carried by sea in Cheng Ho's time to South China. Thus we have the strange experience of finding some of our own finest fairy-tales in almost the same form in South China.

Indo-China and south-west China remained, however, sources of unrest throughout the Ming epoch; we hear especially of many native risings in the present provinces of Kweichow, Kwangsi, and Kwangtung; the first of them came as early as 1372. The philosopher and army commander Wang Yang-ming became famous in the native wars at the beginning of the sixteenth century. These wars were connected with the extension of Chinese settlement in those provinces. At that time the forests of northern and central China had been almost entirely cut down; but timber was needed for building, especially in the Yangtze region, in great quantities, for Chinese architecture is mainly of timber and frame-work. Recourse had therefore to be made to the forests of south-west and south China. Great numbers of Chinese woodmen and contractors went into those regions and began to cut down the forests that were the natives' homes. The result was continual unrest and warfare.

8 *Struggles between cliques*

Yung Lo's successor died early. Under the latter's son, the emperor Hsüan Tsung (1426–1435; reign name Hsüan-tsu), fixed numbers of candidates were assigned for the State examinations. It had been found that almost the whole of the gentry in the Yangtze region sat at the examinations; and that at these examinations their representatives made sure, through their mutual relations, that only their members should pass, so that the candidates from the north were virtually excluded. The important military clique in the north protested against this, and a compromise was arrived at: at every examination one-third of the candidates must come from the north and two-thirds from the south. This system lasted for a long time, and led to many disputes.

At his death Hsüan Tsung left the empire to his eight-year-old son Ying Tsung (1436–49 and 1459–64), who was entirely in the hands of the Yang clique, which was associated with his grandmother. Soon, however, another clique, led by the eunuch Wang Chen, gained the upper hand at court. The Mongols were very active at this time, and made several raids on the province of Shansi; Wang Chen proposed a great campaign against them, and in

14 Aborigines of South China, of the 'Black Miao' tribe, at a festival. China-ink drawing of the eighteenth century.

Collection of the Museum für Völkerkunde, Berlin. No. 1*D* 8756, 68.

15 Pavilion on the 'Coal Hill' at Peking, in which the last Ming emperor committed suicide.
Photo Eberhard.

this campaign he took with him the young emperor, who had reached his twenty-first birthday in 1449. The emperor had grown up in the palace and knew nothing of the world outside; he was therefore glad to go with Wang Chen; but that eunuch had also lived in the palace and also knew nothing of the world, and in particular of war. Consequently he failed in the organization of reinforcements for his army, some 100,000 strong; after a few brief engagements the Mongol general Yeh-hsien (Yesen) had the imperial army surrounded and the emperor a prisoner. The eunuch Wang Chen came to his end, and his clique, of course, no longer counted. The Mongols had no intention of killing the emperor; they proposed to hold him to ransom, at a high price. The various cliques at court cared little, however, about their ruler. After the fall of the Wang clique there were two others, of which one, that of General Yü, became particularly powerful, as he had been able to repel a Mongol attack on Peking. Yü proclaimed a new emperor—not the captive emperor's son, a baby, but his brother, who became the emperor Ching Tsung. The Yang clique insisted on the rights of the imperial baby. From all this the Mongols saw that the Chinese were not inclined to spend a lot of money on their imperial captive. Accordingly they made an enormous reduction in the ransom demanded, and fairly forced the Chinese to take back their former emperor. The Mongols hoped that this would at least produce political disturbances by which they might profit, once the old emperor was back in Peking. And this did soon happen. At first the ransomed emperor was pushed out of sight into a palace, and Ching Tsung continued to reign. But in 1456 Ching Tsung fell ill, and a successor to him had to be chosen. The Yü clique wanted to have the son of Ching Tsung; the Yang clique wanted the son of the deposed emperor Ying Tsung. No agreement was reached, so that in the end a third clique, led by the soldier Shih Heng, who had helped to defend Peking against the Mongols, found its opportunity, and by a *coup d'état* reinstated the deposed emperor Ying Tsung.

This was not done out of love for the emperor, but because Shih Heng hoped that under the rule of the completely incompetent Ying Tsung he could best carry out a plan of his own, to set up his own dynasty. It is not so easy, however, to carry a conspiracy to success when there are several rival parties, each of which is ready to betray any of the others. Shih Heng's plan became known before long, and he himself was beheaded (1460).

The next forty years are filled with struggles between cliques, which steadily grew in ferocity, particularly since a special office, a sort of secret police headquarters, was set up in the palace, with functions which it extended beyond the palace, with the result that many people were arrested and disappeared. This office was set up by the eunuchs and the clique at their back, and was the first dictatorial organ created in the course of a fascistization of the State that made steady progress in these years.

In 1505 Wu Tsung came to the throne, an inexperienced youth of fifteen who was entirely controlled by the eunuchs who had brought him up. The leader of the eunuchs was Liu Chin, who had the support of a group of people of the gentry and the middle class. Liu Chin succeeded within a year in getting rid of the eunuchs at court who belonged to other cliques and were working against him. After that he proceeded to establish his power. He secured in entirely official form the emperor's permission for him to issue all commands himself; the emperor devoted himself entirely to his pleasures, and care was taken that they should keep him sufficiently occupied to have no chance to notice what was going on in the country. The first important decree issued by Liu Chin resulted in the removal from office or the punishment or murder of over three hundred prominent persons, the leaders of the cliques opposed to him. He filled their posts with his own supporters, until all the higher posts in every department were in the hands of members of his group. He collected large sums of money, which he quite openly extracted from the provinces as a special tax for his own benefit. When later his house was searched there were found 240,000 bars and 57,800 pieces of gold (a bar was equivalent of ten pieces), 791,800 ounces and 5,000,000 bars of silver (a bar was five ounces), three bushels of precious stones, two gold cuirasses, 3,000 gold rings, and much else—of a total value exceeding the annual Budget of the State! The treasure was to have been used to finance a revolt planned by Liu Chin and his supporters.

Among the people whom Liu Chin had punished were several members of the former clique of the Yang, and also the philosopher Wang Yang-ming, who later became so famous, a member of the Wang family, which was allied to the Yang. In 1510 the Yang won over one of the eunuchs in the palace, and so became acquainted with Liu Chin's plans. When a revolt broke out in western China, this eunuch (whose political allegiance was, of course, unknown to Liu Chin) secured appointment as army commander. With the army intended for the crushing of the revolt, Liu Chin's palace was attacked when he was asleep, and he and all his supporters were arrested. Thus the other group came into power in the palace, including the philosopher Wang Yang-ming. Liu Chin's rule had done great harm to the country, as enormous taxation had been expended for the private benefit of his clique. On top of this had been the young emperor's extravagance: his latest pleasures had been the building of palaces and the carrying out of military games; he constantly assumed new military titles, and was burning to go to war.

9 *Risings*

He might have had a good opportunity for this, for his misrule had resulted in a great popular rising, which began in the west, in Szechwan, and then spread to the east. As always, the rising was joined by some ruined scholars, and the movement, which had at first been directed against the gentry as such, was turned into a movement against the government of the moment. No longer were all the wealthy and all officials murdered, but only those who did not join the movement. In 1512 the rebels were finally overcome, not so much by any military capacity of the government armies as through the loss of the rebels' fleet of boats in a typhoon.

In 1517 a new favourite of the emperor's induced him to make a great tour in the north, to which the favourite belonged. The tour and the hunting greatly pleased the emperor, so that he continued his journeying. This was the year in which the Portuguese Fernão Pires de Andrade landed in Canton—the first modern European to enter China.

In 1518 Wang Yang-ming, the philosopher general, crushed a rising in Kiangsi. The rising had been the outcome of years of unrest, which had had two causes: native risings of the sort we described above, and loss due to the transfer of the capital. The province of Kiangsi was a part of the Yangtze region, and the great landowners there had lived on the profit from their supplies to Nanking. When the capital was moved to Peking, their takings fell. They placed themselves under a prince who lived in Nanking. This prince regarded Wang Yang-ming's move into Kiangsi as a threat to him, and so rose openly against the government and supported the Kiangsi gentry. Wang Yang-ming defeated him, and so came into the highest favour with the incompetent emperor. When peace had been restored in Nanking, the emperor dressed himself up as an army commander, marched south, and made a triumphal entry into Nanking.

Wang Yang-ming became acquainted as early as 1519 with the first European guns, imported by the Portuguese who had landed in 1517. (The Chinese then called them Fu-lang-chi, meaning Franks. Wang is the first Chinese who speaks of the "Franks".) The Chinese had already had mortars which hurled stones, as early as the second century A.D. In the seventh or eighth century their mortars had sent stones of a couple of hundredweights some four hundred yards. There is mention in the eleventh century of cannon which apparently shot with a charge of a sort of gunpowder. The Mongols were already using true cannon in their sieges. In 1519, however, when the Chinese emperor came to Nanking, the first Portuguese were presented to him, and entertained for about a year in a hostel. Lin Hsün learned about guns from them, and copied the guns for Wang Yang-ming. The Chinese, however, had in general no respect for the Europeans, whom they described as "bandits" who had expelled the lawful king of Malacca and had now come to China as its representatives. Later they were regarded as a sort of Japanese, because they, too, practised piracy.

10 *Machiavellianism*

All medieval Chinese philosophy was based on one of the two ancient philosophers, Confucius or Lao Tzŭ; Wang Yang-ming's philosophy followed Confucius. He liberated himself, however, from the tendency started in the Sung epoch, which continued to rule in China in his time and after him; he introduced into philosophy the conception of "intuition". He regarded intuition as the decisive philosophic experience; only through intuition could man come to true knowledge. This may contain an element of meditative Buddhism; we may say that the Sung philosophy was the product of a synthesis of Confucianism and the Buddhism of the monasteries, while Wang Yang-ming aimed at a synthesis of Confucianism and meditative Buddhism, reviving the ideas of the philosopher Lu Hsiang-shan, to whom little attention had been paid in the Sung epoch. The introduction, however; of the conception of intuition, a highly subjective conception, into the system of a practical State philosophy like Confucianism could not but lead in the practice of the statesman to machiavellianism. The statesman who followed the teaching of Wang Yang-ming had the opportunity of justifying whatever he did by his intuition.

Wang Yang-ming failed to gain acceptance for his philosophy. After carrying on great campaigns against southern Chinese natives, he died in 1529. He may have had an intention of himself seizing power. His disciples also failed to establish his doctrine in China, because it served the interests of an individual despot against those of the gentry as a class, and the middle class, which might have formed a counterweight against them, was not yet politically ripe for the seizure of the opportunity here offered to it. In Japan, however, Wang's doctrine gained many followers, because it admirably served the dictatorial State system which had developed in that country.

11 *Foreign policy in the sixteenth century*

The feeble emperor Wu Tsung died in 1521, after an ineffective reign, without leaving an heir. The clique then in power at court looked round the possible pretenders for the one who seemed least likely to do anything, and their choice fell on the fifteen-year-old Shih Tsung, who was made emperor. The forty-five years of his reign are filled in home affairs with intrigues between the cliques at court, with growing distress in the country, and with revolts on a larger and larger scale. Abroad there were wars with Annam, increasing raids by the Japanese, and, above all, long-continued fighting against the famous Mongol ruler Yen-ta, from 1549 onward. At one time Yen-ta reached Peking and laid siege to it. The emperor, who had no knowledge of affairs, and to whom Yen-ta had been represented as a petty bandit, was utterly dismayed and ready to do whatever Yen-ta asked; in the end he was dissuaded from this, and an agreement was arrived at with Yen-ta for State-controlled markets to be set up along the frontier, where the Mongols could dispose of their goods against Chinese goods on very favourable terms. After further difficulties lasting many years, a compromise was arrived at: the Mongols were earning good profits from the markets, and in 1571 Yen-ta accepted a Chinese title. On the Chinese side, this Mongol trade, which continued in a rather different form in the Manchu epoch, led to the formation of a merchant class in the frontier province of Shansi, with great experience in credit business; later the first Chinese bankers came almost entirely from this quarter.

After a brief interregnum there came once more to the throne a ten-year-old boy, the emperor Shen Tsung (reign name Wan Li; 1573–1619). He, too, was entirely under the influence of various cliques, at first that of his tutor, the scholar Chang Chü-chan. About the time of the death, in 1583, of Yen-ta we hear for the first time of a new people. In 1581 there had been unrest in southern Manchuria. The Mongolian Tümet attacked China, and there resulted collisions not only with the Chinese but between the different tribes living there. In southern and central Manchuria were remnants of the Tungus Juchên (Djurdjen). The Mongols had subjugated the Juchên, but the latter had virtually become independent after the collapse of Mongol rule over China. They had formed several tribal alliances, but in 1581–83 these had fought each other, so that the union had to all intents been destroyed. The Chinese intervened as mediators in these struggles, and drew a demarcation line between the territories of the various Tungus tribes. All this is only worth mention because it was from these tribes that there later developed the tribal league of the Manchus, who were then to rule China for some three hundred years.

In 1592 the Japanese invaded Korea. This was their first real effort to set foot on the continent, a purely imperialistic move. Korea, as a Chinese vassal, appealed for Chinese aid. At first the Chinese army had no success, but in 1598 the Japanese were forced to abandon Korea. They revenged themselves by intensifying their raids on the coast of central China; they often massacred whole towns, and burned down the looted houses. The fighting in Korea had its influence on the Tungus tribes: as they were not directly involved, it contributed to their further strengthening.

The East India Company was founded in 1600. At this time (1594–1604), while the English were trying to establish themselves in India, the Chinese tried to gain increased influence in the south by wars in Annam, Burma, and Siam. These were Chinese colonial wars, similar to the English fighting in India. But there began to be defined at that time in the south of Asia the relation between States that exists in fact or in aspiration at the present time. Burma later recovered its independence, with little more than the shadow of Chinese overlordship, but the

Chinese regarded it as a Chinese vassal. They considered the British occupation of the country to be illegal, and to this day the Chinese claim that after its liberation from the Japanese it should have the status of a Chinese protectorate. In 1601 the first European, the Jesuit Matteo Ricci, succeeded in gaining access to the Chinese court, through the agency of a eunuch. He made some presents, and the Chinese regarded his visit as a mission from Europe bringing tribute. Ricci was therefore permitted to remain in Peking. He was an astronomer, and was able to demonstrate to his Chinese colleagues the superiority of European astronomy. In 1613, after Ricci's death, the Jesuits and some Chinese whom they had converted were commissioned to reform the Chinese calendar. In the time of the Mongols, Arabs had been at work in Peking as astronomers, and their influence had continued under the Ming until the Europeans came. By his astronomical labours Ricci won a place of honour in Chinese literature; he is the European most often mentioned. The missionary work was less effective. The missionaries penetrated by the old trade routes from Canton and Macao into the province of Kiangsi and then into Nanking. Kiangsi and Nanking were their chief centres. They soon realized that missionary activity that began in the lower strata would have no success; it was necessary to work from above, beginning with the emperor, and then the whole country could be converted to Christianity. When later the emperors of the Ming dynasty were expelled and fugitives in South China, one of the pretenders to the throne was actually converted—but it was politically too late. The missionaries had, moreover, mistaken ideas as to the nature of Chinese religion; we know to-day that a universal adoption of Christianity in China would have been impossible even if an emperor had personally adopted that foreign faith: there were emperors who had been interested in Buddhism or in Taoism, but that had been their private affair and had never prevented them, as heads of the State, from promoting the religious system which politically was the most expedient—that is to say, usually Confucianism. What we have said here in regard to the Christian mission at the Ming court is applicable also to the missionaries at the court of the first Manchu emperors, in the seventeenth century. Early in the eighteenth century missionary activity was prohibited—not for religious but for political reasons, and only under the pressure of the Capitulations in the nineteenth century were the missionaries enabled to resume their labours.

12 *External and internal perils*

Toward the end of the reign of Wan Li, about 1620, the danger that threatened the empire became more and more evident. The Manchus complained, no doubt with justice, of excesses on the part of Chinese officials; the friction constantly increased, and the Manchus began to attack the Chinese cities in Manchuria. In 1616, after his first considerable successes, their leader Nurhachu assumed the imperial title; the name of the dynasty is Tai Ch'ing (interpreted as "The great clarity", but probably a transliteration of a Manchurian word meaning "hero"). In 1618, the year in which the Thirty Years' War started in Europe, the Manchus conquered the greater part of Manchuria, and in 1621 their capital was Liaoyang, then the largest town in Manchuria.

But the Manchu menace was far from being the only one. On the south-east coast a pirate made himself independent; later, with his family, he dominated Formosa and fought many battles with the Europeans there (European sources call him Koxinga). In western China there came a great popular rising, in which some of the natives joined, and which spread through a large part of the southern provinces. This rising was particularly sanguinary, and when it was ultimately crushed by the Manchus the province of Szechwan, formerly so populous, was almost depopulated, so that it had later to be resettled. And in the province of Shantung in the east there came another great rising, also very sanguinary, that of the secret society of the "White Lotus". We have already pointed out that these risings of secret societies were always a sign of intolerable conditions among the peasantry. This was now the case once more. All the elements of danger which we mentioned at the outset of this chapter began during this period, between 1610 and 1640, to develop to the full.

Then there were the conditions in the capital itself. The struggles between cliques came to a climax. On the death of Shen Tsung (or Wan Li; 1573–1619), he was succeeded by his son, who died scarcely a month later, and then by his sixteen-year-old grandson. The grandson had been from his earliest youth under the influence of a eunuch, Wei Chung-hsien, who had castrated himself. With the emperor's nurse and other people, mostly of the middle class, this man formed a powerful group. The moment the new emperor ascended the throne, Wei was all-powerful. He began by murdering every eunuch who did not belong to his clique, and then murdered the rest of his opponents. Meanwhile the gentry had concluded among themselves a defensive alliance that was a sort of party; this party was called the Tung-lin Academy. It was confined to literati among the gentry, and included in particular the literati who had failed to make their way at court, and who lived on their estates in Central China and were trying to gain power themselves. This group was opposed to Wei Chung-hsien, who ruthlessly had every discoverable member murdered. The remainder went into hiding and organized themselves secretly under another name. As the new emperor had no son, the attempt was made to foist a son upon him; at his death in 1627, eight women of the harem were suddenly found to be pregnant! He was succeeded by his brother, who was one of the opponents of Wei Chung-hsien and, with the aid of the opposing clique, was able to bring him to his end. The new emperor tried to restore order at court and in the capital by means of political and economic decrees, but in spite of his good intentions and his unquestionable capacity he was unable to cope with the universal confusion. There was insurrection in every part of the country. The gentry, organized in their "Academies", and secretly at work in the provinces, no longer supported the government; the central power no longer had adequate revenues, so that it was unable to pay the armies that should have marched against all the rebels and also against external enemies. It was clear that the dynasty was approaching its end, and the only uncertainty was as to its successor. The various insurgents negotiated or fought with each other; generals loyal to the government won occasional successes against the rebels; other generals went over to the rebels or to the Manchus. The two most successful leaders of bands were Li Tzŭ-ch'êng and Chang Hsien-chung. Li came from the province of Shensi; he had come to the fore during a disastrous famine in his country. The years around 1640 brought several widespread droughts in North China, a natural phenomenon that was repeated in the nineteenth century, when unrest again ensued. Chang Hsien-chung returned for a time to the support of the government, but later established himself in western China. It was typical, however, of all these insurgents that none of them had any great objective in view. They wanted to get enough to eat for themselves and their followers; they wanted to enrich themselves by conquest; but they were incapable of building up an ordered State system. Li ultimately made himself "king" in the province of Shensi and called his dynasty "Shun", but this made no difference to the fact that there was no administrative system in existence; there was no distribution of land among the peasants serving in Li's army; no plan was set into operation for the collection of taxes; not one of the pressing problems was faced.

Meanwhile the Manchus were gaining support. Almost all the Mongol princes voluntarily joined them and took part in the raids into North China. In 1637 the united Manchus and Mongols conquered Korea. Their power steadily grew. What the insurgents in China failed to achieve, the Manchus achieved with the aid of their Chinese advisers: they created a new military organization, the "Banner Organization". The men fit for service were distributed among eight "banners", and these banners became the basis of the Manchu State administration. By this device the Manchus emerged from the stage of tribal union, just as before them Turks and other northern peoples had several times abandoned the traditional authority of a hierarchy of tribal leaders, a system of ruling families, in favour of the authority, based on efficiency, of military leaders. At the same time the Manchus set up a central government with special ministries on the Chinese model. In 1638 the Manchus appeared before Peking, but they retired once more. Manchu armies even reached the province of Shantung. They were hampered by the death at the critical moment of the Manchu ruler Abahai (1626–1643). His son Fu Lin was not entirely normal and was barely six years old; there was a regency of princes, the most prominent among them being Prince Dorgon.

Meanwhile Li Tzŭ-ch'êng broke through to Peking. The city had a strong garrison, but owing to the disorganization of the government the different commanders were working against each other; and the soldiers had no fighting spirit because they had had no pay for a long time. Thus the city fell, on April 24th, 1644, and the last Ming emperor killed himself. A prince was proclaimed emperor; he fled through western and southern China, continually trying to make a stand, but it was too late; without the support of the gentry he had no resource, and ultimately, in 1659, he was compelled to flee into Burma.

Thus Li Tzŭ-ch'êng was now emperor. It should have been his task rapidly to build up a government, and to take up arms against the other rebels and against the Manchus. Instead of this he behaved in such a way that he was unable to gain any support from the existing officials in the capital; and as there was no one among his former supporters who had any positive, constructive ideas, just nothing was done.

This, however, improved the chances of all the other aspirants to the imperial throne. The first to realize this clearly, and also to possess enough political sagacity to avoid alienating the gentry, was General Wu San-kui, who was commanding on the Manchu front. He saw that in the existing conditions in the capital he could easily secure the imperial throne for himself if only he had enough soldiers. Accordingly he negotiated with the Manchu Prince Dorgon, formed an alliance with the Manchus, and with them entered Peking on June 6th, 1644. Li Tzŭ-chêng quickly looted the city, burned down whatever he could, and fled into the west, continually pursued by Wu San-kui. In the end he was abandoned by all his supporters and killed by peasants. The Manchus, however, had no intention of leaving Wu San-kui in power: they established themselves in Peking, and Wu became their general.

Chapter XII

THE MANCHU DYNASTY (1644-1911)

1 *Installation of Manchus*

THE Manchus had gained the mastery over China owing rather to China's internal situation than to their military superiority. How was it that the dynasty could endure for so long, although the Manchus were not numerous, although the first Manchu ruler (Fu Lin, known as Emperor Shun Chih; 1644–1662) was a psychopathic youth, although there were princes of the Ming dynasty ruling in South China, and although there were strong groups of rebels all over the country? The Manchus were aliens; at that time the national feeling of the Chinese had already been awakened; aliens were despised. In addition to this, the Manchus demanded that as a sign of their subjection the Chinese should wear pigtails and assume Manchurian clothing (law of 1645). Such laws could not but offend national pride. Moreover, marriages between Manchus and Chinese were prohibited, and a dual government was set up, with Manchus always alongside Chinese in every office, the Manchus being of course in the superior position. The Manchu soldiers were distributed in military garrisons among the great cities, and were paid State pensions, which had to be provided by taxation. They were the master race, and had no need to work. Manchus did not have to attend the difficult State examination which the Chinese had to pass in order to gain an appointment. How was it that in spite of all this the Manchus were able to establish themselves?

The conquering Manchu generals first went south from eastern China, and in 1645 captured Nanking, where a Ming prince had ruled. (Meanwhile Wu San-kui went to the west and conquered western China—not, however, for the Manchus, but for himself. Nominally he remained loyal to the Manchus at first, and they took no notice of him.) The region round Nanking was the economic centre of China. Soon the Manchus were in the adjoining southern provinces, and thus they conquered the whole of the territory of the landowning gentry, who after the events of the beginning of the seventeenth century had no longer trusted the Ming rulers. The Ming prince in Nanking was just as incapable, and surrounded by just as evil a clique, as the Ming emperors of the past. The gentry were not inclined to defend him. A considerable section of the gentry were reduced to utter despair; they had no desire to support the Ming any longer; in their own interest they could not support the rebel leaders; and they regarded the Manchus as just a particular sort of "rebels". Many thousands of officials, scholars, and great landowners committed suicide. Many books, often really moving and tragic, are filled with the story of their lives. Some of them tried to form insurgent bands with their peasants and went into the mountains, but they were unable to maintain themselves there. The great bulk of the gentry soon brought themselves to collaborate with the conquerors when they were offered tolerable conditions. In the end the Manchus did not interfere in the ownership of land in central China.

At the time when in Europe Louis XIV was reigning, the Thirty Years' War was coming to an end, and Cromwell was carrying out his reforms in England, the Manchus conquered the whole of China. Chang Hsien-chung and Li Tzŭ-ch'êng were the first to fall; the pirate Koxinga lasted a little longer and was even able to plunder Nanking in 1659, but in 1661 he had to retire to Formosa. Wu San-kui, who meanwhile had conquered western China, saw that the situation was becoming difficult for him. His task was to drive out the last Ming pretenders for the Manchus. As he had already been opposed to the Ming in 1644, and as the Ming no longer had any following among the gentry, he could not suddenly work with them against the Manchus. He therefore handed over to the Manchus the last Ming prince, whom the Burmese had delivered up to him in 1661. Wu San-kui's only possible allies against the Manchus were the gentry. But in the west, where he was in power, the gentry counted for nothing; they had in any case been weaker in the west, and they had been decimated by the insurrection of Chang Hsien-chung. Thus Wu San-kui was compelled to try to push eastwards, in order to unite with the gentry of the Yangtze region against the Manchus. The Manchus, of whom the famous K'ang Hsi become emperor in 1663, guessed Wu San-kui's plan, and in 1673, after every effort at accommodation had failed, open war came. Wu San-kui made himself emperor, and the Manchus marched against him. Meanwhile, the Chinese gentry of the Yangtze region had come to terms with the Manchus, and they gave Wu San-kui no help. He was able to hold his own until his death, though, with the loss of the support of the gentry, he had had no prospect of final success. Not until 1681 was his successor, his grandson Wu Shih-fan, defeated. Wu San-kui vegetated in the south-west, a region too poor to maintain an army that could conquer all China, and too small to enable him to last indefinitely as an independent power. With the end of the rule of Wu San-kui and his successor came the end of the national governments of China; the whole country was now under alien domination, for the simple reason that all the opponents of the Manchus had failed. Only the Manchus were accredited with the ability to bring order out of the universal confusion, so that there was clearly no alternative but to put up with the many insults and humiliations they inflicted—with the result that the national feeling that had just been aroused died away, except where it was kept alive in a few secret societies. There will be much, however, to say about this, once the works which were suppressed by the Manchus are published.

In the first phase of the Manchu conquest the gentry had refused to support either the Ming princes or Wu San-kui, or any of the rebels, or the Manchus themselves. A second phase began about twenty years after the capture of Peking, when the Manchus won over the gentry by desisting from any interference with the ownership of land, and by the use of Manchu troops to clear away the "rebels" who were hostile to the gentry. A reputable government was then set up in Peking, free from eunuchs and from all the old cliques; in their place the government looked for Chinese scholars for its administrative posts. Literati and scholars streamed into Peking, especially members of the "Academies" that still existed in secret, men who had been the chief sufferers from the conditions at the end of the Ming epoch. The young emperor K'ang Hsi (1663–1722; K'ang Hsi is the name by which he was known as emperor, not his personal name) was keenly interested in Chinese culture, and gave privileged treatment to the scholars of the gentry who came forward. A rapid recovery quite clearly took place. The disturbances of the years that had passed had got rid of the worst enemies of the people, the formidable rival cliques and the individuals lusting for power; the gentry had become more considerate in their attitude to the peasants; and bribery had been largely stamped out. Finally, the empire had been greatly expanded. All these things helped to stabilize the régime of the Manchus.

2 *Decline in the eighteenth century*

The improvement continued until the middle of the eighteenth century. About the time of the French Revolution there began a continuous decline, slow at first and then gathering speed. The European works on China offer various reasons for this: the many foreign wars of the emperor Ch'ien Lung (to which we shall refer later), his craze for building, and the irruption of the Europeans into Chinese trade. In the eighteenth century the court surrounded itself with great splendour, and countless palaces and other luxurious buildings were erected, but it must be borne in mind that so great an empire as the China of that day possessed very considerable financial strength, and could support this luxury. The wars were certainly not inexpensive, as they took place along the Russian frontier and entailed expenditure on the transport of reinforcements and supplies; the wars against Turkestan and Tibet were carried on with relatively small forces. This expenditure should not have been beyond the resources of an ordered

Budget. The decline of the Manchu dynasty began at a time when the European trade was almost insignificant, and not after 1842, when China had had to submit to the foreign Capitulations. These cannot, therefore, have been the true cause of the decline. Above all, the decline was not so noticeable in the state of the Exchequer as in a general impoverishment of China. The number of really wealthy persons among the gentry diminished, but the middle class, that is to say the people who had education but little or no money and property, grew steadily in number.

The deeper reason for the decline of the Manchu dynasty lies in the enormous increase in the population with unaltered conditions of production and technique. Here are a few Chinese statistics:

Year	*Population*				
1578 (before the Manchus)	10,621,463	families or	60,692,856	individuals	
1662	19,203,233	,,	100,000,000	,,	*
1710	23,311,236	,,	116,000,000	,,	*
1729	25,480,498	,,	127,000,000	,,	*
1741			143,411,559	,,	
1754			184,504,493	,,	
1778			242,965,618	,,	
1796			275,662,414	,,	
1814			374,601,132	,,	
1850			414,493,899	,,	

* Approximately

It may be objected that these figures are incorrect and exaggerated. Undoubtedly they contain large errors; in those times it was certainly impossible to secure a comprehensive and accurate census. But the first figure (for 1578) of some sixty millions is in close agreement with all other figures of early times; the last (for 1850) seems high, but cannot be far wrong, for even after the great T'ai P'ing Rebellion of 1850, which, together with its after-effects, cost the lives of countless millions, and undoubtedly produced a decline in the population, all statisticians of to-day estimate the population of China at more than four hundred millions. Thus some trust may be placed in our statistics. In the later eighteenth and the early nineteenth century, therefore, we find an enormous increase in the population. There was a similar movement in nineteenth-century Europe. The causes and the results, however, in the two cases were entirely different. In Europe, technical advance and the growth of industry created new conditions of production through which greatly increased populations could be fed. In China the increase in the population came through the long period of internal peace since about 1720. From that time onwards, all China's wars were fought at so great a distance from China proper that the population was not directly affected. Moreover, in the seventeenth and eighteenth centuries the Manchus saw to the maintenance of the river dykes, so that the worst inundations were prevented. Thus there were not so many of the floods which had often cost the lives of many million people in China; and there were no internal wars, with their heavy cost in lives. But while the population increased the tillage failed to increase in the needed proportion. In regard to this I have, unfortunately, no statistics for the later periods; but the general tendency is shown by the following table:

Date	*Cultivated area* *Ch'ing*
1578 (pre-Manchu)	7,013,976
1662	5,311,358
1719	6,631,132
1729	8,781,760

A ch'ing is 100 mou; a mou is about 6 ares, or one-seventh of an acre. As a family required 70 mou of land to be able to live, the relation between tillage and population in 1578 was normal. At the 1578 level, the surplus production needed for the government could be produced. In 1729, about 150 years later, with the doubled population there should have been some 15 million ch'ing to maintain the same satisfactory relation, but the total tillage was only 8.8 millions. There had been no fundamental improvement in methods of tillage, and consequently the general standard of living of the population was bound to fall.

In China it is difficult to secure a technical improvement in agriculture. In central and southern China, which possessed the bulk of the population, rice is cultivated. To this day no means has been found of increasing the yield by the introduction of machinery. In North China an improvement could only be secured by means of great systems of canals and dykes; and this would have been impracticable even with the means of European engineering in the nineteenth century. At most some improvement in production might have been attained by means of improved manuring. At that time there could scarcely be any question of the importation of foodstuffs from abroad; not until late in the nineteenth century did considerable food imports, especially from Indo-China, begin.

It may be asked, why was there no growth of industry in China as in Europe? It was in the eighteenth century that industrialization began in Europe; and it was in that century that the problem of population began to be urgent in China. There was no growth, however, of industry to absorb the excess population. In Europe the handicrafts-men, the "bourgeoisie", turned to industry, building the first factories, in the eighteenth century; the Chinese artisans continued in bondage and dependence on the dominant gentry. The gentry had invested their wealth in land and when the land per head grew less and the population greater, the gentry were not prepared to permit the growth of industry.

On the contrary, wherever opportunities existed for the development of industry, the gentry placed obstacles in its way. There were mines and foundries, there were also porcelain factories, carpet-weaving sheds, and other industries. The gentry, in their capacity of officials, placed all the restrictions they could on these works, most of which were State concerns, and put all possible difficulties in their way. These difficulties consisted not only in the prevention of production on an increased scale and in the imposition of enormous taxes (official and private), but also in interference with transport and so with marketing. Finally there was a lack of one more element that was of importance to the growth of industry in Europe—a perfected credit system. Banks and similar institutions had gradually developed in China, especially in the province of Shansi; but they had little capital, and this they invested more generally in direct trade than in credit business. Thus there was no growth of industry down to the time of the Capitulations in China.

To sum up, owing to the long period of peace the population grew greatly; it was impossible, however, for the area under cultivation to grow correspondingly, or even to any great extent, because central China was already very closely settled; and it was made impossible for industry to develop. Inevitably, therefore, poverty became general, and in consequence there came a decline in the political power of the Manchu dynasty. This decline began at the end of the eighteenth century. The numbers of the gentry fell, more and more of the gentry being reduced to the status of the middle class. This middle class was the first to be affected later by Europeanization, and it was the main support of the anti-Manchu movement and of republicanism. Already, however, the middle class, as the class that furnished the lower ranks of officialdom, showed the evil picture, familiar in the Ming epoch, of growing corruption. This brief survey should suffice to make clear the general course of internal and external events in the history of China down to the middle of the nineteenth century. We will now deal briefly with these events in detail.

3 *Expansion in Central Asia; the first State treaty*

The rise of the Manchu dynasty actually began under the emperor K'ang Hsi (1663–1722). He had three tasks. The first was the removal of the last supporters of the Ming dynasty, and the generals, such as Wu San-kui, who had tried to make themselves independent. This necessitated a long series of campaigns, most of them in the south-west or south of China; these scarcely affected the population of China proper. In 1683 Formosa was occupied and the last of the insurgent army commanders was defeated. It was shown above that the situation of all these people became hopeless as soon as the Manchus had occupied the rich Yangtze region and the intelligentsia and the gentry of that region had gone over to them.

A quite different type of insurgent commander was the Mongol prince Galdan. He, too, planned to make himself independent of Manchu overlordship. At first the Mongols had readily supported the Manchus, when the latter were making raids into China and there was plenty of booty. Now, however, the Manchus, under the influence of the Chinese gentry whom they brought, and could not but bring, to their court, were rapidly becoming Chinese. Even in the time of K'ang Hsi the Manchus began to forget Manchurian; they brought tutors to court to teach the young Manchus Chinese. Later even the emperors did not understand Manchurian! As a result of this process, the Mongols became alienated from the Manchurians, and the situation began once more to be the same as at the time of the Ming rulers. Thus Galdan tried to found an independent Mongol realm, free from Chinese influence.

The Manchus could not permit this, as such a realm would have threatened the flank of their homeland, Manchuria, and would have attracted those Manchus who objected to sinification. Between 1690 and 1696 there were battles, in which the emperor actually took part in person. Galdan was defeated. In 1715, however, there were new disturbances, this time in western Mongolia. Tsewang Rabdan, whom the Chinese had made khan of the Olet, rose against the Chinese. The wars that followed, extending far into Turkestan and also bringing in its Turkish population together with the Dzungars, ended with the Chinese conquest of the whole of Mongolia and of parts of eastern Turkestan. And as Tsewang Rabdan had tried to extend his power as far as Tibet, a campaign was undertaken into Tibet, Lhasa was occupied, a new Dalai Lama was installed there as supreme ruler, and Tibet was made into a protectorate. Since then Tibet has remained to this day a sort of dependency of China.

This penetration of the Chinese into Turkestan took place just at the time when the Russians were enormously expanding their empire in Asia. And this formed the third problem for the Manchus. In 1650 the Russians had established a fort by the river Amur. The Manchus regarded the Amur (which they called the "River of the Black Dragon") as part of their own territory, and in 1685 they destroyed the Russian settlement. After this there were negotiations, which culminated in 1689 in the Treaty of Nerchinsk. This treaty was the first concluded by the Chinese State with a European Power. Jesuit missionaries played a part in the negotiations as interpreters. Owing to the difficulties of translation the text of the treaty, in Chinese, Russian, and Manchurian, contained some obscurities, particularly in regard to the frontier line. Accordingly, in 1727 the Russians sent Count Ravusinsky to Peking to negotiate a revision of the old treaty. The Chinese emperor, Yung Cheng, arranged for the negotiations to be carried on at the frontier, in the town of Kyakhta, in Mongolia, where after long discussions a new treaty was concluded. Under this treaty the Russians received permission to set up a legation and a commercial agency in Peking, and also to maintain a church. This was the beginning of the foreign Capitulations. From the Chinese point of view there was nothing special in a facility of this sort. For some fifteen centuries all the "barbarians" who had to bring tribute had been given houses in the capital, where their envoys could wait until the emperor would receive them—usually on New Year's Day. The custom had sprung up at the reception of the Huns. Moreover, permission had always been given for envoys to be accompanied by a few merchants, who during the envoy's stay did a certain amount of business. And finally the time had been when the Uighurs were permitted to set up a temple of their own. At the same time as the permission given to the Russians to set up a "legation", a similar office was set up (in 1729) for "Uighur" peoples (meaning Mohammedans), again under instructions from the Chinese Foreign Ministry (which was called the Office for Regulation of Barbarians!). The Mohammedan office was placed under two Mohammedan leaders, who lived in Peking. The Europeans, however, had quite different ideas about a "legation", and about the significance of permission to trade. They regarded this as the opening of diplomatic relations between States on an equality, and the carrying on of trade as a special privilege, a sort of Capitulation. This reciprocal misunderstanding produced in the nineteenth century a number of serious political conflicts. The Europeans charged the Chinese with breach of treaties, failure to meet their obligations, and other such things, while the Chinese considered that they had acted with perfect correctness.

4 *Culture*

In this K'ang Hsi period culture began to flourish again. The emperor had attracted the gentry, and so the intelligentsia, to his court because his uneducated Manchus could not alone have administered the enormous empire; and he showed great interest in Chinese culture, himself delved deeply into it, and had many works compiled, especially works of an encyclopaedic character. The encyclopaedias enabled information to be rapidly gained on all sorts of subjects, and thus were just what an interested ruler needed, especially when, as a foreigner, he was not in a position to gain really thorough instruction in things Chinese. The Chinese encyclopaedias of the seventeenth and especially of the eighteenth century were thus the outcome of the initiative of the Manchurian emperor, and were compiled for his information; they were not due, like the French encyclopaedias of the eighteenth century, to a movement for the spread of knowledge among the people. For this latter purpose the gigantic encyclopaedias of the Manchus, each of which fills several bookcases, were much too expensive and were printed in much too limited editions. The compilations begin with the great geographical encyclopaedia of Ku Yen-wu (1613–1682), and attain their their climax in the gigantic eighteenth-century encyclopaedia *T'u-shu chi-ch'eng*, scientifically impeccable in the accuracy of its references to sources. Here were already the beginnings of the "Archaeological School", built up in the course of the eighteenth century, a school which is entitled to be regarded as the predecessor of present-day sinological archaeology. To-day, making use of all archaeological material and inscriptions, and subjecting the classics to fresh study, the students of Chinese archaeology have been trying to gain more accurate knowledge, in order to be able at last to sweep away the long obsolete traditional ideas of the scholars of the past.

For the rest, the most famous literary works of the Manchu epoch belong once more to the field which Chinese do not regard as that of true literature—the novel, the short story, and the drama. Poetry does exist, but it keeps to the old paths and has few fresh ideas. All the various forms of the Sung period are made use of. The essayists, too, offer nothing new, though their number is legion. One of the best known is Yüan Mei (1716–1797), who was also the author of the collection of short stories *Tse-pu-yü* ("The Master did not tell"), which is regarded very highly by the Chinese. The volume of short stories entitled *Liao-chai chich-i*, by P'u Sung-lin (1640–1715?), is world-famous and has been translated into every civilized language. Both collections are distinguished by their practised style. The short story was popular among the greater gentry; it abandoned the popular style it had had in the Ming epoch, and adopted the polished language of scholars.

The Manchu epoch has left to us what is by general consent the finest novel in Chinese literature, *Hung-lou-meng* ("The Dream of the Red Room"), by Ts'ao Hsüeh-ch'in, who died in 1763. It describes the downfall of a rich and powerful family from the highest rank of the gentry, and the decadent son's love of a young and emotional lady of the highest circles. The story is clothed in a mystical garb that does something to soften its tragic ending. The interesting novel *Ju-lin wai-shih* ("Private Reports from the Life of Scholars"), by Wu Ching-tzŭ (1701–1754), is a mordant criticism of Confucianism with its rigid formalism, of the social system, and of the examination system. Social criticism is the theme of many novels. The most modern in spirit of the works of this period is perhaps the treatment of feminism in the novel *Ching-hua-yüan*, by Li Yu-chên

(d. 1830), which demanded equal rights for men and women.

The drama developed quickly in the Manchu epoch, particularly in quantity, especially since the emperors greatly appreciated the theatre. A catalogue of plays compiled in 1781 contains 1,013 titles! Some of these dramas were of unprecedented length. One of them was played in 26 parts containing 240 acts; a performance took two years to complete! Probably the finest dramas of the Manchu epoch are those of Li Yü (d. 1611), who also became the first of the Chinese dramatic critics. What he has to say about the art of the theatre, and about aesthetics in general, is still worth reading.

About the middle of the nineteenth century the influence of Europe became more and more marked. Translation began with Yen-fu (1853–1921), who translated the first philosophical and scientific books and books on social questions, and who made his compatriots acquainted with Western thought. At the same time Lin Shu (1852–1924) translated the first Western short stories and novels. With these two began the new style, which was soon elaborated by Liang Ch'i-ch'ao, a collaborator of Sun Yat-sen's, and by others, and which ultimately produced the "literary revolution" of 1917. Translation has continued to this day; almost every book of outstanding importance in European and American literature is translated within a few months of its appearance, and on the average these translations are of a fairly high level.

Particularly fine work was produced in the field of porcelain in the Manchu epoch. In 1680 the famous kilns in the province of Kiangsi were reopened, and porcelain that is among the most artistically perfect in the world was fired in them. Among the new colours were especially green shades (one group is known as *famille verte*), and also black and yellow compositions. Monochrome porcelain also developed further, including very fine dark blue, brilliant red (called "ox-blood"), and white. In the eighteenth century, however, there began an unmistakable decline, which has continued to this day, although there are still a few craftsmen and a few kilns that produce outstanding work (usually attempts to imitate old models), often in small factories in Manchuria.

In painting, European influence soon shows itself. The best-known example of this is Lang Shih-ming, an Italian missionary whose original name was Giuseppe Castiglione (1688–1766); he began to work in China in 1715. He learned the Chinese method of painting, but introduced a number of technical tricks of European painters, which were adopted in general practice in China, especially by the official court painters: the painting of the scholars who lived in seclusion remained uninfluenced. Dutch flower-painting also had some influence in China as early as the eighteenth century.

The missionaries played an important part at court. The first Manchu emperors were as generous in this matter as the Mongols had been, and allowed the foreigners to work in peace. They showed special interest in the European science introduced by the missionaries; they had less sympathy for their religious message. The missionaries, for their part, sent to Europe enthusiastic accounts of the wonderful conditions in China, and so helped to popularize the idea that was being formed in Europe of an "enlightened", a constitutional, monarchy. The leaders of the Enlightenment read these reports with enthusiasm, with the result that they had an influence on the French Revolution. Confucius was found particularly attractive, and was regarded as a forerunner of the Enlightenment. The "Monadism" of the philosopher Leibnitz was influenced by these reports.

The missionaries gained a reputation at court as "scientists", and in this they were of service both to China and to Europe. The behaviour of the European merchants who followed the missions, spreading gradually in growing numbers along the coasts of China, was not by any means so irreproachable. The Chinese were certainly justified when they declared that European ships often made landings on the coast and simply looted, just as the Japanese had done before them. Reports of this came to the court, and as captured foreigners described themselves as "Christians" and also seemed to have some connexion with the missionaries living at court, and as disputes had broken out among the missionaries themselves in connexion with papal ecclesiastical policy, under the emperor Yung Chêng (1723–1736; name as emperor, Shih Tsung) Christianity was placed under a general ban, being regarded as a secret political organization.

5 *Relations with the outer world*

During the reign of Yung Chêng there was long-continued guerrilla fighting with natives in south-west China. The pressure of population in China sought an outlet in emigration. More and more Chinese moved into the south-west, and took the land from the natives, and the fighting was the consequence of this. This fighting has continued from time to time down to the present day. As recently as 1937 there were long reports in the newspapers of fighting with the natives of southern China. The reason has always been the same. Until the end of the nineteenth century these regions were the only fields of emigration for the Chinese. Only after that was Manchuria opened to immigration. The Chinese emigrants, both from northern and from central China, had always gone to the south. This had been so for more than a thousand years, and most families of North China had relatives in the south, who could help them if they migrated. Only when the south became absolutely unable to absorb any more immigrants did the current of North Chinese emigration turn to the almost unpopulated Manchuria, which the alien rulers of China had regarded as their homeland, and from which they had excluded the Chinese. That current of emigration grew in the twentieth century to the greatest mass migration in history, to the number of over 25,000,000 human beings in a few decades.

At the beginning of the reign of Ch'ien Lung (1736–1796), fighting started in Turkestan. Mongols, or more precisely Kalmuks, defeated by the Chinese, had migrated to the Ili region, where after heavy fighting they gained supremacy over some of the Kazaks and other Turkish peoples living there and in western Turkestan. Some Kazak tribes went over to the Russians, and in 1735 the Russians founded the town of Orenburg in the western Kazak region. The Kalmuks fought the Chinese without cessation until in 1739 they entered into an agreement under which they ceded half their territory to Manchu China, retaining only the Ili region. The Kalmuks subsequently reunited with other sections of the Kazaks against the Chinese. In 1754 peace was again concluded with China, but it was followed by raids on both sides, so that the Manchus determined to enter on a great campaign against the Ili region. This ended with a decisive victory for the Chinese (1755). In the years that followed, however, the Chinese began to be afraid that the various Kazak tribes might unite in order to occupy the territory of the Kalmuks, which was almost unpopulated owing to the mass slaughter of Kalmuks by the Chinese. Unrest began among the Mohammedans throughout the neighbouring western Turkestan, and the same Chinese generals who had fought the Kalmuks marched into Turkestan and captured the Mohammedan city States of Uch, Kashgar, and Yarkand.

The reinforcements for these campaigns, and for the garrisons which in the following decades were stationed in the Ili region and in the west of eastern Turkestan, marched along the road from Peking that leads northward through Mongolia to the far distant Uliassutai and Kobdo. The cost of transport for one *shih* (about 66 lb.) amounted to 120 pieces of silver. In 1781 certain economies were introduced, but between 1781 and 1791 over 30,000 tons, making some 8 tons a day, was transported to that region. The cost of transport for supplies alone amounted in the course of time to the not inconsiderable sum of 120,000,000 pieces of silver. In addition to this there was the cost of the transported goods and of the pay of soldiers and of the administration. These figures apply to the period of occupation, of relative peace: during the actual wars of conquest the expenditure was naturally far higher. Thus these campaigns, though I do not think they brought actual economic ruin to China, were nevertheless a costly enterprise, and one which produced little positive advantage.

In addition to this, these wars brought China into conflict with the European Powers. In the years during which the Chinese armies were fighting in the Ili region, the Russians were putting out their feelers in that direction, and the Chinese annals show plainly how the Russians intervened in the fighting with the Kalmuks and Kazaks. The Ili region remained thereafter a bone of contention between China and Russia, until it finally went to Russia, bit by bit, between 1847 and 1881. The Kalmuks and Kazaks played a special part in Russo-Chinese relations. The Chinese had sent a mission to the Kalmuks farthest west, by the lower Volga, and had entered into relations with them, as early as 1714. As Russian pressure on the Volga region continually grew, these western Kalmuks (called Turgut by the Chinese) decided to migrate eastwards into Chinese territory (1771). During this enormously difficult migration, almost entirely through hostile territory, a large number of the Turgut perished; 70,000, however, reached the Ili region, where they were settled by the Chinese on the lands of the eastern Kalmuks, who had been largely exterminated. There they live to this day.

In the south, too, the Chinese came into direct touch with the European Powers. In 1757 the English occupied Calcutta, and in 1766 the province of Bengal. In 1767 a Manchu general, Ming Jui, who had been victorious in the fighting for eastern Turkestan, marched against Burma, which was subjugated once more in 1769. And in 1790–1791 the Chinese conquered Nepal, south of Tibet, because Nepalese had made two attacks on Tibet. Thus English and Chinese political interests came here into contact.

For Ch'ien Lung's many wars of conquest there seem to have been two main reasons. The first was the need for security. The Mongols had to be overthrown because otherwise the homeland of the Manchus was menaced; in order to make sure of the suppression of the eastern Mongols, the western Mongols (Kalmuks) had to be overthrown; to make them harmless, Turkestan and the Ili region had to be conquered; Tibet was needed for the security of Turkestan and Mongolia—and so on. Vast territories, however, were conquered in this process which were of no economic value, and most of which actually cost a great deal of money and brought nothing in. They were conquered simply for security. That advantage had been gained: an aggressor would have to cross great areas of unproductive territory, with difficult conditions for reinforcements, before he could actually reach China. In the second place, the Chinese noticed the efforts that were being made by the European Powers, especially Russia and England, to divide Asia among themselves, and accordingly they made sure of their own good share.

6 *Decline; revolutions*

The period of Ch'ien Lung is not only that of the greatest expansion of the Chinese Empire, but also that of the greatest prosperity under the Manchu régime. But there began at the same time to be signs of internal decline. If we are to fix a particular year for this, perhaps it should be the year 1774, in which came the first great popular rising, in the province of Shantung. In 1775 there came another popular rising, in Honan—that of the "Society of the White Lotus". This society, which had long existed as a secret organization and had played a part in the Ming epoch, had been reorganized by a man named Liu Sung. Liu Sung was captured and was condemned to penal servitude. His followers, however, regrouped themselves, particularly in the province of Anhui. These risings had been produced, as always, by excessive oppression of the people by the government or the governing class. As, however, the anger of the population was naturally directed also against the idle Manchus of the cities, who lived on their State pensions, did no work, and behaved as a ruling class, the government saw in these movements a nationalist spirit, and took drastic steps against them. The popular leaders now altered their programme, and acclaimed a supposed descendant from the Ming dynasty as the future emperor. Government troops caught the leader of the "White Lotus" agitation, but he succeeded in escaping. In the regions through which the society had spread, there then began a sort of Inquisition, of exceptional ferocity. Six provinces were affected, and in and around the single city of Wuchang in four months more than 20,000 people were beheaded. The cost of the rising to the government ran into millions. In answer to this oppression, the popular leaders tightened their organization and marched north-west from the western provinces of which they had gained control. The rising was suppressed only by a very big military operation, and not until 1802. There had been very heavy fighting between 1793 and 1802—just when in Europe, in the French Revolution, another oppressed population won its freedom.

Ch'ien Lung abdicated on New Year's Day, 1795, after ruling for sixty years. He died in 1799. His successor was Jen Tsung (1796–1821; reign name, Chia Ch'ing). In the course of his reign the rising of the "White Lotus" was suppressed, but in 1813 there began a new rising, this time in North China—again that of a secret organization, the "Society of Heaven's Law". One of its leaders bribed some eunuchs, and penetrated with a group of followers into the palace; he threw himself upon the emperor, who was only saved through the intervention of his son. At the same time the rising spread in the provinces. Once more the government succeeded in suppressing it and capturing the leaders. But the memory of these risings was kept alive among the Chinese people. For the government failed to realize that the actual cause of the risings was the general impoverishment, and saw in them a nationalist movement, thus actually arousing a national consciousness, stronger than in the Ming epoch, among the middle and lower classes of the people, together with hatred of the Manchus. They were held responsible for every evil suffered, regardless of the fact that similar evils had existed earlier and that their causes lay in maladministration.

16 The imperial summer palace of the Manchu rulers, at Jehol.
Photo H. Hammer-Morrisson.

17 Tower on the city wall of Peking.
Photo H. Hammer-Morrisson.

7 *European Imperialism in the Far East*

With the emperor Tao Kuang (1821–1850) begins a new period in Chinese history, which came to an end, for the time being, only in 1911.

In foreign affairs these ninety years are marked by the steadily growing influence of the Western Powers, aimed at turning China into a colony. Culturally this period was that of the gradual infiltration of Western civilization into the Far East; it was recognized in China that it was necessary to learn from the West. In home affairs we see the collapse of the dynasty and the destruction of the unity of the empire; of four great civil wars, one almost brought the dynasty to its end. North and South China, the coastal area and the interior, developed in different ways.

Great Britain had made several attempts to improve her trade relations with China, but the mission of 1793 had no success, and that of 1816 also failed. English merchants, like all foreign merchants, were only permitted to settle in a small area adjoining Canton and at Macao, and were only permitted to trade with a particular group of monopolists, known as the "Hong". The Hong had to pay taxes to the State, but they had a wonderful opportunity of enriching themselves. The Europeans were entirely at their mercy, for they were not allowed to travel inland, and they were not allowed to try to negotiate with other merchants, to secure lower prices by competition.

The Europeans concentrated especially on the purchase of silk and tea; but what could they import into China? The higher the price of the goods and the smaller the cargo space involved, the better were the chances of profit for the merchants. It proved, however, that European woollens or luxury goods or industrial equipment could not be sold; the Chinese would probably have been glad to buy food, but transport was too expensive to permit profitable business. Thus a new article was soon discovered—opium, carried from India to China: the price was high and the cargo space involved was very small. The Chinese were familiar with opium, and bought it readily. Accordingly, from 1800 onwards opium became more and more the chief article of trade, especially for the English, who were able to bring it conveniently from India. Opium is harmful to the people; the opium trade resulted in certain groups of merchants being inordinately enriched; a great deal of Chinese money went abroad. The government became apprehensive, and sent Lin Tsê-hsü as its commissioner to Canton. In 1839 he prohibited the opium trade and burned the chests of opium found in British possession. The British view was that to tolerate the Chinese action might mean the destruction of British trade in the Far East, and that, on the other hand, it might be possible by active intervention to compel the Chinese to open other ports to European trade and to shake off the monopoly of the Canton merchants. In 1840 British ships-of-war appeared off the south-eastern coast of China and bombarded it. In 1841 the Chinese opened negotiations and dismissed Lin Tsê-hsü. As the Chinese concessions were regarded as inadequate, hostilities continued; the British entered the Yangtze estuary and threatened Nanking. In this first armed conflict with the West, China found herself defenceless owing to her lack of a navy, and it was also found that the European weapons were far superior to those of the Chinese. In 1842 China was compelled to capitulate: under the Treaty of Nanking Hong Kong was ceded to Great Britain, a war indemnity was paid, certain ports were thrown open to European trade, and the monopoly was brought to an end. A great deal of opium came, however, into China through smuggling—regrettably, for the State lost the Customs revenue!

This treaty introduced the period of the Capitulations. It contained the dangerous clause which added most to China's misfortunes—the Most Favoured Nation clause, providing that if China granted any privilege to any other State, that privilege should also automatically be granted to Great Britain. In connexion with this treaty it was agreed that the Chinese Customs should be supervised by European Consuls; and a trade treaty was granted. Similar treaties followed in 1844 with France and the United States.

The missionaries returned; until 1860, however, they were only permitted to work in the treaty ports. Shanghai was thrown open in 1843, and developed with extraordinary rapidity from a small and unimportant Chinese town to a city of a million and a centre of world-wide importance.

The terms of the Nanking Treaty were not observed by either side; both evaded them. In order to facilitate the smuggling, the British had permitted certain Chinese junks to fly the British flag. This also enabled these vessels to be protected by British ships-of-war from pirates, which at that time were very numerous off the southern coast owing to the economic depression. The Chinese, for their part, placed every possible obstacle in the way of the British. In 1856 the Chinese held up a ship sailing under the British flag, pulled down its flag, and arrested the crew on suspicion of smuggling. In connexion with this and other events, Britain decided to go to war. Thus began the "Lorcha War" of 1857, in which France joined for the sake of the booty to be expected. Britain had just ended the Crimean War, and was engaged in heavy fighting against the Moguls in India. Consequently only a small force of a few thousand men could be landed in China; Canton, however, was bombarded, and also the forts of Tientsin. There still seemed no prospect of gaining the desired objectives by negotiation, and in 1860 a new expedition was fitted out, this time some 20,000 strong. The troops landed at Tientsin and marched on Peking; the emperor fled to Jehol and did not return; he died in 1861. The new Treaty of Tientsin (1860) provided for (a) the opening of further ports to European traders; (b) the session of Kowloon, the strip of land lying opposite Hong Kong; (c) the establishment of a British Legation in Peking; (d) freedom of navigation along the Yangtze; (e) permission for British subjects to purchase land in China; (f) the British to be subject to their own Consular courts and not to the Chinese courts; (g) missionary activity to be permitted throughout the country. In addition to this, the commercial treaty was revised, the opium trade was permitted once more, and a war indemnity was to be paid by China. In the eyes of Europe, Britain had now succeeded in turning China not actually into a colony, but at all events into a semi-colony; China must be expected soon to share the fate of India. China, however, with her very different conceptions of intercourse between States, did not realize the full import of these terms; some of them were regarded as concessions on unimportant points, which there was no harm in granting to the trading "barbarians", as had been done in the past; some were regarded as simple injustices, which at a given moment could be swept away by administrative action.

But the result of this European penetration was that a great deal of money, especially silver, flowed abroad from China. China's balance of trade was adverse, and became more and more so, as under the commercial treaties she could neither stop the importation of European goods nor set a duty on them; and on the other hand she could not compel foreigners to buy Chinese goods. This efflux of silver brought general impoverishment to China, widespread financial stringency to the State, and continuous financial crises and inflation. China had never had much liquid capital, and she was soon compelled to take up foreign loans in order to pay her debts. At that time internal loans were out of the question (the first internal loan was floated in 1894): the population had scarcely any capital and did not even know what a State loan meant; consequently the loans had to be issued abroad. This, however, entailed the giving of securities, generally in the form of economic privileges. Under the Most Favoured Nation clause, however, these privileges had then to be granted to other States which had made no loans to China. Clearly a vicious spiral, which in the end could only bring disaster.

The only exception to the general impoverishment, in which not only the peasants but the old upper classes were involved, was a certain section of the trading community and the middle class, which had grown rich through its dealings with the Europeans. These people now accumulated capital, became Europeanized with their staffs, acquired land from the impoverished gentry, and sent their sons abroad to foreign universities. They founded the first industrial undertakings, and learned European capitalist methods. This class was, of course, to be found mainly in the Treaty Ports in the south and in their environs. The south, as far north as Shanghai, became more modern, and more advanced; the north made no advance. In the south, European ways of thought were learnt, and Chinese and European theories were compared. Criticism began. The first revolutionary societies were formed in this atmosphere in the south.

8 *Risings in Turkestan and within China: the T'ai P'ing Rebellion*

But the emperor Tao Kuang, a man in poor health though not without ability, had much graver anxieties than those caused by the Europeans. He did not yet fully realize the seriousness of the European peril.

In Turkestan, where Turkish Mohammedans lived under Chinese rule, conditions were far from being as the Chinese desired. The Chinese, a fundamentally rationalistic people, regarded religion as a purely political matter, and accordingly required every citizen to take part in the official form of worship. Subject to that, he might privately belong to any other religion. To a Mohammedan, this was impossible and intolerable. The Mohammedans were only ready to practise their own religion, and absolutely refused to take part in any other. The Chinese also tried to apply to Turkestan in other matters the same legislation that applied to all China, but this proved irreconcilable with the demands made by Islam on its followers. All this produced continual unrest.

Turkestan had had a feudal system of government with a number of feudal lords (*beg*), who tried to maintain their influence and who had the support of the Mohammedan population. The Chinese had come to Turkestan as soldiers and officials, to administer the country. They regarded themselves as the lords of the land and occupied themselves with the extraction of taxes. Most of the officials were also associated with the Chinese merchants who travelled throughout Turkestan and as far as Siberia. The conflicts implicit in this situation produced great Mohammedan risings in the nineteenth century. The first came in 1825–1827; in 1845 a second rising flamed up, and thirty years later these revolts led to the temporary loss of the whole of Turkestan.

In 1848, native unrest began in the province of Hunan, as a result of the constantly growing pressure of the Chinese settlers on the native population; in the same year there was unrest farther south, in the province of Kwangsi, this time in connexion with the influence of the Europeans. The leader was a quite simple man, Hung Hsiu-ch'üan, who gathered the impoverished peasants round him as every peasant leader had done in the past. Very often the nucleus of these peasant movements had been a secret society with a particular religious tinge; this time the peasant revolutionaries came forward as at the same time the preachers of a new religion of their own. Hung had heard of Christianity from missionaries, and he mixed up Christian ideas with those of ancient China and proclaimed to his followers a doctrine that promised the Kingdom of God on earth. He called himself "Christ's younger brother", and his kingdom was to be called *T'ai P'ing* ("Supreme Peace"). He made his colleagues, his first comrades, into kings, and made himself emperor. At bottom the movement, like all similar ones before it, was not religious but social; and it produced a great response from the peasants. Hung redistributed the land and expelled the officials, especially the aliens, the Manchus. His followers had lived in the utmost poverty, for the bad effects of the trade with Europe had been felt especially in South China; now they obtained land, and also wealth from captured cities. A large part of the officials, and particularly of the soldiers sent against them, were Manchus, and consequently the movement very soon became a nationalist movement, much as the popular movement at the end of the Mongol epoch had done. Hung made rapid progress; in 1852 he captured Hankow, and in 1853 Nanking, the important centre in the east. With clear political insight he made Nanking his capital. In this he returned to the old traditions of the beginning of the Ming epoch, no doubt expecting in this way to attract support from the eastern Chinese gentry, who had no liking for a capital far away in the north. He made a parade of adhesion to the ancient Chinese tradition: his followers cut off their pigtails and allowed their hair to grow as in the past.

He did not succeed, however, in carrying his reforms from the stage of sporadic action to a systematic reorganization of the country, and he also failed to enlist the elements needed for this as for all other administrative work, so that the good start made soon degenerated into a terrorist régime.

Hung's followers pressed on from Nanking, and in 1853–1855 they advanced nearly to Tientsin; but they failed to capture Peking itself.

The new T'ai P'ing State faced the Europeans with big problems. Should they work with it or against it? The T'ai P'ing always insisted that they were Christians; the missionaries hoped now to have the opportunity of converting all China to Christianity. The T'ai P'ing treated the missionaries well. After long hesitation and much vacillation, however, the Europeans placed themselves on the side of the Manchus. Not out of any belief that the T'ai P'ing movement was without justification, but because they had concluded treaties with the Manchu government and given loans to it, of which nothing would have remained if the Manchus had fallen; because they preferred the weak Manchu government to a strong T'ai P'ing government; and because they disliked the socialistic element in many of the measures adopted by the T'ai P'ing.

At first, however, it seemed as if the Manchus would be able to cope unaided with the T'ai P'ing. The same thing happened as at the end of the Mongol rule: the imperial armies, consisting of the "banners" of the Manchus, the Mongols, and some Chinese, had lost their military skill in the long years of peace; they had lost their old fighting spirit and were glad to be able to live in peace on their

State pensions. Now three men came to the fore—a Mongol named Seng-ko-lin-hsin, a man of great personal bravery, who defended the interests of the Manchu rulers; and two Chinese, Tsêng Kuo-fan and Li Hung-chang, who were in the service of the Manchus but used their position simply to further the interests of the gentry. The Mongol saved Peking from capture by the T'ai P'ing. The two Chinese were living in central China, and there they recruited, Li at his own expense and Tsêng out of the resources at his disposal as a provincial governor, a sort of militia, the first national Chinese army, consisting of peasants out to protect their country from destruction by the rebel peasants of the T'ai P'ing. Thus the peasants of central China, all suffering from impoverishment, divided into two groups, one following the T'ai P'ing, the other following Tsêng Kuo-fan. Tsêng's army, too, might be described as a "national" army, because Tsêng was not fighting for the interests of the Manchus. Thus the peasants, all anti-Manchu, could choose between two sides, between the T'ai P'ing and Tsêng Kuo-fan. Although Tsêng represented the gentry and was thus against the simple common people, peasants fought in masses on his side, for he paid better, and especially more regularly. Tsêng, being a good strategist, won successes and gained adherents. Thus by 1856 the T'ai P'ing were pressed back on Nanking and some of the towns round it.

While in the central provinces the T'ai P'ing rebellion was raging, China was suffering grave setbacks owing to the Lorcha War of 1856; and there were also great and serious risings in other parts of the country. In 1855 the Yellow River had changed its course, entering the sea once more at Tientsin, to the great loss of the regions of Honan and Anhui. In these two central provinces the peasant rising of the so-called "Nien Fei" had begun, but it only became formidable after 1855, owing to the increasing misery of the peasants. This purely peasant revolt was not suppressed by the Manchu government until 1868, after many collisions. Then, however, there began the so-called "Mohammedan risings". Here there are, in all, five movements to distinguish: (1) the Mohammedan rising in Kansu (1864–5); (2) the Salar movement in Shensi; (3) the Mohammedan revolt in Yunnan (1855–1873); (4) the rising in Kansu (1895); (5) the rebellion of Yakub Beg in Turkestan (from 1866 onward).

While we are fairly well informed about the other popular risings of this period, the Chinese sources say next to nothing about the Mohammedan revolts. The reports are vague and scanty. We know from unofficial accounts that these risings were suppressed with great brutality. To this day there are many Mohammedans in, for instance, Yunnan, but the revolt there is said to have cost a million lives. The figures all rest on very rough estimates: in Kansu the population is said to have fallen from fifteen millions to one million; the Turkestan revolt is said to have cost ten million lives. There are no reliable statistics; but it is understandable that at that time the population of China must have fallen considerably, especially if we bear in mind the equally ferocious suppression of the risings of the T'ai P'ing and the Nien Fei within China, and smaller risings of which we have made no mention.

The Mohammedan risings were not elements of a general Mohammedan revolt, but separate events only incidentally connected with each other. The risings had different causes. An important factor was the general distress in China. This was partly due to the fact that the officials were exploiting the peasant population more ruthlessly than ever. In addition to this, owing to the national feeling which had been aroused in so unfortunate a way, the Chinese felt a revulsion against non-Chinese, such as the Salars, who were of Turkish race. Here there were always possibilities of friction, which might have been removed with a little consideration but which swelled to importance through the tactless behaviour of Chinese officials. Finally there came divisions among the Mohammedans of China which led to fighting between themselves.

All these risings were marked by two characteristics. They had no general political aim such as the founding of a great and universal Islamic State. Separate States were founded, but they were too small to endure; they would have needed the protection of great States. But they were not moved by any pan-Islamic idea. Secondly, they all took place on Chinese soil, and all the Mohammedans involved, except in the rising of the Salars, were Chinese. These Chinese who became Mohammedans are called Dungans. The Dungans are, of course, no longer pure Chinese, because Chinese who have gone over to Islam readily form mixed marriages with Islamic non-Chinese, that is to say with Turks and Mongols.

The revolt, however, of Yakub Beg in Turkestan had a quite different character. Yakub Beg (his Chinese name is An Chi-yeh) had risen to the Chinese governorship of Kuruma when he made himself ruler of Kashgar. In 1866 he began to try to make himself independent of Chinese control. He conquered Ili, and then in a rapid campaign made himself master of all Turkestan.

His State had a much better prospect of endurance than the other Mohammedan States. He had full control of it from 1874. Turkestan was connected with China only by the few routes that led between the desert and the Tibetan mountains. The State was supported against China by Russia, which was continually pressing eastward, and in the south by Great Britain, which was pressing toward Tibet. Farther west was the great Ottoman empire; the attempt to gain direct contact with it was not hopeless in itself, and this was recognized at Istanbul. Missions went to and fro, and Turkish officers came to Yakub Beg and organized his army; Yakub Beg recognized the Turkish sultan as Khalif. He also concluded treaties with Russia and Great Britain. But in spite of all this he was unable to maintain his hold of Turkestan. In 1877 the famous Chinese general Tso Tsung-t'ang (1812–1885), who had fought against the T'ai P'ing and also against the Mohammedans in Kansu, marched into Turkestan and ended Yakub Beg's rule.

Yakub was defeated, however, not so much by Chinese superiority as by a combination of circumstances. In order to build up his kingdom he was compelled to impose heavy taxation, and this made him unpopular with his own followers: they had had to pay taxes under the Chinese, but the Chinese collection had been much less rigorous than that of Yakub Beg. It was technically impossible for the Ottoman empire to give him any aid, even had its internal situation permitted it. Britain and Russia would probably have been glad to see a weakening of the Chinese hold over Turkestan, but they did not want a strong new State there, once they had found that neither of them could control the country while it was in Yakub Beg's hands. In 1881 Russia occupied the Ili region, Yakub's first conquest. In the end the two Great Powers considered it better for Turkestan to return officially into the hands of the weakened China, hoping that in practice they would be able to bring Turkestan more and more under their control. Consequently, when in 1880, three years after the removal of Yakub Beg, China sent a mission to Russia with the request for the return of the Ili region to her, Russia gave way, and the Treaty of Ili was concluded, ending for the time the Russian penetration of Turkestan. In 1882 the Manchu government raised Turkestan to a "foreign country" with a special administration.

This process of foreign penetration of Turkestan is still going on. Until the end of the first world war there was no fundamental change in the situation in the country, owing to the rivalry between Great Britain and Russia. But after 1920 a period began in which Turkestan became almost independent, under a number of rulers of parts of the country. Then, from 1928 onward, a more and more thorough penetration by Russia began, so that by 1940 Turkestan could be described as a Soviet Republic. The second world war diverted Russian attention to the West, and at the same time compelled the Chinese to retreat into the interior from the Japanese; there came, therefore, a mass immigration of Chinese into Turkestan and at the same time a weakening of Russian influence, so that by 1943 the country was more firmly held by the Chinese government than it had been for seventy years. In spite of this, there has as yet been no success in composing the differences between Chinese and the Mohammedan Turks.

9 *Collision with Japan; further Capitulations*

The reign of the incapable Wen Tsung (reign name Hsien Feng: 1851–1861) was marked throughout by the T'ai P'ing and other rebellions and by wars with the Europeans, and that of Mu Tsung (or T'ung Chih: 1862–1874) by the great Mohammedan disturbances. There began also a conflict with Japan which lasted until 1945. T'ung Chih came to the throne as a child of five, and never played a part of his own. It had been the general rule for princes to serve as regents for minors on the imperial throne, but this time the princes concerned won such notoriety through their intrigues that the Peking court circles decided to entrust the regency to two concubines of the late emperor. One of these, called Tzu Hsi (b. 1835), of the Manchu tribe of the Yehe-Nara, quickly gained the upper hand. She had the support of a man of her tribe, the eunuch Yung Lu. The empress Tzu Hsi is one of the strongest personalities of the later nineteenth century who played an active part in Chinese political life. She played a more active part than any emperor had played for many decades.

Meanwhile great changes had taken place in Japan. The restoration of the Meiji had ended the age of feudalism, at least on the surface. Japan rapidly became Europeanized, and at the same time entered on an imperialist policy. Her aims from 1868 onward were clear, and remained unaltered until the end of the second world war: she was to be surrounded by a wide girdle of territories under Japanese domination, in order to prevent the approach of any enemy to the Japanese homeland. This girdle was divided into several zones—(1) the inner zone with the Kurile Islands, Sakhalin, Korea, the Ryukyu archipelago, and Formosa; (2) the outer zone with the Marianne, Philippine, and Caroline Islands, eastern China, Manchuria, and eastern Siberia; (3) the third zone, not clearly defined, including especially the Netherlands Indies, Indo-China, and the whole of China, a zone of undefined extent. The outward form of this subjugated region was to be that of the Greater Japanese Empire, described as the Imperium of the Yellow Race (the main ideas were contained in the Tanaka Memorandum and in the Tada Interview of 1936). Round Japan, moreover, a girdle was to be created of producers of raw materials and purchasers of manufactures, to provide Japanese industry with a market. Japan had sent a delegation of amity to China as early as 1869, and a first Sino-Japanese treaty was signed in 1871; from then on, Japan began to carry out her imperialistic plans. In 1874 she attacked the Ryukyu islands and Formosa on the pretext that some Japanese had been murdered there. Under the treaty of 1874 Japan withdrew once more, only demanding a substantial indemnity; but in 1876, in violation of the treaty and without a declaration of war, she annexed the Ryukyu Islands. In 1876 began the Japanese penetration into Korea; by 1885 she had reached the stage of a declaration that Korea was a joint sphere of interest of China and Japan; until then China's protectorate over Korea had been unchallenged. At the same time (1876) Great Britain had secured further Capitulations in the Chefoo Convention; in 1862 France had acquired Cochin China, in 1864 Cambodia, in 1874 Tongking, and in 1883 Annam. This led in 1884 to war between France and China, in which the French did not by any means gain an indubitable victory; but the Treaty of Tientsin left them with their acquisitions.

Meanwhile, at the beginning of 1875, the young emperor died of smallpox, without issue. Under the influence of the two empresses, who still remained regents, a cousin of the dead emperor, the three-year-old prince Tsai T'ien (reign name Kuang Hsü: 1875–1909) was chosen as emperor. He came of age in 1889 and took over the government of the country. The empress Tzu Hsi retired, but did not really relinquish the reins.

In 1894 the Sino-Japanese War broke out over Korea, as an outcome of the undefined position that had existed since 1885 owing to the imperialistic policy of the Japanese. China had created a North China squadron, but this was all that can be regarded as Chinese preparation for the long-threatened war. The Governor General of Chihli (now Hopei—the province in which Peking is situated), Li Hung-chang, was a general who had done good service, but he lost the war, and at Shimonoseki (1895) he had to sign a treaty on very harsh terms, in which China relinquished her protectorate over Korea and lost Formosa. The intervention of France, Germany, and Russia compelled Japan to content herself with these acquisitions, abandoning her demand for South Manchuria.

10 *Russia in Manchuria*

After the Crimean War, Russia had turned her attention once more to the East. There had been hostilities with China over eastern Siberia, which were brought to an end in 1858 by the Treaty of Aigun, under which China ceded certain territories in northern Manchuria. This made possible the founding of Vladivostok in 1860. Russia received Sakhalin from Japan in 1875 in exchange for the Kurile Islands. She received from China the important Port Arthur as a leased territory, and then tried to secure the whole of South Manchuria. This brought Japan's policy of expansion into conflict with Russia's plans in the Far East. Russia wanted Manchuria in order to be able to pursue a policy in the Pacific; but Japan herself planned to march into Manchuria from Korea, of which she already had possession. This imperialist rivalry made war inevitable: Russia lost the war; under the Treaty of Portsmouth in 1905 Russia gave Japan the main railway through Manchuria, with adjoining territory. Thus Manchuria became Japan's sphere of influence and was lost to the Manchus without their being consulted in any way. The Japanese penetration of Manchuria then proceeded stage by stage, not without occasional setbacks, until she had occupied the whole of Manchuria and set up the "Empire of Manchukuo", which endured as a Japanese protectorate from 1932 to 1945. After the end of the second world war, Manchuria was returned to China, but the existing agreements make certain reservations in favour of the Soviet Union, which recall the situation of 1904.

11 *Reform and reaction: the Boxer Rising*

China had lost the war with Japan because she was entirely without modern armament. While Japan went to work at once with all her energy to emulate European industrialization, the ruling class in China had shown a marked repugnance to any modernization; and the centre of this conservatism was the dowager empress Tzu Hsi. She was a woman of strong personality, but too uneducated—in the modern sense—to be able to realize that modernization was an absolute necessity for China if it was to remain an independent State. The empress failed to realize that the Europeans were fundamentally different from the neighbouring tribes or the pirates of the past; she had not the capacity to acquire a general grasp of the realities of world politics; she still thought, as the ancient Chinese had done, that China was the centre of the world, surrounded by barbarians. She felt instinctively that Europeanization would wreck the foundations of the power of the Manchus and the gentry, and would bring another class, the middle class and the merchants, into power.

There were reasonable men, however, who had seen the necessity of reform—especially Li Hung-chang, who has already been mentioned. In 1896 he went on a mission to Moscow, and then toured Europe. The reformers were, however, divided into two groups. One group advocated the acquisition of a certain amount of technical knowledge from abroad and its introduction by slow reforms, without altering the social structure of the State or the composition of the government. The others held that the State needed fundamental changes, and that superficial instruction from Europe was not enough. The failure in the war with Japan made the general desire for reform more and more insistent not only in the country but in Peking. Until now Japan had been despised as a barbarian State; now Japan had won! The Europeans had been despised; now they were all cutting bits out of China for themselves, extracting from the government one privilege after another, and quite openly dividing China into "spheres of interest", obviously as the prelude to annexation of the whole country.

In Europe at that time the question was being discussed over and over again, why Japan had so quickly succeeded in making herself a modern power, and why China was not succeeding in doing so; the Japanese were praised for their capacity and the Chinese blamed for their lassitude. Both in Europe and in Chinese circles it was overlooked that there were fundamental differences in the social structure of the two countries. The basis of the modern capitalist States of the West is the middle class. Japan had for centuries had a middle class (the merchants) that had entered into a symbiosis with the feudal lords. For the middle class the transition to modern capitalism, and for the feudal lords the way to Western imperialism, was easy. In China there was only a young and weak middle class, vegetating under the dominance of the gentry; the middle class had still to gain the strength to liberate itself before it could become the support for a capitalistic State. And the gentry were still strong enough to maintain their dominance and so to prevent a radical reconstruction; all they would agree to were a few reforms from which they might hope to secure an increase of power for their own ends.

In 1895 and in 1898 a scholar, Ch'ang Yo-wei, who was admitted into the presence of the emperor, submitted to him memoranda in which he called for radical reform. Ch'ang was a scholar who belonged to the positivist school of philosophy of the early Manchu period (the so-called Han school). He was a man of strong and persuasive personality, and had such an influence on the emperor that in 1898 the emperor issued several edicts ordering the fundamental reorganization of education, law, trade, communications, and the army. These laws were not at all bad in themselves; they would have paved the way for a liberalization of Chinese society. But they aroused the utmost hatred in the conservative gentry and also in the moderate reformers among the gentry. Ch'ang Yo-wei and his followers, to whom a number of well-known contemporary scholars belonged, had strong support in South China.

We have already mentioned that owing to the increased penetration of European goods and ideas, South China had become more progressive than the north; this had added to the tension already existing for other reasons between north and south. In foreign policy the north was more favourable to Russia and radically opposed to Japan and Great Britain; the south was in favour of co-operation with Britain and Japan, in order to learn from those two States how reform could be carried through. In the north the men of the south were suspected of being anti-Manchu and revolutionary in feeling. This was to some extent true, though Ch'ang Yo-wei and his friends were as yet largely unconscious of it.

When the empress Tzu Hsi saw that the emperor was actually thinking about reforms, she went to work with lightning speed. Very soon the reformers had to flee; those who failed to make good their escape were arrested and executed. The emperor was made a prisoner in a palace near Peking, and remained a captive until his death; the empress resumed her regency on his behalf. The period of reforms lasted only for a few months of 1898. A leading part in the extermination of the reformers was played by troops from Kansu under the command of a Mohammedan, Tung Fu-hsiang. General Yuan Shih-k'ai, who was then stationed at Tientsin in command of 7,000 troops with modern equipment, the only ones in China, could have removed the empress and protected the reformers; but he was already pursuing a personal policy, and thought it safer to give the reformers no help.

There now began, from 1898, a thoroughly reactionary rule of the dowager empress. But China's general situation permitted no breathing-space. In 1900 came the so-called Boxer Rising, a new popular movement against the gentry and the Manchus similar to the many that had preceded it. The Peking government succeeded, however, in negotiations that brought the movement into the service of the government and directed it against the foreigners. This removed the danger to the government and at the same time helped it against the hated foreigners. But incidents resulted which the Peking government had not anticipated. An international army was sent to China, and marched from Tientsin against Peking, to liberate the besieged European legations and to punish the government. The Europeans captured Peking (1900); the dowager empress and her prisoner the emperor had to flee; some of the palaces were looted. The peace treaty that followed exacted further concessions from China to the Europeans and enormous war indemnities, the payment of which continued for more than forty years, though most of the States receiving them applied them to Chinese education. When in 1902 the dowager empress returned to Peking and put the emperor back into his palace-prison, she was forced by what had happened to realize that at all events a certain measure of reform was necessary. The reforms, however, which she decreed, mainly in 1904, were very modest and were never actually carried out. They were only intended to make an impression on the outer world and to appease the continually growing body of supporters of the reform party, especially numerous in South China. The south remained, nevertheless, a focus of hostility to the Manchus. After his failure in 1898, Ch'ang Yo-wei went to Europe, and no longer played any important political part. His place was soon taken by a young Chinese physician who had been living abroad, Sun Yat-sen, who turned the reform party into a middle-class revolutionary party.

12 *End of the dynasty*

Meanwhile the dowager empress held her own, mainly with the aid of her eunuch Yung Lu. General Yüan Shih-k'ai, who had played so dubious a part in 1898, was not impeccably loyal to her, and remained unreliable. He was beyond challenge the strongest man in the country, for he possessed the only modern army; but he was still biding his time.

In 1908 the dowager empress fell ill; she was seventy-four years old. When she felt that her end was near, she seems to have had the captive emperor Kuang Hsü assassinated (at 5 p.m. on November 14th); she herself died next day (November 15th, 2 p.m.): she was evidently determined that this man, whom she had ill-treated and oppressed all his life, should not regain independence. As Kuang Hsü had no children, she nominated on the day of her death the two-year-old prince P'u Yi as emperor (reign name Hsüan T'ung, 1909–1911).

The fact that another child was to reign and a new regency to act for him, together with all the failures in home and foreign policy, brought further strength to the revolutionary party. The government believed that it could only maintain itself if it allowed Yüan Shih-k'ai, the commander of the modern troops, to come to power. The chief regent, however, worked against Yüan Shih-k'ai and dismissed him at the beginning of 1909; Yüan's supporters remained at their posts. Yüan himself now entered into relations with the revolutionaries, whose centre was Canton, and whose undisputed leader was now Sun Yat-sen. At this time Sun and his supporters had already made attempts at revolution, but without success, as his following was as yet too small. It consisted mainly of young intellectuals who had been educated in Europe and America; the great mass of the Chinese people remained unconvinced: the common people could not understand the new ideals, and the middle class did not entirely trust the young intellectuals.

The state of China in 1911 was as lamentable as could be: the European States, America, and Japan regarded China as a field for their own plans, and in their calculations paid scarcely any attention to the Chinese government. Foreign capital was penetrating everywhere in the form of loans or railway and other enterprises. If it had not been for the mutual rivalries of the Powers, China would long ago have been annexed by one of them. The government needed a great deal of money for the payment of the war indemnities, and for carrying out the few reforms at last decided on. In order to get money from the provinces, it had to permit the governors and viceroys even more freedom than they already possessed. The result was a spectacle altogether resembling that of the end of the T'ang dynasty, about A.D. 900: the various governors were trying to make themselves independent. In addition to this there was the revolutionary movement in the south.

The government made some concession to the progressives, by providing the first beginnings of parliamentary rule. In 1910 a national assembly was convoked. It had a Lower House with representatives of the provinces (provincial diets were also set up), and an Upper House, in which sat representatives of the imperial house, the nobility, the gentry, and also the protectorates. The members of the Upper House were all nominated by the regent. It very soon proved that the members of the Lower House, mainly representatives of the provincial gentry, had a much more practical outlook than the routineers of Peking. Thus the Lower House grew in importance, a fact which, of course, brought grist to the mills of the revolutionary movement.

In 1910 the first risings directed actually against the regency took place, in the province of Hunan. In 1911 the "railway disturbances" broke out in western China as a reply of the railway shareholders in the province of Szechwan to the government decree of nationalization of all the railways. The modernist students, most of whom were sons of merchants who owned railway shares, supported the movement, and the government was unable to control them. At the same time a great anti-Manchu revolution began in Wuchang, one of the cities of which Wuhan, on the Yangtze, now consists. The revolution was the result of government action against a group of terrorists. Its leader was an officer named Li Yüan-hung. The Manchus soon had some success in this quarter, but the other provincial governors now rose in rapid succession, repudiated the Manchus, and declared themselves independent. Most of the Manchu garrisons in the provinces were murdered. The governors remained at the head of their troops in their provinces, and for the moment made common cause with the revolutionaries, from whom they meant to break free at the first opportunity. The Manchus themselves failed at first to realize the gravity of the revolutionary movement; they then fell into panic-stricken desperation. As a last resource, Yüan Shih-k'ai was recalled (November 10th, 1911) and made Prime Minister.

Yüan's excellent troops were loyal to his person, and he could have made use of them in fighting on behalf of the dynasty. But a victory would have brought no personal gain to him; for his personal plans he considered that the anti-Manchu side provided the springboard he needed. The revolutionaries, for their part, had no choice but to win over Yüan Shih-k'ai for the sake of his troops, since they were not themselves strong enough to get rid of the Manchus, or even to wrest concessions from them, so long as the Manchus were defended by Yüan's army. Thus Yüan and the revolutionaries were forced into each other's arms. He then began negotiations with them, explaining to the imperial house that the dynasty could only be saved by concessions. The revolutionaries—apart from their desire to neutralize the Prime Minister and general, if not to bring him over to their side—were also readier than ever to negotiate, because they were short of money and unable to obtain loans from abroad, and because they could not themselves gain control of the individual governors. The negotiations, which had been carried on at Shanghai, were broken off on December 18th, 1911, because the revolutionaries demanded a Republic, but the imperial house was only ready to grant a constitutional monarchy.

Meanwhile the revolutionaries set up a provisional government at Nanking (December 29th, 1911), with Sun Yat-sen as president and Li Yüan-hung as vice-president. Yüan Shih-k'ai now declared to the imperial house that the monarchy could no longer be defended, as his troops were too unreliable, and he induced the Manchu government to issue an edict on February 12th, 1912, in which they renounced the throne of China and declared the Republic to be the constitutional form of State. The young emperor Hsüan T'ung (P'u Yi), after the Japanese conquest of Manchuria in 1931, was installed there by the Japanese as emperor of "Manchukuo", which had become a Japanese protectorate. He was, however, entirely without power during the melancholy years of his nominal rule, which lasted until 1945.

In 1912 the Manchu dynasty came in reality to its end. On the news of the abdication of the imperial house, Sun Yat-sen resigned in Nanking, and recommended Yuan Shih-k'ai as president.

Chapter XIII

THE REPUBLIC (Since 1912)

1 *Social and intellectual position*

IN order to understand the period that now followed, let us first consider the social and intellectual position in China in the period between 1911 and 1927. The Manchus were no longer there, nor were there any remaining real supporters of the old dynasty. The class of gentry, however, still existed. Alongside it was a still numerically small middle class, with little political education or enlightenment.

The political interests of these two groups were obviously in conflict. But in this period there had been big changes. The gentry were largely divided among themselves. They still possessed the basis of their existence, their land, but the land was falling in value, as there were now other opportunities of capital investment, such as industrial undertakings, export, or shareholding in foreign banks; and especially because there was after all not much capital to invest. In addition to this, cheaper rice and other foodstuffs were streaming from abroad into China, bringing the prices for Chinese foodstuffs down to the world market prices, another painful business blow to the gentry. Silk had to meet the competition of Japanese silk and especially of rayon; the Chinese silk was of very unequal quality and sold with difficulty. On the other hand, through the influence of the Western capitalistic system, which was penetrating more and more into China, land itself became "capital" once more. And an object of speculation for people with capital; its value no longer depended entirely on the rents it could yield but, under certain circumstances, on quite other things—the building of railways or public buildings, and so on. These changes impoverished and demoralized the gentry, who in the course of the past century had grown fewer in number. For the gentry were not in a position to take part in the capitalist manipulations, because they had never possessed capital; their wealth had lain entirely in their land, and the income from their rents was consumed quite unproductively in luxurious living.

Moreover, the class solidarity of the gentry was dissolving. In the past politics had been carried on by cliques of gentry families, with the emperor at their head as an unchangeable institution. This edifice had now lost its summit; the struggles between cliques still went on, but entirely without the control which the emperor's power had after all exercised, as a sort of regulative element in the play of forces among the gentry. The arena for this competition had been the court. After the destruction of the arena, the field of play lost its boundaries: the struggles between cliques no longer had a definite objective; the only objective left was the maintenance or securing of any and every hold on power. Under the new conditions cliques or individuals among the gentry could only ally themselves with the possessors of military power, the generals or governors. In this last stage the struggle between rival groups turned into a rivalry between individuals, and for the securing of the aim in view any means were considered justifiable. Never was there such bribery and corruption among the officials as in the years after 1912. This period, until 1927, may therefore be described as a period of dissolution and destruction of the social system of the gentry.

Over against this dying class of the gentry stood, broadly speaking, a tripartite opposition. To begin with, there was the new middle class, divided and without clear political ideas; antidynastic of course, but undecided especially as to the attitude it should adopt toward the peasants. And to this day the peasants form the great bulk of the Chinese population. The middle class consisted mainly of traders and bankers, whose aim was the introduction of Western capitalism in association with foreign Powers. There were also young students, some of whom had been educated abroad, and had absorbed the ideals of democracy, but had too little accurate knowledge of the complicated onditions within China to be able to realize that in China's xisting position those ideals were impracticable.

In the second place, there was a relatively very small genuine proletariat, the product of the first activities of big capitalists in China; the aims of the proletariat were naturally opposed to those of the capitalists. Thirdly, and inally, there was a gigantic peasantry, uninterested in politics and uneducated, but ready to give unthinking allegiance to anyone who promised to make an end of the intolerable conditions in the matter of rents and taxes, conditions that were growing steadily worse with the decay of the gentry. These peasants were thinking of popular risings on the pattern of all the risings in the history of China—attacks on the towns and the killing of the hated landowners, officials, and moneylenders, that is to say of the gentry.

Such was the picture of the middle class and those who were ready to support it, a group with widely divergent interests, held together only by its opposition to the gentry system and the monarchy. It could not but be extremely difficult, if not impossible, to achieve political success with such a group. Sun Yat-sen, the "Father of the Republic", accordingly laid down three stages of progress in his many works, of which the best-known are *San-min chu-i*, ("The Three Principles of the People"), and *Chien-küo fang-lüeh* ("Plans for the Building up of the Realm"). The three phases of development through which Republican China had to pass were: the phase of struggle against the old system, the

phase of educative rule, and the phase of truly democratic government. The phase of educative rule was to be a sort of authoritarian system with a democratic content, under which the people should be familiarized with democracy and enabled to grow politically ripe for true democracy.

Difficult as was the internal situation from the sociological point of view, it was no less difficult in economic respects. China had recognized that she must at least adopt Western technical and industrial progress in order to continue to exist as an independent State. But the building up of industry demanded large sums of money. The existing Chinese banks were quite incapable of providing the capital needed; but the acceptance of capital from abroad led at once, every time, to further political capitulations. The gentry, who had no capital worth mention, were violently opposed to the capitalization of their properties, and were in favour of continuing as far as possible to work the soil in the old style. Quite apart from all this, all over the country there were generals who had come from the ranks of the gentry, and who collected the whole of the financial resources of their region for the support of their private armies. Investors had little confidence in the Republican government so long as they could not tell whether the government would decide in favour of its Right or of its Left wing.

No less complicated was the intellectual situation at this time. Confucianism, and the whole of the old culture and morality bound up with it, was unacceptable to the middle-class element. In the first place, Confucianism rejected the principle, required at least in theory by the middle class, of the equality of all people; secondly, the Confucian great-family system was irreconcilable with middle-class individualism, quite apart from the fact that the Confucian form of State could only be a monarchy. Every attempt to bolster up Confucianism in practice or theory was bound to fail and did fail. Even the gentry could scarcely offer any real defence of the Confucian system any longer. With Confucianism went the moral standards especially of the upper classes of society. Taoism was out of the question as a substitute, because of its anarchistic and egocentric character. Consequently, in these years, part of the gentry turned to Buddhism and part to Christianity. Some of the middle class who had come under European influence also turned to Christianity, regarding it as a part of the European civilization they had to adopt. Others adhered to modern philosophic systems such as pragmatism and positivism. Marxist doctrines spread rapidly.

Education was secularized. Great efforts were made to develop modern schools, though the work of development was continually hindered by the incessant political unrest. Only at the universities, which became foci of republican and progressive opinion, was any positive achievement possible. Many students and professors were active in politics, organizing demonstrations and strikes. They pursued a strong national policy, often also socialistic. At the same time real scientific work was done; many young scholars of outstanding ability were trained at the Chinese universities, often better than the students who went abroad. There is a permanent disagreement between these two groups of young men with a modern education: the students who return from abroad claim to be better educated, but in reality they often have only a very superficial knowledge of things modern and none at all of China, her history, and her special circumstances. These returned students are therefore generally a disturbing influence in politics. The students of the Chinese universities have been much better instructed in all the things that concern China, and most of them are in no way behind the returned students in the modern sciences. They are therefore a much more serviceable element.

The main achievement of the young scholars was the so-called "literary revolution" (1917–1919), the logically necessary application of the political revolution in the field of education. The new "vernacular" took place of the old "classical" literary language. The language of the classical works is so remote from the language of daily life that no uneducated person can understand it. A command of it requires a full knowledge of all the ancient literature, entailing decades of study. The gentry had elaborated this style of speech for themselves and their dependants; it was their monopoly; nobody who did not belong to the gentry and had not attended its schools could take part in literary or in administrative life. The literary revolution, the leader of which was Professor Hu Shih, introduced the language of daily life, the language of the people, into literature: newspapers, novels, scientific treatises, translations, appeared in the vernacular, and could thus be understood by anyone who could read and

write, even if he had no other Confucianist educatio[n.]
This movement has had and continues to have enormou[s]
results. To-day public opinion is divided into two mai[n]
groups, one of which (politically on the Left) advocate[s]
the general introduction and use of the vernacular i[n]
every branch of writing; the other is for retaining th[e]
vernacular only in parts of the newspaper, but for th[e]
rest advocates a modernized literary language, simplifie[d]
and brought nearer to the vernacular, to be the languag[e]
of essays and poems and official publications, and also o[f]
the news columns. They claim that a radical adoptio[n]
of the vernacular would be inartistic, and would als[o]
reveal local differences, and finally, and especially, tha[t]
it is too long-winded and would waste much space an[d]
paper. The literary language with its great concisenes[s]
does in fact use only half the space needed for the vernacular.

In any case, it may be said that the literary revolution has achieved its main objects. As a consequence of it, a great quantity of new literature has been published. Not only is every important new book that appears in the West published in translation within a few months, but modern novels and short stories and poems have been written, some of them of high literary value.

At the same time as this revolution there took place another fundamental change in the language. It was necessary to take over a vast number of new scientific and technical terms. As Chinese, owing to the character of its script, is unable to adopt foreign words, and can do no more than provide a rather rough paraphrase, the practice was started of expressing all new ideas by newly formed native words. Thus modern Chinese had no foreign words, and yet it has all the new ideas. For example, a telegram is a "lightning-letter"; a wireless telegram is a "not-have-wire-lightning-communication"; a fountain-pen is a "self-flow-ink-water-brush"; a typewriter is a "strike-letter-machine". Most of these neologisms are similar in the modern languages of China and Japan.

There had been several proposals in recent decades to

o away with the Chinese characters and to introduce an lphabet in their place. They have all failed so far, because ie character of the Chinese language is unsuited to an lphabetical script. They would also destroy China's ultural unity: there are many dialects in China that iffer so greatly from each other that, for instance, a man rom Canton cannot understand a man from Shanghai. f Chinese were written with European letters, the result vould be a Canton literature and another literature conined to Shanghai, and China would break up into a number f areas with different languages. The old Chinese writing s independent of pronunciation. A Cantonese and a Pekinger can read each other's newspapers without difficulty. They pronounce the words quite differently, but the neaning is unaltered. Even a Japanese can read a Chinese newspaper without special study of Chinese, and a Chinese vith a little preparation can read a Japanese newspaper vithout understanding a single word of Japanese.

The aim of modern education in China is to work toward the establishment of "High Chinese", the former official (Mandarin) language, throughout the country, and to set limits to the use of the various dialects. Once this has been done, it will be possible to proceed to a reform of the script without running the risk of political separatist movements, which are always liable to spring up, and also without leading, through the adoption of various dialects as the basis of separate literatures, to the break-up of China's cultural unity.

2 *Fighting between generals*

The situation of the Republic after its foundation was far from hopeful. Republican feeling existed only among the very small groups of students who had been educated in Europe or by Europeans, and a few traders, in other words, among the "middle class". And even in the revolutionary party to which these groups belonged there were the most various conceptions of the form of republican State to be aimed at. The Left wing of the party, mainly intellectuals and manual workers, had in view more or less vague socialistic institutions; the Liberals, for instance the traders thought of a liberal democracy, more or less on the American pattern; and the nationalists merely wanted the removal of the alien Manchu rule. The three groups had come together for the practical reason that only so could they get rid of the dynasty. They gave unreserved allegiance to Sun Yat-sen as their leader, although he belonged rather to the Left. He succeeded in mobilizing the enthusiasm of continually widening circles for action, not only by the integrity of his aims but also because he was able to present the new socialistic ideology in an alluring form. The anti-republican gentry, however, whose power was not yet entirely broken, took a stand against the party. The generals who had gone over to the Republicans had not the slightest intention of founding a Republic, but only wanted to get rid of the rule of the Manchus and to step into their place. This was true also of Yüan Shih-k'ai, who in his heart was entirely on the side of the gentry, although the European press especially had always energetically defended him. In character and capacity he stood far above the other generals, but he was no republican.

Thus the first period of the Republic, until 1927, was marked by incessant attempts by individual generals to make themselves independent. The Government could not depend on its soldiers, and so was impotent. The first risings of military units began at the outset of 1912. The governors and generals who wanted to make themselves independent sabotaged every decree of the central government; especially they sent it no money from the provinces and also refused to give their assent to foreign loans. The province of Canton, the actual birthplace of the republican movement and the focus of radicalism, declared itself in 1912 an independent Republic. In the western provinces of Shensi and Kansu the Mongol Hsiung-yün ruled as viceroy with the support of the native Mohammedans (Dungans); he was entirely against the government, and only after long negotiations did it become possible to conclude a sort of armistice with him.

Within the Peking government matters soon came to a limax. Yüan Shih-k'ai and his supporters represented he Conservative view, with the unexpressed but obvious im of setting up a new imperial house and continuing the ld gentry system. Most of the members of Parliament ame, however, from the middle class and were opposed o any reaction of this sort. One of their leaders was murlered, and the blame was thrown upon Yüan Shih-k'ai; here then came, in the middle of 1912, a new revolution, n which the radicals made themselves independent and ried to gain control of South China. But Yüan Shih-k'ai ommanded better troops and won the day. At the end of October 1912 he was elected, against the Opposition, s president of China, and the new State was recognized y foreign countries.

China's internal difficulties reacted on the border States, n which the European Powers were keenly interested. The Powers considered that the time had come to begin the definitive partition of China. Thus there were long negotiations and also hostilities between China and Tibet, which was supported by Great Britain. The British demanded the complete separation of Tibet from China, but the Chinese rejected this (1912); the rejection was supported by a boycott of British goods. In the end the Tibet question was left undecided. Tibet remained until recent years almost independent of China, but was able to elude repeated British attempts at bringing influence to bear, countering them by coming closer to China. The changes resulting from the war with Japan (1937–1945) ultimately brought a Sino-Tibetan *rapprochement*. The eastern part of Tibet became a Chinese province (Sikang); it has attracted a great number of Chinese settlers, and no doubt will soon be a purely Chinese territory. This, however, has brought Tibet herself closer to China than before 1912.

In Outer Mongolia Russian interests predominate. In 1911 there were diplomatic incidents in connexion with the Mongolian question. At the end of 1911 the Hutuktn of Urga declared himself independent, and the Chinese were expelled from the country. A secret treaty was cor cluded in 1912 with Russia, under which Russia recognize the independence of Outer Mongolia, but was accorde an important part as adviser and helper in the develop ment of the country. In 1913 a Russo-Chinese treaty wa concluded, under which the autonomy of Outer Mongoli was recognized, but Mongolia became a part of the Chines realm. After the Russian revolution had begun, revolutio broke out also in Mongolia. The country suffered all th horrors of the struggles between White Russians (Genera Ungern-Sternberg) and the Reds; there were also Chines attempts at intervention, though without success, unti in the end Mongolia became an independent Soviet Repub lic. As such she is closely associated with Soviet Russia Nationalist China, however, did not recognize Mongolia's independence, and in his work *China's Destiny* (1944) Chiang Kai-shek insisted that China's aim remains the recovery of the frontiers of 1840, which means among other things the recovery of Outer Mongolia. In spite of this, after the second world war Chiang Kai-shek had to renounce *de jure* all rights in Outer Mongolia. Inner Mongolia was always united to China much more closely; only for a time during the war with Japan did the Japanese maintain there a puppet government ("Mongukuo"). The disappearance of this government was almost unnoticed. The Nationalist government of Chiang Kai-shek and its satellites made a brief attempt to recover Inner Mongolia, and it then came under the domination of Communist China.

At the time when Russian penetration into Mongolia began, Japan had entered upon a similar course in Manchuria, which she regarded as her "sphere of influence". On the outbreak of the first world war Japan occupied the former German-leased territory of Tsingtao, at the extremity of the province of Shantung, and from that point she occupied the railways of the province. Her plan was to make the whole province a protectorate; Shantung is rich in coal and especially in metals. Japan's plans were revealed in the notorious "Twenty-one Demands"

1915). Against the furious opposition especially of the students of Peking, Yüan Shih-k'ai's government accepted the greater part of these demands. In negotiations with Great Britain, in which Japan took advantage of the British commitments in Europe, Japan had to be conceded the predominant position in the Far East.

Meanwhile Yüan Shih-k'ai had made all preparations for turning the Republic once more into an empire, in which he would be emperor; the empire was to be based once more on the gentry group. In 1914 he secured an amendment of the Constitution under which the governing power was to be entirely in the hands of the president; at the end of 1914 he secured his appointment as president for life, and at the end of 1915 he induced the Parliament to resolve that he should become emperor.

This naturally aroused the resentment of the republicans, but it also annoyed the generals belonging to the gentry, who had had the same ambition. Thus there were disturbances, especially in the south, where Sun Yat-sen with his followers agitated for a democratic republic. Foreign Powers intervened. Japan recognized that a divided China would be much easier to penetrate and annex than a united China, and accordingly she opposed Yüan Shih-k'ai. At the beginning of 1916 the monarchy was brought again to an end. Shortly after this Yüan Shih-k'ai was assassinated, at the hands, it was rumoured, of agents of Japan.

He was succeeded as president by Li Yüan-hung. Meanwhile five provinces had declared themselves independent. Foreign pressure on China steadily grew. She was forced to declare war on Germany, and though this made no practical difference to the war, it enabled the European Powers to penetrate further into China. Difficulties grew to such an extent in 1917 that a dictatorship was set up (that of Sü Shi-ch'ang), and soon after came actually the recall of the Manchus and the reinstatement of the deposed emperor (July 1st–8th, 1917).

This led to various risings of generals, each aiming simply at the satisfaction of his thirst for personal power.

Ultimately the victorious group of generals, headed b; Tuan Ch'i-jui, secured the election of Fêng Kuo-chang i place of the retiring president. Fêng was succeeded at th end of 1918 by Hsü Shih-ch'ang, who held office unti 1922. Hsü, as a former ward of the emperor, was a typica representative of the gentry, and was opposed to all repub lican reforms.

The south held aloof from these northern governments In Canton an opposition government was set up, formed mainly of followers of Sun Yat-sen; the Peking governmen was unable to remove the Canton government. But the Peking government and its president scarcely counted any longer even in the north. All that counted were the generals, the most prominent of whom were: (1) Chang Tso-lin, who had control of Manchuria and had made certain terms with Japan, but who was ultimately murdered by the Japanese (1928); (2) Wu P'ei-fu, who held North China; (3) the so-called "Christian general", Fêng Yü-hsiang, and (4) Ts'ao K'un, who became president in 1923.

At the end of the first world war Japan had a hold over China amounting almost to military control of the country. China did not sign the Treaty of Versailles, because she considered that she had been duped by Japan, since Japan had driven the Germans out of China but had not returned the liberated territory to the Chinese. In 1921 peace was concluded with Germany, the German privileges being abolished. The same applied to Austria. Russia, immediately after the setting up of the Soviet government, had renounced all her rights under the Capitulations. This was the first step in the gradual rescinding of the Capitulations; the last of them went only in 1943, as a consequence of the difficult situation of the Europeans and Americans in the Pacific produced by the second world war.

At the end of the first world war the foreign Powers revised their attitude toward China. The idea of territorial partitioning of the country was replaced by an attempt at financial exploitation; military friction between the Western Powers and Japan was in this way to be minimized. Financial control was to be exercised by an international banking consortium (1920). It was necessary for political reasons that this committee should be joined by Japan. After her Twenty-one Demands, however, Japan was hated throughout China. During the world war she had given loans to the various governments and rebels, and in this way had secured one privilege after another. Consequently China declined the banking consortium. She tried to secure capital from her own resources; but in the existing political situation and the acute economic depression internal loans had no success.

In an agreement between the United States and Japan in 1917, the United States, in consequence of the war, had had to give their assent to special rights for Japan in China. After the war the international conference at Washington (November 1921–February 1922) tried to set narrower limits to Japan's influence over China, and also to re-determine the relative strength in the Pacific of the four Great Powers (America, Britain, France, Japan). After the failure of the banking plan this was the last means of preventing military conflicts between the Powers in the Far East. This brought some relief to China, as Japan had to yield for the time to the pressure of the Western Powers.

The years that followed until 1927 were those of the complete collapse of the political power of the Peking government—years of entire dissolution. In the south Sun Yat-sen had been elected Generalissimo in 1921. In 1924 he was re-elected with a mandate for a campaign against the north. In 1924 there also met in Canton the first general congress of the Kuomintang ("People's Party"). From the middle-class parties of the south a new party, the Chinese Communist Party, had broken away; it joined the Kuomintang, so that a "Popular Front" was created. The Kuomintang (in 1929 it had 653,000 members, or roughly 0.15 per cent. of the population!) is the continuation of the Komingtang ("Revolutionary Party") founded by Sun Yat-sen, which as a middle-class party had worked for the removal of the dynasty. The new Kuomintang was much more socialistic, as is shown by its admission of the Communists.

At the end of 1924 Sun Yat-sen with some of his followers went to Peking, to discuss the possibility of a reunion between north and south on the basis of the programme of the People's Party. There, however, he died at the beginning of 1925 (he was born in 1866), before any definite results had been attained; there was no prospect of achieving anything by the negotiations, and the south broke them off. But the death of Sun Yat-sen had been followed after a time by tension within the party between its Right and Left wings. The southern government had invited a number of Russian advisers in 1923 to assist in building up the administration, civil and military, and on their advice the system of government had been reorganized on lines similar to those of the soviet and commissar system. This change had been advocated by an old friend of Sun Yat-sen, Chiang Kai-shek, who later married Sun's sister-in-law. Chiang Kai-shek, who was born in 1886, was the head of the military academy at Whampoa, near Canton, where Russian instructors were at work. The new system was approved by Sun Yat-sen's successor, Hu Han-min (who died in 1936), in his capacity of party leader. It was opposed by the elements of the Right, who at first had little influence. Chiang Kai-shek soon became one of the principal leaders of the south, as he had command of the efficient troops of Canton, who had been organized by the Russians.

The People's Party of the south and its governments, at that time fairly radical in politics, were disliked by the foreign Powers; only Japan supported them for a time, owing to the anti-British feeling of the South Chinese and in order to further her purpose of maintaining disunion in China. The first serious collision with the outer world came on May 30th, 1925, when British soldiers shot at a crowd demonstrating in Shanghai. This produced a widespread boycott of British goods in Canton and in British Hong Kong, inflicting an enormous loss on British trade with China and bringing great advantages in consequence to Japanese trade and shipping: from the time of this boycott began the Japanese grip on Chinese coastwise shipping.

The second party congress was held in Canton in 1926.

Chiang Kai-shek already played a prominent part. The Communists were expelled from the party; on the other hand, the Right wing held a separate congress in Shanghai. The remainder of the Cantonese People's Party, with the support of the Communists, began the great campaign in the north under Chiang Kai-shek. At first it had good success: the various provincial governors and generals and the Peking government were played off against each other, and in a short time one leader after another was defeated. The Yangtze was reached, and in 1926 the southern government moved to Hankow. All over the southern provinces there now came a genuine rising of the masses of the people, mainly the result of Communist propaganda and of the government's promise to give land to the peasants, to set limits to the big estates, and to bring order into the taxation. In spite of its Communist element, at the beginning of 1927 the southern government was essentially one of the middle class and the peasantry, with a socialistic tendency.

3 *The re-unification of China*

With the continued success of the northern campaign, and with Chiang Kai-shek's southern army at the gates of Shanghai (March 21st, 1927), a decision had to be taken. Should the Left wing be allowed to gain the upper hand, and the great capitalists of Shanghai be expropriated as it was proposed to expropriate the gentry? Or should the Right wing prevail, an alliance be concluded with the capitalists, and limits be set to the expropriation of landed estates? Chiang Kai-shek, through his marriage with Sun Yat-sen's wife's sister, had become allied with one of the greatest banking families. In the days of the siege of Shanghai Chiang, together with his closest colleagues (with the exception of Hu Han-min and Wang Ch'ing-wei, a leader who will be mentioned later), decided on the second alternative. As a result Shanghai came into his hands without a struggle, and the capital of the Shanghai financiers, and soon foreign capital as well, was placed at his disposal, so that he was able to pay his troops and finance his administration. At the same time the Russian advisers were dismissed or executed.

The decision arrived at by Chiang Kai-shek and his friends did not remain unopposed. The "Left group" parted from him (1927) and formed a rival government in Hankow, while Chiang Kai-shek made Nanking the seat of his government (April 1927). In that year Chiang not only concluded peace with the financiers and industrialists, but also a sort of "armistice" with the landowning gentry. "Land reform" still stood on the party programme, but nothing was done, and in this way the confidence and co-operation of large sections of the gentry was secured. This made it possible to enter into negotiation with the generals belonging to the northern gentry, and Chiang began these in 1927. The choice of Nanking as the new capital pleased both the industrialists and the agrarians: the great bulk of China's young industries lay in the Yangtze region, and that region was still the principal one for agricultural produce; the landowners of the region were also in a better position with the great market of the capital in their neighbourhood.

The Left wing remained in Hankow, in the centre of the Yangtze region. There were long and tedious negotiations, in which Wang Ch'ing-wei, who had returned from abroad, took part (with Hu Han-min and Chiang Kai-shek he had been a fellow-worker of Sun Yat-sen's since 1906). Wang's position now was that of a middle-class Socialist. Owing to the increasing pressure, however, of the Nanking government, which was gradually finding more and more support from the gentry and the middle class of Hankow, that city had to be given up. The Left government at Hankow, which had now become yet more radical, withdrew into the province of Kiangsi; there a Socialist State was founded, and land reform received special attention. There were constant struggles, until in 1934 the pressure became so strong that Kiangsi had to be abandoned, and in an adventurous march the "Red Army" fought its way right through western China into the province of Shensi. There a new Socialist State was founded, with Yenan as its capital.

Meanwhile the Nanking government had succeeded in carrying its dealings with the northern generals to a point at which they were largely out-manoeuvred and became ready for some sort of collaboration (1928). There were now four supreme commanders—Chiang Kai-shek, Fêng Yü-hsiang (the "Christian general"), Yen Hsi-shan, the very successful governor of Shansi, and Li Chung-yen. Naturally this was not a permanent solution; not only did Chiang Kai-shek's three rivals try to free themselves from his ever-growing influence and to gain full power themselves, but various groups under military leadership rose again and again, even in the home of the Republic, Canton itself. These struggles, which were carried on more by means of diplomacy and bribery than at arms, lasted until 1936. Chiang Kai-shek, as by far the most skilful player in this gigantic game, and at the same time the man who had the support of the foreign governments and of the financiers of Shanghai, gained the victory. China was unified under his dictatorship.

As early as 1928, when there seemed a possibility of uniting China, with the exception of the "Communist" Kiangsi and of Manchuria, which was dominated by Japan, and when the European Powers began more and more to support Chiang Kai-shek, Japan felt that her interests in North China were threatened, and landed troops in Shantung. There was hard fighting on May 3rd, 1928. General Chang Tso-lin, in Manchuria, who was allied to Japan, endeavoured to secure a cessation of hostilities, but he fell victim to a Japanese assassin; his place was taken by his son, Chang Hsüeh-liang, who pursued an anti-Japanese policy. The Japanese recognized, however, that in view of the international situation the time had not yet come for intervention in North China. In 1929 they withdrew their troops and concentrated instead on their plans for Manchuria.

Until the time of the "Manchurian incident" (1931), the Nanking government steadily grew in strength. It gained the confidence of the Western Powers, who proposed to make use of it in opposition to Japan's policy of expansion in the Pacific sphere. On the strength of this favourable situation in its foreign relations, the Nanking government succeeded in getting rid of one after another of the Capitulations. Above all, the administration of the "Marine Customs", that is to say of the collection of duties on imports and exports, was brought under the control of the Chinese government: until then it had been under foreign control. Now that China could act with more freedom in the matter of tariffs, the government had greater financial resources, and through this and other measures it became financially more independent of the provinces. It succeeded in building up a small but thoroughly modern army, entirely loyal to the government and superior to the still existing provincial armies. This army gained its military experience in skirmishes with the Communists and the remaining generals.

It is true that when in 1931 the Japanese occupied Manchuria, Nanking was helpless, since Manchuria was only loosely associated with Nanking, and its governor, Chang Hsüeh-liang, had tried to remain independent of it. Thus Manchuria was lost almost without a blow. On the other hand, the fighting with Japan that broke out soon afterwards in Shanghai brought credit to the young Nanking army, though owing to its numerical inferiority it was unsuccessful. China protested to the League of Nations against its loss of Manchuria. The League sent a commission (the Lytton Commission), which condemned Japan's action, but nothing further happened, and China indignantly broke away from her association with the Western Powers (1932–1933). In view of the tense European situation (the beginning of the Hitler era in Germany, and the Italian plans of expansion), the Western Powers did not want to fight Japan on China's behalf, and without that nothing more could be done. They pursued, indeed, a policy of playing off Japan against China, in order to keep those two Powers occupied with each other, and so to divert Japan from Indo-China and the Pacific.

China had thus to be prepared for being involved one day in a great war with Japan. The Communist view was that the sooner the war came the better. The Japanese would undoubtedly succeed in conquering eastern China, and so in throwing Chiang Kai-shek out of his strong position; this would alter the balance of power in their favour, and with Russia's aid they might be able to build up a unified Left-wing China and to lead it against Japan. Chiang Kai-shek, on the other hand, wanted to postpone war as long as possible. He wanted time to establish his power more thoroughly within the country, and to strengthen his army. In regard to external relations, the great Powers would have to decide their attitude sooner or later. America could not be expected to take up a clear attitude: she was was for peace and commerce, and she made greater profits out of her relations with Japan than with China; she sent supplies to both (until 1941). On the other hand, Britain and France were more and more turning away from Japan, and Russo-Japanese relations were at all times tense. Japan tried to emerge from her isolation by joining the Axis Powers (1936); but it was still doubtful whether the Western Powers would proceed with Russia, and therefore against Japan, or with the Axis, and therefore in alliance with Japan.

Japan for her part considered that if she was to raise the standard of living of her large population and to remain a world power, she must bring into being her "Greater East Asia", so as to have the needed raw material sources and export markets in the event of a collision with the Western Powers; in addition to this, she needed a security girdle as extensive as possible in case of a conflict with Russia. In any case, "Greater East Asia" must be secured before the European conflict broke out.

4 *The Sino-Japanese war* (1937–1945)

Accordingly, from 1933 onward Japan followed up her conquest of Manchuria by bringing her influence to bear in Inner Mongolia and in North China. She succeeded first, by means of an immense system of smuggling, currency manipulation, and propaganda, in bringing a number of Mongol princes over to her side, and then (at the end of 1935) in establishing a semi-dependent government in North China. Chiang Kai-shek took no action.

The signal for the outbreak of war was an "incident" by the Marco Polo Bridge, south of Peking (July 7th, 1937). The Japanese government profited by a quite unimportant incident, undoubtedly provoked by the Japanese, in order to extend its dominion a little further. China still hesitated; there were negotiations. Japan brought up reinforcements and put forward demands which China could not be expected to be ready to fulfil. Japan then occupied Peking and Tientsin and wide regions between them and south of them. The Chinese soldiers stationed there withdrew almost without striking a blow, but formed up again and began to offer resistance. In order to facilitate the planned occupation of North China, including the province of Shantung, Japan decided on a diversionary campaign against Shanghai. The Nanking government sent its best troops to the new front, and held it for nearly three months against superior forces; but meanwhile the Japanese steadily advanced in North China. On November 9th Nanking fell into their hands. By the beginning of January 1938, the province of Shantung had also been conquered.

Chiang Kai-shek and his government fled to Ch'ung-k'ing (Chungking), the most important commercial and financial centre of the interior after Hankow, which was soon threatened by the Japanese fleet. By means of a number of landings the Japanese soon conquered the whole coast of China, so cutting off all supplies to the country; against hard fighting in some places they pushed inland along the railways and conquered the whole eastern half of China, the richest and most highly developed part of the country. Chiang Kai-shek had the support only of the agriculturally rich province of Szechwan, and of the scarcely developed provinces surrounding it. Here there was as yet no industry. Everything in the way of machinery and supplies that could be transported from the hastily dismantled factories was carried westwards. Students and professors went west with all the contents of their universities, and worked on in small villages under very difficult conditions—one of the most memorable achievements of this war for China! But all this was by no means enough for waging a defensive war against Japan. Even the famous Burma Road could not save China.

The Communists in the north-west were in a similar plight. They, too, fought well against the Japanese, and by the guerrilla warfare which they soon started they inflicted great losses on them. But they, too, were without an industry of their own; the road to Russia through Mongolia was cut by the Japanese, and the route through Turkestan was too difficult to be able to influence the conduct of the war. China's situation was made worse by the antagonism between Chiang Kai-shek and the Communists; both sides would probably have been glad to make some sort of peace between them, but each distrusted the other and both were simply waiting for a chance, in spite of the war, to pay off old scores. Thus Chiang Kai-shek kept a large part of his best troops throughout the war on the line of demarcation facing the Communists, without using them against the Japanese.

By 1940–1941 Japan had attained her war aim: China was no longer a dangerous adversary. She was still able to engage in small-scale fighting, but could no longer secure any decisive result. Puppet governments were set up in Peking, Canton, and Nanking, and the Japanese waited for these governments gradually to induce supporters of Chiang Kai-shek to come over to their side. Most was expected of Wang Ching-wei, who headed the new Nanking government. He was one of the oldest followers of Sun Yat-sen, and was regarded as a democrat. In 1925, after Sun Yat-sen's death, he had been for a time the head of the Nanking government, and for a short time in 1930 he had led a government in Peking that was opposed to Chiang Kai-shek's dictatorship. Beyond any question Wang still had many followers, including some in the highest circles at Chungking, men of eastern China who considered that collaboration with Japan, especially in the economic field, offered good prospects. Japan paid lip service to this policy: there was talk of sister peoples, which could help each other and supply each other's needs. There was propaganda for a new "Greater East Asian" philosophy, *Wang-tao*, in accordance with which all the peoples of the East could live together in peace under a thinly disguised dictatorship. What actually happened was that everywhere Japanese capitalists established themselves in the former Chinese industrial plants, bought up land and securities, and exploited the country for the conduct of their war.

After the great initial successes of Hitlerite Germany in 1939–1941, Japan became convinced that the time had come for a decisive blow against the positions of the Western European Powers and the United States in the Far East. Lightning blows were struck at Hong Kong and Singapore. at French Indo-China, and at the Netherlands East Indies. The American navy seemed to have been eliminated by the attack on Pearl Harbour, and one group of islands after another fell into the hands of the Japanese. Japan was at the gates of India and Australia. Russia was carrying on a desperate defensive struggle against the Axis, and there was no reason to expect any intervention from her in the Far East. Greater East Asia seemed assured against every danger.

The situation of Chiang Kai-shek's Chungking government seemed hopeless. Even the Burma Road was cut, and supplies could only be sent by air; there was shortage of everything. With immense energy small industries were begun all over western China, often organized as co-operatives; roads and railways were built—but with such resources would it ever be possible to throw the Japanese into the sea? Everything depended on holding out until a new page was turned in Europe. Infinitely slow seemed the progress of the first gleams of hope—the steady front in Burma, the reconquest of the first groups of islands; the first bomb attacks on Japan itself. Even in May, 1945, with the war ended in Europe, there seemed no sign of its ending in the Far East. Then came the atom bomb, bringing the collapse of Japan; the Japanese armies receded from China, and suddenly China was free, mistress once more in her own country as she had not been for decades.

5 *The outlook*

Yet all the problems had not been solved. A war solves no problems, especially to-day, when there is no longer any country living in isolation, and every event anywhere in the world affects us all.

In spite of all the loss of human lives, all the misery and want and destruction, the war had its good side: the undeveloped west of China had awakened. Chinese capitalists had invested in the west the resources they brought from the east, and new industries had started there. Never again will the west be the mere hinterland of the coast that it was, even if part of the capital should flow back into the liberated east.

The question is, will it be used for the good of this sorely tried and desperately poor country? This depends on several things. China has always been without sufficient capital, and has always had difficulty in balancing its Budget. The war accelerated inflation, that dangerous specific of all governments that think only of short-term results. The Chinese dollar had for years been slowly falling in value; Chiang Kai-shek's government, inefficient and corrupt, allowed it to become a worthless paper. Millions of foreign loans disappeared without any visible effect on the Budget or the financing of the war. Will a sound and stable currency be successfully built up in the near future, and will it be possible to find means of investing foreign loans with as much benefit to China as the Marshall aid has brought to some European countries? Or will China, under Communist rule, try to find a new way of building up a modern State without capital and loans?

Chiang Kai-shek has had to leave Nanking and his "People's Party". Will that child of his, which has unfortunately inherited many of the qualities of Chiang and his clique, be able to reform itself and become progressive, efficient, and incorruptible; or will all China come under a Communist régime? Even in this case, Mao Tse-tung and his friends will be faced with the same problem. They might be backed by active Russian intervention, just as Chiang had American help, but this alone cannot solve their problems.

If what happened in China in 1946–48 had happened two or more centuries ago, our judgment would have been quite clear: it would have been that Nationalist China collapsed because its internal problems, especially the land problem, had proved insoluble. Revolt came as a result, and the revolutionaries succeeded because they made a new division of the land, eliminated the corrupt officials, and, at first at all events, replaced them by honest and relatively efficient ones. But the present movement is no longer a simple popular uprising of the type of the T'ai P'ing rebellion of the nineteenth century. The Communist movement, dating from the separation in 1927 of the Left from the Right wing of the People's Party, has relations with Russia. It is not merely a popular rising of Chinese peasants, but also part of an international movement.

Some may say: "Just as the United States are bound to help any Liberal or Right-wing government in China, just as it helped Chiang Kai-shek in spite of the bitter criticism which in America followed the wartime enthusiasm for China, so now Russia is bound to assist the Communist government of China. China is a tool in either case." But that is over-simplifying the issue. China has problems of her own, and those problems demand specific solutions. Even within the general framework of Communism, those solutions will be Chinese, even more than Yugoslavia's solutions have been her own. China has to be modernized, to be industrialized. In the years ahead of us Russia will be much too absorbed in her own reconstruction to be able to send machinery to China on any reasonably adequate scale. How, then, can China be industrially equipped? She has also to undergo a land reform. Even the members of the People's Party have been well aware of that. But land redistribution will not alone suffice. Even if the thirty per cent. of China's peasants who are tenant cultivators become the owners of their holdings once more, they will remain almost as poor as before. Nor can salvation be expected from organizing them in collective farms.

China does not produce enough. Who will send her rice and grain, and what will she be able to export in payment? Every change in the social order at first tends to diminish production. Indo-China used to export to China, but she is in turmoil and cannot export now. Russia cannot export, quite apart from the immense difficulties of transportation. Whoever becomes the ruler of China will have to find a solution for her practical problems; whoever it may be, they will be the same problems, and he will perforce be more concerned with the finding of practical solutions for them than with following any sort of ideological theory. Here, I think, is a key to the understanding of China's immediate future.

BIBLIOGRAPHICAL NOTES

These notes are not a bibliography; they are intended merely to give the student the opportunity of pursuing further the questions touched on in this book. References to the well-known Chinese sources, mainly the "Twenty-four Annals" are not given. In special cases these can be found in my other publications which are mentioned below.

Chapter 1

The way has been paved for the true valuation of the Chinese accounts of the earliest period by the Chinese scholar Ku Chieh-kang (*Ku-shih-pien, Discussions on Ancient History*, 7 volumes, in Chinese) and by H. Maspero ("Les légendes mythologiques dans le Chou king", *Journal Asiatique* 1924). Chinese legends have recently also been studied by B. Karlgren ("Legends and Cults in Ancient China", *Bulletin of the Museum of Far Eastern Antiquities* No. 18, Stockholm 1946; cf. *Artibus Asiae*, vol. 9, 1946, pp. 355–364).

The demonstration that the dates given in regard to the earliest period in the Chinese sources are wrong, and were calculated at a later time, has been given long ago by the Japanese scholars Ijima Tadao and Shinjô Shinzô (for a bibliography cf. *Asia Major*, vol. 9, 1933, pp. 597–611) and in my article "Der Beginn der Chou-Zeit" (*Sinica* 1933, pp. 182–188). These results are still disregarded by Chinese astronomers and historians such as Liu Ch'ao-yang (*Studia Serica, Monographs, Series B*, No. 2 and No. 3, Ch'eng-tu 1944 and 1945) and Fu Szû-nien. See my review in *Orians* (vol. 2, No. 1, Leiden 1950).

On the Peking Man and the paleolithic age we have now the comprehensive books of H. L. Movins ("The Lower Palaeolithic Cultures of Southern and Eastern Asia", *Transact. American Philosoph. Society*, vol. 38, part 4, 1948) and W. W. Howells: *Early Man in the Far East* (Stud. in Physical Anthropology No. 1, Detroit 1949). The results of these books modify certain details of our description which was based mainly upon the researches of H. Weidenreich (see, f.i., his article in the *American Anthropologist*, vol. 42, pp. 375–383) and of Teilhard de Chardin (see, f.i., his article in *L'Anthropologie*, vol. 35, pp. 201 sqq. and his later works). For the regions bordering on North China and for the province of Shantung the works of Riuzô Torii (in the *Journal of the College of Science, Imp. University of Tôkyô*, vol. 36, No. 4 and later) and Ichiro Yawata ("Contribution to the Prehistoric Archaeology of Southern Jehol", *Report of the First Scientific Expedition to Manchukuo* 1933, Section 6, Part 1, Tôkyô 1935) are useful.

For the neolithic age there is now the standard work of J. G. Andersson (*Researches into the Prehistory of the Chinese*, Stockholm 1943) with its references to further literature.

Theories on the origin of Chinese civilization, taking into account the results of excavations, have been put forward especially by O. Menghin (*Die Weltgeschichte der Steinzeit*, Wien 1933), R. Heine-Geldern (in his article in the *Anthropos* 1932, pp. 559 sqq.), C. W. Bishop (*Origin of Far Eastern Civilization*, Washington 1942) and W. Eberhard ("Early Chinese Cultures and their Development", *Smithsonian Report for* 1937, and in a revised form in *Lokalkulturen im alten China*, 2 volumes, Leiden and Peking 1943).

The obsolete theories, no longer tenable, on the Hsia dynasty are still to be found in many books and articles (a typical example is A. Forke: "Yao, Schun und Yü", *Asia Major, Neue Folge*, vol. 1, pp. 1–55, Leipzig 1944). Of importance is the article by E. Erkes ("Ist die Hsia-Dynastie géschichtlich?" *T'oung Pao* 1937, pp. 34 sqq.). A new start has been made by Ku Chieh-kang ("Three Papers on the History of Hsia", *Historical Annual*, vol. 2, No. 3, Peiping 1936; in Chinese).

Chapter 2

For this period, H. G. Creel's book (*The Birth of China*, New York 1935) is still a classic. All earlier books on this period are entirely out of date. Of great importance in regard to the Shang bronzes are the special articles by B. Karlgren (in the *Bulletin of the Museum of Far Eastern Antiquities*, vol. 8 and later volumes) and M. Loehr (in *Oriental Art*, vol. 1, No. 3, London 1948 and in *Artibus Asiae*, vol. 12, No. 1/2, Ascona 1949). All earlier works on the ancient bronzes and their origin should be used only with the greatest caution. The principal work on the significance of the ornamentation of the bronzes are C. Hentze's books (such as *Die Sakralbronze und ihre Bedeutung in den frühchinesischen Kulturen*, Antwerpen 1941 and his earlier books); his conclusions deserve attention but will certainly be modified and cannot be regarded as conclusive yet.

Chapter 3

For the beginning of the Chou dynasty H. G. Creel's work, mentioned above, should be used. The description in McNair's *China* (United Nations Series, Berkeley 1947) is very valuable as for the first time the attempt is made to make use of the historical data found in Chou inscriptions. The descriptions of H. Maspero (*La Chine Antique*, Paris 1927) and O. Franke (*Geschichte des Chinesichen Reiches*, vol. 1, Berlin 1930) are now antiquated.

Our account of ethnic conditions is based on preliminary studies by G. Haloun ("Contributions to the History of Clan Settlement in Ancient China", *Asia Major* 1924, pp. 76–111 and pp. 587–623) and especially M. Granet (*Festivals and Songs of Ancient China*, London 1932; *Danses et légendes de la Chine ancienne*, Paris 1926; his *Catégories matrimoniales et relations de proximité dans la Chine ancienne*, Paris 1939 has to be read with precaution. It is Granet's weakest work). For an understanding of Chou feudalism, H. Maspero's essay (in the *Revue de l'Institut de Sociologie* 1936, vol. 16, pp. 37–70) is by far better than f.i. Ch'i Ssu-ho's recent study ("A comparison between Chinese and European Feudal Institutions" in the *Yen-ching Journal of Social Studies*, vol. 4, No. 1, 1948, pp. 1–13). In this book, the word "feudalism" is used as H. Maspero or F. Michael (*The Origin of Manchu Rule in China*, Baltimore 1942, p. 48) use it. This means that we do not accept the much broader Marxist definition (see f.i. S. Dubrowsky: "Über das Wesen des Feudalismus" in *Agrarprobleme*, Moscow

1929, p. 214) nor that we accept the theory that the Chou social system was a "proto-feudal society" (see Chen Hanseng: *Frontier Land Systems in Southernmost China*, New York 1949).

For the philosophy of Confucius and Lao-tse, out of the countless works that of Fung Yu-lan (*History of Chinese Philosophy*, London 1937; a second volume is in preparation) is by far the best, though it takes up a "conservative" attitude and makes no attempt at sociological interpretation. The translations of Lao-tse's work are innumerable. A. Waley (*The Way and its Power*, London 1934) deserves special attention for its new interpretation. The question of the age of Lao-tse and his book has been discussed by H. H. Dubs (*JAOS* vol. 61, pp. 215–221) and D. Bodde (*JAOS* vol. 62, pp. 8–13 and vol. 64, pp. 24–27). Some remarks of a sociological nature are to be found in my *Das Tobareich Nordchinas* (Leiden 1949). A different view of the chronological and social question is taken by E. Erkes (in his review of Waley in *Artibus Asiae* vol. 5, 1935, pp. 288–307).

For the period of the Contending States and the transformation then in progress, see M. Granet (*La civilisation chinoise*, Paris 1929 and his *La pensée chinoise*, Paris 1930). The problem of the agrarian system of Late Chou has often been discussed. There was no satisfactory solution. Now, Hsü Chung-shu has offered a new interpretation ("A study on the Ching T'ien System", *Bulletin of Chinese Studies*, vol. 4, part 1, Ch'eng-tu 1944, pp. 121–156; in Chinese) which is the key to the whole agrarian question, including the problem of the legal status of the farmer. Hsü T'ung-hsin (in *Historical Annual*, vol. 1, No. 2, pp. 161–164) gives a good explanation of the origin of family names and the change of the meaning of the term "po-hsing", but so far, the problem of the dissolution of the clans into joint families during the Chou period and the spread of the use of family names has not yet been extensively studied.

We have now a number of good studies on Taoist and other Secret Societies in modern times (f.i. Ch'en Yüan: "New Taoist Societies in the Northern Provinces at the beginning of the Southern Sung Dynasty", *Catholic University of Peking*

Book Series No. 8, 1941, and Li Shih-yü: "Religions secrète contemporianes dans le Nord de la Chine.', *Studia Serica Monographs, Series B. No.* 4, Ch'eng-tu 1948; both in Chinese), but still practically nothing about the early secret societies. Some remarks only in my *Lokalkulturen im alten China* (Leiden and Peking 1943) and some articles by H. H. Dubs (in McNair: *China*, Berkeley 1947 and in *ISIS*, vol. 38, part 1, 1947, pp. 62–86 in his discussion of Chinese alchemy).

Chapter 5

The only reliable book on this period is still D. Bodde's *China's First Unifier* (Leiden 1938). His remarks on the system of administration are especially valuable if short. D. Bodde's later book (*Statesman, Patriot, and General in Ancient China*, New Haven 1940) is also of importance for this period.

In this and the following chapter my theory on the origin of Chinese medieval society or "Gentry society" is given. More can be found in my *Das Tobareich Nordchinas* (Leiden 1949). This theory differs from the concept of an "Oriental Society" or "Asiatic government" as it was called first by K. Marx (in the *New York Daily Tribune*, June 25, 1853). Our criticism is the same as that of A. Bonné (*State and Economics in the Middle East*, London 1948). The main publications on the theory of "Oriental Society" are written by K. A. Wittfogel ("Foundations and stages of Chinese Economic History", *Zeitschr. f. Sozialforschung*, vol. 4, 1935; "Die Theorie der orientalischen Gesellschaft", *Zeitschr. f. Sozialforschung*, vol. 7, 1938; "The Society of Prehistoric China", *Zeitschr. f. Sozialforschung*, vol. 8, 1939) and Ch'i Ch'ao-ting (*Key Economic Areas in Chinese History*, London 1936). O. Lattimore's theories are related but original (f.i. his *Inner Asian Frontiers of China*, New York 1940, a book which gives a good interpretation for the relations between China and its nomadic northern neighbours). The history of these northern neighbours has been dealt with in recent years by W. M. MacGovern (*The Early Empires of Central Asia*, Chapel Hill 1939) and R. Grousset (*L'Empire des Steppes*, Paris 1939), but both books are not yet fully satisfactory. Some materials on the tribes in the Far East and their cultural relations to

China are collected in my *Kultur und Siedlung der Randvölker Chinas* (Leiden 1942).

Chapter 6

For this period there are now at least partial translations of the official Chinese annals (H. H. Dubs: *The History of the Former Han Dynasty*, Baltimore 1938 and 1944; further volumes in preparation). For the first part of the Han period and also the preceeding periods there is also the earlier translation by E. Chavannes (*Mémoires historiques de Szu-ma Ts'ien*, 5 vols., Paris 1895–1905). Both works have a special value by their extensive explanations and notes. The best general account of the history of the Han period is O. Franke's *Geschichte des chinesischen Reiches* (vol 1).

On Li K'ui, the creator of Chinese law, see P. Pelliot (*Bull. Ec. fr. d'Extrème-Orient*, vol. 9, p. 124) and O. Franke ("Staatssozialistische Versuche im alten und mittelalterlichen China", *Sitzber. d. Pr. Ak. d. Wiss., phil.-hist. Klasse* 1931, No. 13, p. 226). Franke's article also deals with the economic reforms of Wang Mang. These are described in detail by Hu Shih (in the *Journal of the North China Branch R. As. Soc.* vol. 59, p. 218 sqq.) and better by H. H. Dubs (in *T'oung Pao*, vol. 35, pp. 219–265).

The importance of Tung Chung-shu was first recognized by O. Franke in connection with his new interpretation of the Ch'un-ch'iu ("Das Problem des Tsch'un'ts'iu und Tung Tschung-schu's Tsch'un-ts'iu fan lu", *Mitt. d. Sem. f. Or. Sprachen*, vol. 21, Abt. 1, 1918). Some further remarks on this philosopher in Lin Mou-sheng: *Men and Ideas. An informal history of Chinese political thought*, New York 1942. On the later periods of Han philsophy see E. Balázs: "La crise sociale et la philosophie politique à la fin des Han", *T'oung Pao*, vol. 39, pp. 83–131.

Social life and social stratification during Han time are described by H. Maspero ("La vie privée en Chine à l'époque des Han", *Revue des Arts Asiatiques*, vol. 7, 1931–2) and M. Wilbur (*Slavery in China during the Former Han Dynasty*, Chicago 1943).

On the astronomy and science of the period see W. Eberhard ("Beitraege zur kosmologischen Spekulation der Chinesen in der Han-Zeit", *Baessler-Archiv* 1933, Berlin 1933 and further articles in the *Harvard Journal of Asiatic Studies*, vol. 1, 1934 and *Monumenta Serica*, vol. 2, pp. 149–164; vol.5, pp. 208–262; vol. 7, pp. 242–266). On the textiles and clothing of the period see A. and W. Eberhard (*Die Mode der Han- und Chin-Zeit*, Antwerpen 1945). On Chinese music see C. Sachs: *The Rise of Music in the Ancient World, East and West* (New York 1943, pp. 105–153). This field is not yet adequately studied, some articles written by Chinese scholars except. On Chinese art the works of O. Sirén (*Histoire des Arts anciens de la Chine*, Paris 1929–30; *Chinese Painting. A history of the development of Chinese painting*, London 1933; *The Chinese on the Art of Painting*, Peking 1936 and other books) contain numerous illustrations. See also articles by B. Karlgren (in the *Bulletin of the Museum of Far Eastern Antiquities*) on Han art. On Chinese literature there is at present no book that can be recommended, but two books are in preparation. The field is, of course, covered by many Chinese "Histories of Literature". The best material contains Cheng Chen-to's work, but a more stimulating interpretation is given by Jung Chao-tsu (*Chung-kuo wen-hsüeh-shih ta-kang*, Peking 1935). On the military system of the Han new material has been brought forward by a study of documents recently excavated in Kansu province (Lao K'an: "The Military System of the Han Dynasty as recorded on Wooden Clips", *Bulletin of the Academia Sinica*, vol. 10, 1948; in Chinese).

Chapter 7

(A) Apart from O. Franke (*Geschichte des chinesischen Reiches*, vol. 2–3) there is no work that gives any adequate account of the events. The introduction of Buddhismus into China has been discussed by H. Maspero ("Le Songe et l'Ambassade de l'Empereur Ming", *Bull. Ec. fr. d'Extr.-Orient*, vol. 10).

(B) This account is based mainly on my own researches, only partly published (f.i. "Chronologische Übersicht über die Geschichte der Hunnen in der spaeteren Han-Zeit",

Belleten No. 16, pp. 387–441, Istanbul 1941; "Die Biographien des Liu Yüan und des Liu Ts'ung", *Sinoloji Enstitüsü nesriyati* No. 4, Ankara 1942).

(C) The political development is given by O. Franke (see above). Of the religious movement in this period a good outline is given in J. R. Ware's translations ("The Wei-shu and the Sui-shu on Taoism", *JAOS*, vol. 53, 1933, pp. 215–250; also the parallel translation on Buddhism in T'oung Pao, 1933). The interesting biography of the monk Fo-t'u-teng has been translated by Arthur F. Wright (in *Harvard Journal of As. Studies*, vol. 11, 1948, pp. 321–371).

(D) The material is presented in detail in my *Das Tobareich Nordchinas* (Leiden 1949). The valuable book of Tsukamoto Zenryû (*Shina bukkyôshi kenkyû*, Tôkyô 1942) gives not only an excellent account of the religious situation but also sociological data. Unfortunately, I was not able to see this book when my own account was written.

(E) Material on the Kök-Turks is collected in Ed. Chavannes book (*Documents sur les T'ou-kiue occidentaux*, St. Petersburg 1903).

(F) Yang Lien-sheng ("Notes on the Economic History of the Chin Dynasty", *Harvard Journal of As. Studies*, vol. 9, pp. 112–119) and Ch'üan Han-sheng (Natural Economy in the Medieval Ages of China, *Bulletin Ac. Sinica*, vol. 10, 1948; in Chinese) give some economic and social data for this period. On the literature of the period important material is given in the translations of E. von Zach (*Übersetzungen aus dem Wen-hsüan*, Batavia 1937), L. Giles (*Gems of Chinese Literature*) and G. Margouliès (*La prose artistique en Chine* and *Le Kou-wên chinois*, Paris 1926).

Chapter 8

The beginning of the T'ang dynasty is described by W. Bingham (*The Founding of the T'ang Dynasty*, Washington 1940). Fundamental for the economic history of this period is St. Balázs, ("Beitraege zur Wirtschaftsgeschichte der T'ang-Zeit", *Mitt. d. Sem. f. Orient, Spr.*, Berlin 1931–33), but meanwhile many details have been studied separately (see f.i. Ts'en Chung-mien: "Price Fluctuations of the T'ang

Dynasty" and "Economic Prosperity and Decadence of Yang-chou in the T'ang and Sung Dynasties", both in *Bulletin Ac. Sin.*, vol. 11, 1947). These and similar recent Chinese studies are important from the point-of-view of collecting material rather than from the viewpoint of theory.

For the administrative system and its history see R. des Rotours ("Les grand fonctionnaires des provinces en Chine sour la dynastie des T'ang", *T'oung Pao*, vol. 25, 1928; *Le traité des examens*, Paris 1932 and his later works). For relations with Western Asia see G. Ferrand (*Relations des voyages et textes géographiques*, Paris 1913–14), A. Kuwabara ("On P'u Shou-keng", *Mem Res. Dept. of the Toyo Bunko*, Tokyo 1928). On life in Turkestan L. Ligeti, is vividly informative, but his book has so far only appeared in Hungarian and Turkish (*Bilinmiyen Ic-Asya, Unknown Asia*, Istanbul 1947). See also W. Barthold (*Turkestan down to the Mongol Invasion*, London 1928, and *Zwölf Vorlesungen über die Geschichte der Türken Mittelasiens*, Berlin 1935). E. Bretschneider's translations are still valuable (*Medieval Researches*, 2 volumes, London 1888).

For the religious problems and the foreign religions see Ed. Chavannes and P. Pelliot ("Un traité Manichéen retrouvé en Chine", *Journal Asiatique* 1913), J. J. M. de Groot (*Sectarianism and Religious Persecution in China*, 2 volumes, Amsterdam 1903–4) and A. C. Moule (*Christians in China before the Year 1550*, London 1930).

Some remarks on the "Social Background of the Revolt of Huang Ch'ao" are made by Li Wen-chih (in *Shih-ta yüeh-k'an*, No. 22, Peking 1935; in Chinese), but an extensive study of this revolt does not yet exist.

Chapter 9

(A) On the history and social structure of the tenth century a book of mine is in preparation. So far some articles have been published (f.i. "Some Sociological Remarks on the System of Provincial Administration during the Period of the Five Dynasties", *Studia Serica*, vol. 7, pp. 1–18; Ch'eng-tu 1949; "Some Cultural Traits of the Sha-t'o Turks", *Oriental Art*, vol. 1, pp. 50–55, London 1948; "The Composition of the Leading Political Group During the Five Dynasties", *Asiatische Studien*, vol. 1, pp. 19–28; Bern 1947; "Die Beziehungen der Staten der T'o-pa und der Shat'o zum Ausland", *Annales de l'Université d'Ankara*, vol. 2, pp. 141–216; Ankara 1948).

(B) For economic questions H. Williamson's book (*Wang An-shih*, 2 volumes, London 1935) is of great importance, as is O. Franke's article on the administrative problems of the time ("Der Bericht Wang Ngan-schis von 1058 über Reform des Beamtentums", *Sitzber. d. Pr. Ak. d. Wiss.*, 1931/2), both books primarily dealing with Wang An-shih (see also E. Haenisch's article in *Asia Major, Neue Folge*, vol. 1, pp. 55–74, Leipzig 1944).

Questions of trade and inflation have been studied lately mainly by Chinese scholars (see Ch'üan Han-sheng: "Price fluctuations during the Northern Sung Period", and "Smuggling Trade between the Sung and Kin Kingdoms", both in *Bull. Ac. Sin.*, vol. 11, 1947).

For philosophic questions the handbooks, such as A. Forke's (*Geschichte der mittelalterlichen chinesischen Philosophie*, Hamburg 1934), but especially more recent researches by Fung Yu-lan ("The Rise of Neo-Confucianism and its Borrowings from Buddhism and Taoism", *Harvard Journal of Asiatic Studies*, vol. 7, 1942, pp. 89–125; "The Philosophy of Chu Hsi", *Harvard Journal*, vol. 7, 1942, pp. 1–51; see also D. Bodde's remarks in the *Review of Religion*, 1942, pp. 369–383). Mention should also be made of Huang Siu-ch'i's book, as we have only briefly mentioned this particular aspect of Sung philosophy (*Lu Hsiang-shan, a twelfth-century Chinese idealist Philosopher*, New Haven 1944).

(C. D. F) For the Northern empires K. A. Wittfogel and Fêng Chia-shêng's book *History of Chinese Society, Liao* (Philadelphia 1949) with its accompanying articles (f.i. "Public Office in the Liao Dynasty and the Chinese Examination System", *Harvard Journal of As. Stud.*, vol. 10, 1947, pp. 13–40) is now the standard work.

(E) Very few articles and books in Western languages deal with this period. Some Chinese articles deserve mention, such as the studies by Hsü I-t'ang ("The Development of Hangchow as a Metropolis during the South Sung Dynasty", *Bull. of Chinese Studies*, vol. 4a, pp. 231–288; Ch'eng-tu 1944, and "The Administration of Social Relief in Peaceful Times during the Sung Dynasty", *Bull. Chin. Studies*, vol. 5, pp. 33–48, 1945) and Liu Ming-shu "Evidences from Chinese scources of Suleiman's Records of his Voyages", *Bull. Chin. Studies*, vol. 4a, pp. 171–230, 1944; "Miscellaneous Notes on the Trade and Commercial Relations between Chinese and the South Seas during the Sung Dynasty", *Bull. Chin. Studies*, vol. 5, pp. 49–84, 1945 and "Laws concerning Publication during the Sung Dynasty", *Bull. Chin. Studies*, vol. 5, pp. 95–114).

Chapter 10

The most important original source for the Mongol time is the "Secret History", now translated by E. Haenisch (*Die geheime Geschichte der Mongolen*, Second ed. Leipzig 1948). There are also translations by Palladius, A. Kozin (both into Russian), Shiratori Kurakishi (into Japanese), A. Temir (into Turkish) and P. Pelliot, and numerous studies in connection with the book. For the social history of the period the works of Meng Szû-liang ("Social Classes under the Yuan Dynasty", *Yenching Journal, Monographs* No. 14, Peking; in Chinese) and B. Vladimirtzov (*Le régime social des Mongols*, Paris 1948) and H. Franke (*Geld und Wirtschaft in China unter der Mongolen-Herrschaft*, Leipzig 1949) are the standard works of reference.

Chapter 11

Little serious work has yet been done in the West on the social history of the Ming period. Among the Chinese studies see Wang Ts'ung-wu for the beginning of Ming rule ("The Up-rising of Ming T'ai-tsu", *Bull. Ac. Sin.*, vol. 10, 1948) and Liang Fang-chung ("The Scope of Land Taxation in the Ming Dynasty", *Academia Sinica, Inst. of Social Science*, 1939).

For early West-Eastern relations see now Fr. Jaeger ("Das Buch von den wunderbaren Maschinen", *Asia Major, Neue Folge*, vol. 1, pp. 78–96, 1944); for influences upon

Chinese folk-lore see W. Eberhard ("Studies of Near Eastern and Chinese Folk-tales", *Sinologica*, vol. 1, Basel 1947; to be continued).

For the art of the period many works could be mentioned. Suffice it to mention O. Sirén (*A History of Later Chinese Painting*, 2 vols., London 1938) and R. L. Hobson (*Handbook of the Pottery and Porcelain of the Far East*, Second edition, London 1937).

The great novels and dramas of the Ming period were first translated into French (M. Bazin: *Le Pi-Pa-Ki, ou l'histoire du luth*, Paris 1841; St. Julien: *Si-siang-ki, ou l'histoire du pavillon d'occident*, Geneva 1872–80; St. Julien: *Hoei-lan-ki, ou l'histoire du cercle de craie*, London 1833 and others), later into German (mostly by Fr. Kuhn) and English (P. Buck: *All Men are Brothers*; A. Waley: *Monkey*, London 1946; C. H. Brewitt-Taylor: *San Kuo, or Romance of the Three Kingdoms*, Shanghai 1925, and others). A good survey of the principal dramas is given by L. C. Arlington (*Famous Chinese Plays*, Peking 1937).

Chapter 12

It is impossible here to indicate the extraordinary number of works on the Manchu period; yet there is still a lack of works on the economic and social history of the period, so that in spite of abundant materials many questions remain unsettled.

For the beginning of the Manchu period are important E. Hauer (*Huang Ts'ing K'ai-kuo Fang-lüeh, die Gründung des Mandschurischen Kaiserreiches*, Berlin 1926) and Fr. Michael (*The Origin of Manchu Rule in China*, Baltimore 1942). O. Lattimore's books mainly deal with Central Asian policy and frontier questions but are not confined to the modern period only (especially *Mongols of Manchuria*, New York 1934, and *Inner Asian Frontiers of China*, New York 1940).

For the history of the period A. W. Hummel's collection of biographies is indispensable (*Eminent Chinese of the Ch'ing Period*, 2 volumes, Washington 1943/4). A good special study of the Opium War is G. W. Overdijking's *Lin Tse-hsü, en biographische schets* (Leiden 1938). The Mohammedan uprisings are dealt with in M. Hartmann (*Zur Geschichte des*

Islam in China, Leipzig 1921), but as with all books so fa[r] published on the T'ai-p'ing rebellion, they lack in objectivity This lacuna will probably be filled soon with the results of the teamwork of the Far Eastern Institute, Univ. of Washington. Meanwhile the books of W. J. Hail (*Tseng Kuo-fan and the T'ai-p'ing Rebellion*, New Haven 1927) and W. L. Bates (*Tso Tsung-t'ang*, Shanghai 1937) should be mentioned. For the last period of the Manchu régime Backhouse and Bland *Annals and Memoirs of the Court of Peking*, London 1914, and the earlier *China under the Empress-Dowager*) give information.

Chapter 13

Information as to the events of recent years is contained in numerous periodicals, notably *Pacific Affairs* (New York), *Far Eastern Quarterly* (both with extensive bibliographies), and also in the *China Yearbook*.

On Sun Yat-sen's and his successors' political doctrines see, f.i., P. M. A. Linebarger (*The Political Doctrines of Sun Yat-sen*, Baltimore 1937) and now D. G. Tewksbury (*Source Book on Asian Ideology*, New York 1949, volume 1 on China and Japan).

On the land problem we have now a very rich literature. Some of these economic and social studies may be mentioned here: (a) J. L. Buck: *Land Utilization in China* (Chicago 1937), (b) R. H. Tawney: *Land and Labor in China* (New York 1932), (c) Ta Chen: *Chinese Migrations with special reference to Labor Conditions* (Bulletin No. 340, U.S. Bureau of Labor Statistics, 1923), (d) J. L. Buck: *Chinese Farm Economy* (Chicago 1930), (e) H. T. Fei: *Peasant Life in China* (London 1938) and *Earthbound China* (Chicago 1945), (f) Chen Han-seng: *Frontier Land Svstems in Southernmost China* (New York 1949), (g) Shih Kuo-heng: *China enters the Machine Age* (Cambridge 1944), (h) J. Doolittle: *Social Life of the Chinese* (2 vols., New York 1865), (i) A. H. Smith: *Village Life in China* (New York 1899), (j) F. H. King: *Farmers of Forty Centuries* (Madison 1911), (k) D. H. Kulp: *Country Life in South China* (New York 1925), (l) M. Yang: *A Chinese Village* (New York 1945), (m) Lin Yüeh-hwa: *The Golden Wing* (New York 1944), (n) F. L. K. Hsü:

Under the Ancestors Shadows (New York 1948), (o) G. F. Winfield: *China, the Land and the People* (New York 1947), (p) L. Highbaugh: *Family Life in West China* (New York 1948) and (q) G. St. Gelder: *The Chinese Communists* (London 1946). A good bibliography on the Land Problems is given in the *Nankai Social and Economic Quarterly* (vol. 8, 1935, pp. 325–384).

INDEX

N